MW01490697

ONE MILE

RUNNING ACROSS AMERICA TO END ABORTION

MORE

ANNA STRASBURG

ONE MILE MORE

RUNNING ACROSS AMERICA TO END ABORTION

By Anna Strasburg

Copyright © 2022 by Anna Strasburg

Editor: Denise Loock

Cover by: Jenneth Dyck

Author photo: Jacqueline Pilar

Interior design by: Ben Wolf (www.benwolf.com/editing-services)

Cover photo by: Andy Gwynn

Paperback ISBN: 979-8-9867348-1-1

Hardcover ISBN: 979-8-9867348-2-8

Ebook ISBN: 979-8-9867348-0-4

All rights reserved. Neither commercial nor noncommercial interests may reproduce any portion of this book without the express written permission of the author.

Scriptures marked ESV are taken from The Holy Bible, English Standard Version® (ESV®), Copyright© 2001 by Crossway, a publishing ministry of Good News Publishers. Used by permission. All rights reserved.

Scripture quotations marked NIV are taken from the Holy Bible, New International Version®, NIV®. Copyright© 1973, 1978, 1984, 2011 by Biblica, Inc. Used by permission of Zondervan. All rights reserved worldwide. www.zondervan.com. "NIV" and "New International Version" are trademarks registered in the United States Patent and Trademark Office by Biblica, Inc.

The events of this book are true, and the author has worked
for complete accuracy throughout the work.

Some names, places, and times have been changed
to protect the privacy of some individuals.

Dear Caroline,

It has been such a blessing having your help sharing my book. I am so excited to be working on the same mission together and proud to be in this calling with someone like you. Keep up the good work!

— Anna Strasburg

To my husband, James, my dearest friend.

CONTENTS

ACKNOWLEDGMENTS

I would like to say thank you first to my team, who believed in our mission so whole-heartedly that they abandoned the comforts of home (showers, beds, and any normalcy) to travel across America to protect the most innocent of our time—the preborn.

Thank you, Sarah-Marie (Hoduski) Sherbon, for being our team's writer, living selflessly, editing my book, and providing unending encouragement about it. Thank you, Nicholas Hoduski, for faithfully coming alongside me to run across America with me, to train me, to believe in me, to encourage me, to challenge me, and to be not only my brother but also my friend. Thank you, Megan Maier, for being the best friend a person could ask for—not only believing in what God had called me to do but also making it possible with impeccable organization, dedication, and sacrifice. I love you all.

I would like to thank my husband, James, for all the sacrifices he has made to help me make time to write this book; without him, I never would have completed it.

I also want to thank my parents, Mark and Jeanne Hoduski, for raising me to be a person of faith. Without them and their incredible example, I never would have answered God's call to run across America.

Also, thank you to all the other people who are not mentioned in this book but helped make this journey and book possible.

PROLOGUE: THE CALL

My worn, aqua-blue running shoes pounded the pavement of Brent Lane and my lungs gasped for air in the Florida humidity. The damp spring air rushed around me as I finished a ten-mile training run with a sprint.

Distance running is a retreat for me—something about it silences everything in my body and helps me find my quiet place with God. This run was no different. I prayed, "God, I am deeply burdened by abortion in our country. Children are dying by the thousands every day, and yet no one seems to care. I want to make a difference, but I have nothing to offer. I'm not a great speaker or a doctor. I'm a simple sophomore math education major with no money."

As I ran, I continued to think about the horrors of abortion. "But what can I do, God?" I pushed through the last few steps of my run and cried out once more to him: "Either take this passion for these children from me or give me a way to live it out." And in that moment God laid the call on my heart: *Run across America to end abortion.*

I went back to my room half-excited and half-terrified about the idea. Over the next few days, I told my closest friends about running across America. Slowly, my courage and confidence in what God had laid on my heart grew. I named the run across the United States *Project If Life* and slowly I planned the route I hoped to run. In one of my college math classes, I calculated the run from the West Coast to the East Coast would be roughly 3,000 miles.

For the rest of that semester, I woke up at 5:00 a.m. every day before my classes to train. I was up before the campus cafeteria opened, so every morning I downed a bowl of oatmeal in the dark dorm room I shared with three other girls before hitting Brent Lane to start my distance run.

One morning, I realized I was eating my last packet of oatmeal. I prayed, "I'm out of oatmeal, and I'll throw up on distance runs if I don't eat. Please provide me with oatmeal, or else I can't train anymore." As I headed out to train, I knew God would provide.

The next day, I entered the college's student lounge. As I walked toward my mailbox, a friend of mine, Jared Cirone, approached me and said, "Hey! I know you've been distance running. I've decided to focus on lifting, and I'm not going to be distance running anymore, so I don't need oatmeal anymore. I have a bunch of it if you want it."

"No way! I literally ran out yesterday and was praying for God to provide more for me. How amazing."

Restocked with oatmeal, I kept training. My younger brother Nick often trained with me. He turned conditioning into an adventure. Cycling or running with him from my college to Pensacola Beach became weekly adventures.

On one early damp run toward the beach, the clouds were rolling in, and a coastal storm was bending the sea grass with stiff winds. As we ran a comfortable distance inland from the rolling waves, we came to the bridge that leads out to Gulf Breeze. A homeless man sat on a retaining wall cooking over a fire he had made with a small cook stove. He motioned us over and said, "Would you like to join me for coffee?"

"Sure," we replied as he filled mismatched cups with coffee that was almost clear from grounds that had been recycled so many times from previous batches. We sipped our drinks, enjoying the adventure.

But not every run was as charming.

A few days later, I headed down Airport Boulevard alone. Nick had class, so he couldn't run with me. I was focused on something other than running when an approaching dark-colored SUV slowed down. The change in speed caught my attention. I looked toward the vehicle and locked eyes with the driver. He stared back at me, inching closer in his SUV. As he drew closer to me, I froze and erupted into unexplainable tears. I looked backward and forward trying to plot an escape route, but I felt trapped.

As I debated my next move, he continued to stare at me. Suddenly, he sped up and ramped his SUV onto the sidewalk beside me. I told my body to run, to move, to flee, to do anything, but I stood there motionless with a steady stream of tears running down my cheeks. I knew he was going to take me, and yet I remained petrified with fear.

He opened his door to get out, and I still stood motionless. A horn blared loudly and caught my attention and his. An elderly lady pulled up just behind the SUV and aggressively honked her horn. Her face was full of fury as she continued to pound on her horn. *She must have seen this man's aggression and blaring her horn is her way of helping me.* I looked back over at the man. The horn must have startled him because he stayed in his SUV.

His hesitancy somehow unfroze my mind and body. *Run! Just run!* My legs obeyed and I dashed toward a more public area. When I reached Brent Lane, I felt safer and then headed back to campus before my mind could fully process what had happened. Once on campus, my lungs gasped for air as my body shook with fear.

5

The fear generated by that brief encounter lasted for months. This actualization of one of my deepest fears was brutal. As I continued my training for the run across America, I battled fear constantly.

I've always struggled with nightmares of predators. As a child, I often awakened my oldest sister, Sarah-Marie, after a bad dream —unwilling to describe what I had seen in my sleep but needing to talk, to be with someone. My nightmares continued into college and the level of terror they created was so real that I asked a group of girls to pray with me about the dreams. With their guidance, I learned to meditate on Psalm 91 when I was afraid. Specifically, I recited verse five and six: "You will not fear the terror of the night, nor the arrow that flies by day, nor the pestilence that stalks in the darkness, nor the plague that destroys at midday" (NIV).

In addition to the running, learning about the pro-life movement was an important part of training for the cross-country trip. I became absorbed by the history, the science, and the medical arguments surrounding abortion. I studied the subject as though I was taking a college class. I made flashcards and read book after book, attempting to gain as much knowledge as I could.

One evening I was at a banquet for Safe Harbor Pregnancy Center with one of my best friends, Megan Maier. The banquet was a fund-raising event so the center could continue to provide free pregnancy tests, ultrasounds, clothes, formula, counseling, and more for women who found themselves pregnant.

At the banquet, we were seated with a few other people for dinner. As we sat down at the table, a man smiled warmly as he introduced himself and his wife. "I'm Dr. William Lile, and this is my lovely wife, Lesley. I'm a local OBGYN, and I speak across the country on the pro-life movement."

"That's amazing," I said, "I am pro-life too. I'm planning to run across the country after I graduate college to help educate and activate people into the movement. I've been studying and reading everything I can, but would you be able to mentor me?" I asked, feeling excited but shy.

"Of course!" he said, without hesitation. "Have you heard of the Drowsy Poet?"

I nodded when he mentioned the delightful coffee shop.

"Lesley and I'll meet you there, and I'll teach you what you need to know."

We set a time and date.

When the day arrived, Megan and I headed to the Drowsy Poet. Dr. And Mrs. Lile were waiting for us. We bought coffee, gathered around a table, and Dr. Lile began teaching me. My mind raced as my pen struggled to keep up with every word he said. At the end of two hours, my hand was sore, but my heart was happy. I had learned so much.

"Thank you!" I said as Megan and I shook hands with him and then hugged his wife. "You have no idea what a blessing this is."

Megan and I headed back to campus. As Megan drove, my stomach sunk as I said, "Megs, you know all about my plan to run across America, better than anyone. Would you come with me? You're so organized and capable."

I searched her face. She flipped her long, curly brown hair to one side, adjusted her thick-rimmed glasses, and kept her eyes unwaveringly on the road.

"I know I could be successful if you were a part of my team," I prompted.

"Let me take the summer to pray about it," she responded.

"Thank you."

The spring semester of my sophomore year came to an end, and I headed back to my home in Kansas. I spent the summer studying and running. Before I knew it, it was time to head back to college for my junior year.

One day my eldest sister, Sarah-Marie, invited me to get some coffee and cookies at McDonalds so we could spend time together before I left.

At McDonalds, our conversation quickly turned to my call to run across America. As I talked, she toyed with a strand of her hair. Her large blue eyes were focused on me while I told her about my call and my passion to speak to people on behalf of the preborn.

After I finished telling her about what God had called me to, she remained silent for another moment before her eyes sparkled with animation.

"Annie, this is incredible. When I was a sophomore in college, I felt God call me to cross the United States writing on behalf of the preborn. I've been waiting five years for God to bring me a partner. We can go together, and I'll write pro-life articles and run the project's website."

My heart was full when I headed back to college for the fall semester of my junior year. Back on campus, I met up with my friend Megan again, and we talked about Project If Life. My stomach churned as I formulated my request once more: "Megan, will you come with me?"

"Yes! I prayed about it all summer, and I feel called to go with you." She barely finished before I hugged her. "I've already been talking about it with my dad, and he has lots of advice. I can keep track of all the details of the trip and be the project manager."

"This is amazing!" I said with a small squeal, then squeezed her hand.

"We need to start telling people and promoting the project. We also need a way to accept donations."

"We could make bracelets and hand them out to people," I said.

"Good idea."

While in college, artist Dave Ham drew me for a contest supporting Project If Life. The contest was used to help get the word out about my run across America.

Megan and I did not have much money, but between the two of us, we managed to purchase bracelets to promote our new ministry. I handed them out across campus, telling everyone I saw about my run across America.

During spring semester, I was working my on-campus job as a barista in the school's coffee shop. One day a college staff member ordered a coffee, then asked me about my bracelet.

"It's for my run across America for the pro-life movement," I explained as I pulled out a bracelet to give him.

"How are you funding it?"

"We've received donations from individuals, and we've been reaching out to churches and other organizations for support too."

"Do you have anyone to handle the legal side of your finances? Someone to make sure everything is above-board?"

"No, but my team and I have been praying for someone"

"I see." He paused. "I'm Dustin McElreath, by the way," he chuckled at the late introduction.

"I'm Anna. Nice to meet you," I shook his hand and then he took his coffee and left.

During my next shift, Dustin returned. "Hi, Anna. I went home and talked to my wife about your run across America. She and I would like to help. We want to start a nonprofit to handle the finances of your ministry."

"That's a huge answer to prayer!" I reached across the counter and shook his hand. "I can't wait to tell my project manager about it."

A few weeks later as I walked through the student lounge, I saw a friend named William Sousa. I wanted to give him a bracelet, and I also noticed he was with a tall redheaded guy named James. I had developed a goofy crush on James years earlier when I heard him sing the Irish ballad "Danny Boy" at a singing contest. My friends and I labeled him our "celebrity crush." Whenever any of us saw him on campus, we joked about the encounter. Though I enjoyed the celebrity sighting tales immensely, it was never more than that in my head.

"This is James Strasburg," William said.

"Nice to meet you," I said, smiling and shaking James's hand, as if I had no idea who he was. I handed bracelets to both, and we chatted a few minutes.

I left thinking the encounter was nothing more than another Irish tenor story to share with my friends.

In the fall semester of my senior year, I plunged into my studies, work, and more running. I had not thought much about James in months, so I was surprised to tap the Messages icon on my computer and discover he had written to me. He asked me to attend a formal concert with him.

When I told Megan and Nick about the invitation, they both had another idea.

"You have to say no unless he sings to you. After all, this may be the only chance you ever get to have him sing for you," Nick said.

"That's what I was thinking." Megan said.

"Very true." I agreed to ask him to sing the invitation.

A couple evenings later, I returned to my room a bit late after a work shift. My room phone light was blinking red, indicating there was a message for me. I pressed the button. To my astonishment, James sang a little ditty and asked me again to attend the formal with him. I smiled as my stomach filled with nervous, happy butterflies. *It's not a real date, just a simple formal. No need to get too excited.*

My friends came over, and we crowded around the phone to hear his beautiful voice as it floated out of the old, dingy room phone.

I opened my computer, messaged him back, and accepted his invitation.

On the night of the concert, he arrived with a gift and a beautifully arranged bouquet, wrapped artistically to match my dress. I took the flowers and smelled them as my stomach danced with butterflies once more. The concert, company, and evening went well, though when it came to an end, and I said goodnight to James, I did not think we would go on another date. His company was wonderful, but he had treated me so much like a friend that I did not even let anything more than friendship cross my mind.

Over the next several weeks, James became a weekly regular at the coffee shop where I worked. Each time he bought a small black coffee, made small talk, and then left. After several visits, he stopped buying coffee and began talking longer on each visit. My stomach fluttered each time he came, but I kept myself from appearing too excited to see him.

One night, I saw his tall, 6' 2" frame enter the shop and come toward me. Butterflies flitted in my stomach once more, and I grabbed a rag to clean an already clean counter.

"Hi, Anna," he said, his voice slightly cracking. He cleared his throat and rubbed his neck nervously.

"Oh, hi, James!" The words tumbled out quickly and betrayed my nervousness. I slowed my speech. "How are you?"

"I'm doing well." He paused, putting his hand up to his mouth as if trying to get words to come out. After a brief pause he continued, "I was just curious. Would you want to have dinner with me tomorrow night?" As he spoke, his cheeks turned bright red all the way to his ears as he feigned confidence.

"I'm sorry, but I already have plans." I smiled again, trying to encourage him, despite my being busy.

"How about the next night?"

"I already have plans with some of my friends." I said, giving him another smile.

"I'll come back tomorrow night and try again."

He left without a date, but I was delighted that he wasn't giving up and I could count on seeing him again so soon.

The next night he came in again to ask me on another date, and we agreed on a night to have dinner. The butterflies in my stomach flitted so much that I couldn't help but smile. Dinner went well, and we agreed to keep seeing each other before we both went home for Christmas break.

Once home, I continued to tell people about my mission to run across America. Many people expressed concern about three girls traveling across the country, so after much deliberation, we decided to buy a German Shepherd puppy for protection. One of my sisters, Natosha, found a litter of German Shepherd puppies for sale. We went right away, chose a chubby, energetic one, and named him Atticus. Sarah-Marie agreed to train him while I went back to college.

Spring semester of my senior year, I plunged into my last course requirements. Megan, Sarah-Marie, and I continued to plan, tell people about our mission, and ask for support. I began officially dating James, studying for school, learning more about the pro-life movement, and continuing with more training runs.

After graduation, Megan, Sarah-Marie, and I headed back to Kansas to begin Project If Life.

We had little money to get us to either coast, so we decided I would run from Kansas to the West Coast. If we completed the first portion of the journey, I'd then do the second portion of the journey—running from Kansas to the East Coast. We set a date for a launch party and invited everyone we knew to come and support our mission.

The day of the launch party finally arrived. A room in the high school I attended was transformed with decorations, along with art, baked goods, and espresso for sale. Most important, friends and family had come to help us launch our journey. I gave a speech, sharing about the faith of Corrie ten Boom and proudly telling my audience that my team and I were starting our trip across America. Like Corrie, we knew God was our provision, and we fully intended to rely on Him to meet all our needs.

After my speech, people approached my team with questions: "Where are you going to stay? What are you going to eat? What are you going to drive?"

I gave the same response to each question: "We don't know, but God has called us to go, so we're going."

When the launch party ended, we counted the donated money, putting the bills in one-hundred-dollar stacks. We had $2,000! We were stunned by God's faithfulness and provision.

Two former teachers, Kathie and Spencer Clarke, approached Sarah-Marie, Megan, and me as we chatted at a table. "We're so excited for your mission to protect God's little ones," Mrs. Clarke said in a high, sweet voice that had been familiar to me since kindergarten.

"We'd like to donate our van for your journey," Mr. Clarke said, drawing out each word as he spoke. "We built a bed in the back for camping. It's a 1989 Ford Econoline."

My team and I exchanged surprised glances. "A van?" I said in disbelief. "That would be the biggest blessing!" I looked toward Megan and Sarah-Marie with wide eyes and said, "This means we can actually leave. We have a vehicle."

We knew God had great things in store for us, and we couldn't wait to actually begin. We had started with nothing, but God was meeting all our needs. We now had an advisory board in place to guide us and pray with us, we had enough money to begin, a vehicle we could travel and live out of, and most of all, we had seen God's provision, once more confirming my calling to run coast-to-coast across America.

1

HEAT, MOSQUITOES, AND HOSPITALITY

I ran down the steps of my childhood home in Kansas, heading to the West Coast—or at least as far as I could make it that day. My pace was steady as my breaths came in a deep, controlled rhythm.

To make me feel like I was in my usual running routine, I styled my dirty-blonde hair into a tight, inside-out French braid and wore my purple CamelBak of water. I felt confident as my distance for the day grew. I didn't let my mind focus on the mileage, but rather on the few steps that lay ahead.

Despite the sweltering July heat of Kansas, I couldn't help but smile. Every step took me one step closer to making me a USA crosser. My team and I set out to fulfill what had been years in the making: a coast-to-coast run across America to save the lives of the preborn.

My route started at the Kansas-Missouri border where my parents lived and would end in California. The second portion would start again at my parents' home, and I would travel east to Washington, DC.

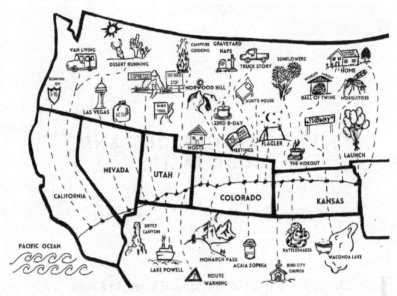

I started running across America from my parents' home in Kansas and headed west. This map shows many of the stops along the way.

My run for the day ended, and I was pleased to find I had covered enough ground to make the commute back to my parents' house too long to consider. My sister Sarah-Marie and I were on our own—a team of two people and a dog—and we would live in our van as I ran across America. Our third teammate, Megan, would join us in a few weeks.

We were full of hope, believing God would provide for each of our needs as we went. And if He didn't, we would know it was time to go home. We each shared a conviction to defend the preborn no matter the cost, and we hoped we could inspire other people to feel the same way.

The next day my feet hit the pavement in a comforting cadence as I covered miles along the right shoulder of Highway 24. I scanned the familiar Kansas scenery: endless fields of corn, wheat, and grass swayed gently and rhythmically. Every few steps, grasshoppers jumped from the grasses beside me in buzzing clouds that rose and fell around me. Many miles passed, and the ninety-degree day slowly wound down to sunset. The fading light of the plains seemed golden as it hit the ongoing fields. With dusk approaching, I wouldn't be able to run much longer. A few minutes later, Sarah-Marie drove toward me in our red van, knowing I never wanted to run after dark because of fear and safety. She pulled over on Highway 24 just ahead of me, and I stopped my Runkeeper GPS as I neared the passenger door of the van. Panting, I smiled at Sarah-Marie through the window, thankful to be picked up and to have finished my run for the day.

I opened the door and wiped the pouring sweat away from my eyes. "I never thought there'd be a difference between running a one-time, high-mileage race and running high mileage day after day, but there sure is!" I panted more, leaning on the van door in happy exhaustion. "I sure could use the comforts of my own bed" —I paused, looking at the sweat pouring down my arms and legs before finishing— "and I sure could use a shower."

"Makes sense with all that sweat." Sarah-Marie laughed. "You wanna find a place to park our van for the night?"

"Definitely." I hopped into the van.

The sun set as we looked for a gas station or park. When we saw one, Sarah-Marie pulled into the parking lot. The gas station's bright floodlights against the darkness of the open countryside made us feel safe. We let Atticus out to use the restroom before coaxing him into his large gray crate for the night.

Sarah-Marie had trained him well, so he was obedient. At nine months old, he had grown into a handsome, fierce-looking, one-hundred-pound German shepherd with a terrifying, growling bark. Although he was a gentle pup, his size, demeanor, and snarl made us feel safer.

After Atticus was loaded, we cleared supplies off the bed in the back to make room for us to sleep. We had overpacked, leaving almost no room to fit in the bed. We rearranged as best we could, and Sarah-Marie crawled into the bed and lay down. I scrambled over our belongings and squeezed in beside her, wedging my shoulder in next to hers to lie on my back. Out of habit, we pulled our blankets over our bodies and tried to fall asleep.

Oppressive, stagnant heat filled the van. Beads of sweat formed on my lips and forehead. My hair stuck to me like paste, and the air felt heavy as I breathed in the humid air. Another bead of sweat formed on my forehead and rolled down my temples. I threw off my blanket in frustration, unstuck my sweaty, sticky arm from Sarah-Marie's, and turned on my side, hoping the night would end soon.

"We need some air," I said with a weary sigh.

"The side windows are already open, but we can open the front windows," Sarah-Marie responded.

"That should help. These side windows are so small they don't provide any ventilation."

Sarah-Marie crawled forward and rolled down the driver-side window, then attempted to lower the one on the passenger side. It refused to budge, so she crawled back to join me. Almost immediately, I felt bursts of fresh air wash over me. I settled in again next to Sarah-Marie with contentment and closed my eyes once more, eager to rest. My mind drifted toward sleep, then I felt a stinging itch on my leg, then another, then another. I sat up and frantically slapped my legs.

"Mosquitoes!" I yelled, wildly smacking myself. "They must have smelled us through the open window. They're pouring in."

Before I could suggest it, Sarah-Marie crawled forward, started the van, and rolled up the window. But it was too late— mosquitoes buzzed everywhere, darting around our van in a bloodthirsty cloud. Blood smears formed on the ceiling and walls as we killed the ravenous insects with a frenzied zeal.

After many minutes of frantic mosquito killing, we concluded that we had killed all the mosquitoes. I surveyed my bites and scanned the van.

Sarah-Marie saw all the blood smears and laughed. "It looks like a crime scene."

"It sure does, and a nasty one at that."

We once more lay down to sleep but, sadly, with the front window closed. An hour passed in hot, restless misery until Sarah-Marie slowly sat up and asked, "Annie, are you still awake?"

"Yes."

"What if we watch a movie until the night cools off enough for us to sleep?"

"Sounds good to me." We pulled out Sarah-Marie's computer and spent a few hours watching a movie, then finally fell asleep.

The next morning, we awoke early, hoping to beat the July heat. The sky's lovely sunrise colors faded into gray. I had slept in my running clothes, so getting ready was quick: I laced up my Saucony shoes and placed my purple CamelBak on my back. I brushed my hair and quickly braided it into a single, inside-out French braid.

As I got out of the van, I said, "I'm going to run with Atticus today for safety."

"Perfect. I'll pick you up when you call." Sarah-Marie pulled out her laptop to work on pro-life articles. As the team's writer and web-content manager, she was eager to get to work. Her work ethic was unbeatable. When she set her mind on a task, the sun could rise and set unnoticed until the job was done.

I hooked Atticus's leash to his collar, started my Runkeeper GPS, and quickly left the van behind me. After only a few steps, Atticus jerked back on his leash, forcing me to stop. I pulled his leash as hard as I could, but he refused to go forward. He whined and whimpered, trying to pull me back to the van. I again pulled tightly on his leash and made him come to me.

Sarah-Marie saw the trouble, rolled down her window, and said, "I don't know if he'll run since he sees the van. I'll drive up the road a mile and meet you there."

The van sputtered as she started it up, and the engine rumbled as it pulled away. I laughed as she drove out of sight. Due to some mechanical problem, the van could hardly stay within the lines on the road. Soon the van was gone, and I was excited to get into my running rhythm. After a few steps, Atticus darted from my right side to my left. I tripped, lurched forward, and almost fell on my face. I ran a few more steps when something on the side of the road grabbed Atticus's attention. He darted after it and pulled me with him. I tripped as he pulled, and my stomach sank as I prepared to hit the ground, but somehow, I managed to keep my balance. My face burned with frustration as I tried to pull him back to me.

We began again. This time I held the leash tight to protect us both. The remainder of the first mile was as painful as the beginning. But up ahead, I could make out the van sitting on the side of the road, and relief filled me. I was almost done with this mile, and then I could put him in his crate. Atticus saw the van just after I did, put his head down, and charged toward the van. I held on as he bolted toward it.

When I got back to the van, Sarah-Marie rolled down her window. "I'm so frustrated. I get that he's a puppy, but he's impossible to run with. I wouldn't mind as much if it were a simple run, but it's not. I'm trying to make ten or fifteen miles today, and I'm already worn out after the first mile because of him!" I finished while gulping for air.

"How about we load Atticus up for today and you run alone? To make sure you're safe, I'll drive up the road and meet you in a mile. When you reach me, I'll do it again until you're done for the day."

"But that means you won't be able to focus on your articles."

"Until Atticus is better at running, I think it's best to make sure you're safe as you run."

"Thank you." I started my Runkeeper GPS again and resumed my pace. The ground was flat, and though it took endurance, the run was fairly easy. After several miles—and several meetings with Sarah-Marie at the van— my legs felt heavy and unwilling to continue. As I neared the van yet again, Sarah-Marie sat in the long grass beside our van where she had parked, playing fetch with Atticus. She threw the stick as far as she could. Atticus bounded away after it with unending energy and a slobbery, open-mouthed puppy grin.

Reaching the van, I leaned against the side and panted as Atticus retrieved the stick and ran back. Sarah-Marie noticed my exhaustion, and with a strong throw, sent Atticus out again after the stick. As he darted after it, Sarah-Marie opened the trunk of our van and rummaged around. She then produced a box.

"What's this?"

"Chocolate milk, your favorite. Full of protein and doesn't need to be refrigerated." Her blue eyes twinkled as she handed me the box.

"Thank you." I popped a straw into the milk and drank it as my heart rate calmed. I felt like I could conquer the world as I sipped my milk. Sarah-Marie had been caring for me in similar ways since my infancy. When I was little, she always picked out my clothes, carried me to bed, and made sure I could keep up with my five siblings. What a blessing to have her company on this journey.

I ran a few more miles that day before Sarah-Marie and I decided to look for a place to eat dinner. Rural Kansas didn't offer a lot of options.

"Let me look for a restaurant," I said as I searched nearby places on my phone. "Looks like there's a Subway. Does that sound good? It's healthy and pretty cheap."

"Yeah, I like Subway." Sarah-Marie started up the van and headed toward the restaurant. As we walked in, Sarah-Marie said, "We should each order a footlong and save the other half for breakfast. It'll be cheaper that way."

"Good thinking," I said, happy to pinch any penny we could.

We ate half our sandwiches and put the other halves in a plug-in cooler in our van. Sarah-Marie drove until we found a place to park and prepare for another hot night.

A daily routine took shape—running, eating Subway, and sleeping in gas station parking lots. One day we stopped in the town of Glasco as evening fell. I sat in the van, looking forward to going to bed for the night when my phone buzzed with a text. Knowing it was James, I pulled my phone out of my pocket as quickly as I could.

He wrote, "My family and I are on our way back home from our trip to Colorado. My dad said we could go a little out of the way and meet up with you briefly. We won't be anywhere near you until midnight, but he said we could stop and say hello quickly before we head to our hotel for the night."

"Sarah-Marie!" I said, nearly squealing. "James is coming back from Colorado, and he and his family want to stop to say hi for a few minutes. Do you mind?"

"Of course not, Annie." Her smile showed how happy she was for me.

Excitement erased my weariness, but it slowed time to an impossible bore. From the passenger seat of the van, I chatted with Sarah-Marie and took in my surroundings. The town of Glasco felt ancient. Historic buildings lined either side of the empty Main Street. The darkness behind the old structures made us feel like we were on the set of a Western movie and added to the feeling of being in the olden days.

Full of eagerness to see James, I reflected on our six months of dating and how seldom I saw him now that I had graduated college. Finally, I made out the headlights of a car as it rambled down Main Street and pulled up next to our van.

I threw open the side door of our van and rushed toward the

car, but my shyness around his family, whom I was still getting to know, checked my desire to jump into his arms. Instead, I tried to appear calm as I half-walked, half-ran to James. I hugged him briefly before hugging each of his family members.

"So good to see you guys again!" came out of my mouth faster than I intended.

"Good to see you too." James reached out to hold my hand. I took it and smiled up at him. James smiled back. His godliness, kindness, and goofiness were the perfect mix with his easy-going yet highly organized personality.

My boyfriend, James Strasburg, and I in Glasco, Kansas in August 2016. His family was on a road trip and drove out of their way to see me since James and I were now distance dating.

"And thank you guys for coming out of your way so James and I could see each other. It means so much to me," I said to his parents.

James tugged at my hand and tilted his head down the street. "Let's go for a walk with the few minutes we have."

We laughed and talked as we walked. I held his hand tightly with both of my hands and drank in his tall frame. His dark green eyes sparkled with happiness, and I admired his dark red hair. I loved the creases that formed beside his eyes every time he smiled. I grinned back up at him and squeezed his hands even tighter between mine.

We walked hand in hand until we were away from his family. He turned me to him, pulled me close, and hugged me tightly. "I've really missed you."

"I've missed you too."

After James and his family left, Sarah-Marie and I once more prepared for a night in our van. We were learning to work our way through the difficulties of living life in a van with a dog, figuring out the tough logistics of high-mileage running, and being away from those we loved.

Just before falling asleep, I whispered to Sarah-Marie, "You know, this journey is turning out a whole lot different than I anticipated. I just assumed we'd have hosts and I'd be giving speeches. I wonder if I'll ever speak, or if our journey will be just like this: van living, running, and simply trusting His provision and timing?"

"It's different than I thought too." A sigh escaped her lips before she was asleep.

2

A STRANGER'S KINDNESS

Neither Sarah-Marie nor I had showered in two weeks, but a lake lay ahead on our route, and that meant one thing—a bath.

Waconda Lake was large, for Kansas. Grass grew right up to its edge, and a few trees provided shade along the shore. The water was dull gray, the surface smooth. Long dirt and gravel driveways led to free campsites. We found a private spot among a few deciduous trees, making us feel as if we had some semblance of a home.

When Sarah-Marie let Atticus out, he sprinted to the water for a drink and swim. My sister and I grabbed our shower stuff and headed to the lake in our running clothes for a much-needed bath. My skin was covered with a thick layer of dirt and sweat, and my French braid no longer hid the excessive oil in my hair. The lake's warm water muddied with each step we took as we waded in. There was an odd contrast between the murky lake water and the shampoo bottle and pink razor I held.

I sat with a happy sigh and leaned backward to wet my hair. I poured an unnecessarily large amount of shampoo in my hand and lathered my hair aggressively. White suds formed on my scalp, slowly releasing the caked grime from my body. I massaged my hair into a pile on my head and slowly exhaled.

"This is the life," I said as the warm water released the tension weeks of running and living in a van had built up.

"No kidding," Sarah-Marie said in an equally relaxed tone.

In my goofy state of contentment, I leaned backward to rinse my mound of soapy, foamy hair and was startled to make eye contact with two fishermen staring in curious confusion. They quickly looked back to their rods. Self-conscious, I rinsed my hair, then picked up my razor to shave but hesitated with embarrassment.

Oh well, just ignore them. I grabbed my razor and slid it across my legs in well-practiced strokes. With a nod toward the fishermen, I said to Sarah-Marie, "That was a bit uncomfortable."

She laughed. "They should mind their own business but feeling clean is so worth it."

"Definitely," I said. A few shared chuckles eased the remaining tension. "But when we planned this run across America, I didn't expect to be living in a van and bathing in the first body of water we came across."

"Me either."

We giggled again. I was happy to have someone as tough and yet feminine as Sarah-Marie by my side.

Refreshed, we loaded Atticus into his crate for the night and climbed into the back of the van to relax. We left the rear doors open and admired the calm lake and darkening sky. As sunset approached, the temperature cooled. A deep stillness surrounded us when the sun was no longer visible.

Out of nowhere, clouds filled the sky and strong winds blew. Gust after gust roared, rattling our van doors on their old hinges and forcing them to slam all the way open. One gust propelled hundreds of tiny grass bugs into our van. I grabbed one door and tried to shut it, but the wind held it open. Sarah-Marie gripped the handle of the other door, and we both yanked against the wind's rising fury. Rain pelted the ground around us as the wind intensified. Each sweep of wind blew rain into our van, almost in waves.

"We need to get these doors shut!" I shouted over the wind. We tugged and pulled as the wind drilled the rain onto our skin, clothes, and hair.

After a short struggle, we pulled the back doors together. They slammed wildly, and rain continued to beat our van in torrential, furious gusts. The trees around the lake bent almost in half under the strength of the raging storm. Everything in the back of the van was drenched. Bugs crawled all over our bed, the seats, and the ceiling. The water outside began to flood around us as the rain continued.

"We need to get to higher ground!" Sarah-Marie shouted. Her blue eyes looked frantic as she stared at the threatening storm.

We crawled forward to the front seats, and Sarah-Marie started the engine. She drove the van about a half mile from the lake. "Do you think this is high enough ground?"

"I sure hope so."

"Okay, then let's spend the night here."

"Great. Now to figure out what to do with the wet bed and the tons of bugs."

We crawled to the back of the van, smashing bugs as we went. Wet and cold, we grabbed dry clothes and changed. As I lay down, the water on the bed soaked into my clothes. Despite the wet bed and my damp hair, I fell asleep as the storm hammered our van.

My eyes slowly opened to warm, gentle sunshine. The storm had passed, leaving little evidence that it had ever raged. It was Thursday, our chosen Sabbath, and the day looked surprisingly beautiful. I sat up. Sarah-Marie was already awake but lying quietly and peacefully.

"Do you want to go to Glenn Elder today?" I yawned.

"Sure. That town is close, and maybe there's something to do there."

We headed to the town and wandered around aimlessly until we saw a large garage sale. I browsed with disinterest because I did not have a single dollar to my name. But then a huge section of makeup caught my eye. I opened drawer after drawer eagerly.

"Wow! This is really nice makeup," I said as I sifted through yet another drawer of the used makeup.

"I can get you whatever you'd like, Annie," Sarah-Marie said.

"Are you sure? I don't know. I don't even wear makeup now that all I do is run." She had little money and shouldn't spend it on me.

"They're only a quarter each. Get whatever you want," she urged. "You'll wear makeup again someday."

After sorting for a while, I filled my hands with several of my favorite items, and we both walked up to the lady running the garage sale to check out.

Once back at the lake, we excitedly applied our new (used) makeup using the side mirrors of our old van. I felt refreshed and lovely as I put on the last few touches.

"Feels good to be clean and dolled up," I said.

"It really does, Annie." She turned to me quickly and said, "How about we get Mexican tonight! It's more expensive than Subway, but let's do something different to celebrate the Sabbath."

"Sure. It beats Subway," I gave her a silly smirk. "And a sit-down restaurant will be a nice way to celebrate."

We spent several more days and nights at the lake using it as a base until the day arrived for our third teammate, Megan, to join us. We waited most of the morning in eager anticipation until a car approached. We were overjoyed to see not just Megan but also our siblings Tessa and Alexander. They had come to drop off Megan and spend a day with us before heading back home. The three newcomers hopped out of the car, and we all hugged.

Megan's long, thick, curly hair was wrapped tightly in a messy bun, and she wore a casual shirt, running shorts, and thick-rimmed glasses. I hugged her extra tight. "I am so glad you're here. I feel so confident in our success with you by my side—"

Megan smiled, but with a look that said I should stop.

But I had to finish. "You're so organized and have so much ability to accomplish things. I'm so thankful to have you as a teammate. We couldn't do this without you."

"Thank you." Her small smile showed she appreciated the compliment but didn't like me saying it publicly.

After we chatted awhile, we took Megan's stuff out of the car and loaded it into our van. Sarah-Marie and I also loaded our extra clothes into the car to downsize our belongings.

"Now that that's done, you guys want to pick up pizza?" I asked, eager to hang out with my siblings and Megan.

"I have a quick errand at Dollar General. Do you mind if I do that before dinner?" Sarah-Marie asked, her face red.

"Of course not," I said as we all got into the car and van. "We can stop there before we get pizza."

Sarah-Marie drove the van, and I rode in the passenger seat. As we headed down the road, the van drifted out of our lane into the left lane. Sarah-Marie's arms tensed as she tried to pull the van back into our lane, but instead it drifted onto the right-hand shoulder.

"What's wrong with the steering? I've been noticing it drifting, but it seems to be getting worse." I clenched the handle on the side door as we drifted.

"I don't know, but it's definitely getting worse, and we need to get it fixed." She turned the van into the Dollar General parking lot.

We were about to walk into the store, when to my surprise, Sarah-Marie pulled out several wrapped gifts and headed into the store alone. She was gone for only a few minutes, then returned from Dollar General empty-handed. "What was that about?" I asked.

"Well, I met a worker the other day, and I asked her how she was doing. It turns out that she's a single mom, and her baby's about to turn one." Sarah-Marie paused. "She had no presents for her baby's first birthday, so I got her some."

Touched by her kindness, I said, "I don't know how you managed to buy and wrap gifts for that lady's baby." Her kindness prompted me to think about how many pro-life people care about children before and after they are born. Providing gifts for that woman's baby so perfectly paralleled what pregnancy resource centers all across America do by providing resources for mothers before and after the baby is born.

Alexander blurted, "Let's go see the world's largest ball of twine."

"See what?" Megan laughed.

"It's one of the seven wonders of Kansas," Tessa said enthusiastically, but with a smug smirk.

"Sounds so impressive," Megan lifted her eyebrows and smiled with fake excitement.

We loaded into the car and van and drove to the famous attraction. We hopped out of our vehicles and before us was a small, roped-off shelter. Under the shelter was a giant ball of rope.

"This is it?" Megan laughed. "Kansas sure has a lot to offer!" The rest of us chuckled.

After a good laugh and some pictures with the twine, we purchased a pizza at a nearby restaurant. Once back at the lake, we started a fire and ate. The moonlight reflected beautifully on the water. Everyone chatted in the warm evening air as we sipped our steaming cocoa. One by one, each of us went to bed—in the van, around the fire, and in our tent.

The next morning, the sun awakened us early. As if by instinct, my siblings and I went in various directions to gather twigs, sticks, and logs for a fire to cook breakfast. I returned and dropped a large armful on the fire, then smirked at Megan as she dropped a few twigs onto our pile.

"I stink at this." She pursed her lips in a pout.

"You'll get better. The rest of us have been camping all our lives, so we're used to gathering wood."

As soon as the fire was going, Sarah-Marie cooked pancakes in one cast-iron skillet as I scrambled eggs in another. Sarah-Marie placed pancakes on each plate, and I followed behind scooping eggs into tortilla shells. Tessa poured each of us some strong, percolator coffee, which made the meal and morning feel complete.

Soon after breakfast ended, Tessa and Alexander prepared to head home. We hugged them and said sad goodbyes before they got in their car and left. Megan, Sarah-Marie, and I cleaned up our campsite and then headed to where I last finished running. When we reached the spot, Sarah-Marie stopped on the roadside. I hopped out of the van, started my Runkeeper GPS, and began yet another run.

After thirteen miles, I was ready for lunch, although still feeling strong. I stopped to text Megan. When she and Sarah-Marie arrived, I climbed into the van.

"Subway?" Sarah-Marie asked.

"I guess." After a pause, I added, "It's getting pretty old, but I don't know where else we could eat."

At Subway, I ordered my sandwich, ate half, and felt refreshed. I was ready to run again. Another several miles passed, then Megan offered to join me. I was grateful for the much-needed company.

As we ran, I told her, "Megs, I've been praying to see a field of sunflowers."

"I'm surprised you haven't seen any. Isn't Kansas supposed to have a lot of them?"

"We're supposed to, but I guess not," I replied between breaths.

"You're getting pretty high mileage."

"Yeah, better than the beginning of Kansas. The lunch break has been giving me more energy. If I cover a lot of ground in the morning, the evening miles feel like a bonus."

"You're amazing."

After my run, we grabbed more Subway for dinner and coffee from a local gas station. Sarah-Marie and Megan poured coffee for themselves as I poured cocoa. We stood in a small circle chatting and laughing as Sarah-Marie added cream to her coffee.

"Do you own the two-toned van out front?" A deep, serious voice came from behind me.

I turned around, startled to see a police officer with a furrowed brow and tight lips. My stomach dropped, and our smiles disappeared. "We do" was our unanimous answer.

"I've received several reports about a two-toned van swerving all over the road," he said. My face felt hot and my palms clammy. Megan crossed her arms and Sarah-Marie twirled a strand of her hair as a moment passed in silence. We stood still, unsure what to say.

"Well, it must be another two-toned van," he said, then chuckled.

He walked away, still chuckling. When he was gone, we looked at one another and laughed in disbelief. Megan stroked her hair back and exhaled slowly before chuckling again. Sarah-Marie still played with her hair, but her face looked less tense as she forced a slight smile.

"He must have seen we weren't crazy or drunks," Megan said.

"Yeah, but we better get that steering problem fixed before we really get in trouble for swerving. Not getting a ticket was a gift from God," Sarah-Marie said as we headed back to the van.

"No kidding," I said.

Back in the van, we headed to a local park to spend the night. Sarah-Marie crawled in first followed by Megan. They giggled as they crawled, finally unwinding from the tension of the confrontation with the officer.

They lay side-by-side as I crawled back to join them. I wedged in beside Megan and our shoulders touched. Sweat beaded on my forehead, then ran down my face. *Another night of this unending heat, but at least we got rid of stuff so the three of us can fit.* I rolled on my side so Megan and I wouldn't be touching. Despite the heat, sleep came quickly.

Early the next morning, I opened the rear door to use the restroom. Mosquitoes rushed in and awakened Sarah-Marie and Megan. Realizing sleep was out of the question, we grabbed our toothbrushes and water bottles, let Atticus out of the van to play, and headed to a water pump in the park.

We filled our water bottles quickly and wet our toothbrushes in the pump water. Our hair was wild and untamed as we stooped at the pump, brushing our dirty teeth, and taking turns swatting one another and ourselves to ward off the pests. I felt sticky and gross from another hot night without a shower.

The breakfast menu that morning was leftover Subway. I grabbed my poorly wrapped sandwich from our cooler and climbed to the back of the van to eat it. Overnight, the bread had become mushy and stuck to the meatballs. I bit into the sandwich and tried to swallow but gagged instead. I wiped the bread off the meatballs and tried another bite. I gagged again and tossed the rest of the sandwich in the trash.

"Ready to run?" Megan asked.

"Yeah, I guess."

Megan started the van and headed to a small coffee shop in Osborne called the Hideout. Sarah-Marie climbed out with her laptop and waved goodbye, eager to get some work done.

As Megan drove me to my run spot, I felt the lack of food in every part of my body. When we reached the spot, she pulled over and waited for me to get out.

"Megs, I feel so sick from not eating my sandwich. I don't want to run, but I know I have to," I said, my hand motionless on the van's door handle.

"You don't have to run if you don't feel well."

"I don't want to waste an entire day." I opened my door and turned to put my feet to the ground. I positioned my purple CamelBak, started my Runkeeper GPS, and headed west. My mind attempted to drift into distance-running mode, but nausea kept me aware of my body's condition.

After two miles, the lack of food overcame my resolve. Weak and dizzy, I called Megan. I stood dazed and nauseated for a few minutes until she arrived.

"What if we get you some food? Would that help?" Megan asked.

"Is there anything but Subway?" I whined.

"I don't think so." Her eyebrows were creased with concern as she spoke.

"Subway it is," I said.

———

We grabbed Subway and met Sarah-Marie back at the Hideout, where we were hit with a refreshing wave of cool air as we walked into the shop.

"How was your morning?" Megan asked Sarah-Marie, her voice chipper as always.

"Good! I almost finished an article. You wouldn't believe how much I can get done with Wi-Fi and a good cup of coffee."

"Glad to hear that." Megan turned to me. "Do you want anything to drink, Anna?"

As she spoke, I was plopping down on a white fluffy couch in the entryway. The couch seemed to envelop me. "Chocolate

34

milk sounds amazing," I responded, trying to keep my eyes open.

From Left to Right: Anna, Megan, Sarah-Marie, and Atticus. Our team stood outside the Hideout Coffee Shop in Osborne, Kansas. We were overjoyed to find good coffee to drink.

The next thing I knew, I was waking up on the same white couch with a huge, thirty-two-ounce, Styrofoam cup of chocolate milk on the table in front of me. My skin was crusty with dried sweat, and I shivered in the cold air of the shop. My limbs were stiff as I sat up, and I wondered how long I had been asleep. *How could I have slept so soundly in public?*

I turned around and saw Sarah-Marie and Megan at the counter talking to a brown-haired lady with a big smile, who was working behind the counter. They were telling her about our journey so far. "Yeah, it's been amazing so far," Sarah-Marie said. "We live in our van as we travel."

I walked up and Megan said, "Anna, this is Rachel Heinen, the owner of the coffee shop."

"Hi," I said, wiping the sleep from my eyes.

"They told me you're running across America to end abortion. What made you care so much?" Rachel asked me.

"Well, I heard about babies in the womb when I was in the fifth grade. My teacher, Mrs. Steinbrink, was so gentle when she explained that we needed to protect them. As I got older, I learned that people were killing preborn children, which horrified me and made me want to stop it. That desire to end abortion stuck with me throughout all my schooling, even through college, so I started to study and learn about abortion. I didn't know how I could help until God called me to run across America."

"There are so many ways people can get involved," Sarah-Marie said with a higher pitch than before, showing her passion. "People can volunteer at their pregnancy resource centers, vote for people who will protect the preborn, speak out against abortion, and pray to end abortion."

"Your journey sounds incredible," Rachel said. "Just out of curiosity, how do you shower?"

Megan fumbled for words, then finally said, "We-we don't. Well, they used a lake for a bath recently."

"We just haven't had hosts," Sarah-Maire added with a side glance at Megan, trying to make our situation sound less mortifying than it was.

"You can come over and use my shower if you'd like. I don't mind."

Again, we paused. Sarah-Marie tried to form words but couldn't. Megan's mouth was open, but she said nothing. I was unsure how to accept such kindness but also felt embarrassed by the need for a shower. "That would be great," Megan finally answered. I could tell she was hesitant to accept, but as our project manager, she was committed to care for the team every way she could.

After eating and napping, I was able to get in a successful, thirteen-mile run. Megan and Sarah-Marie picked me up, and we took a short drive to Rachel's house. I was eager for a shower. Running high mileage and sleeping in a hot van made showers even more of a necessity.

Always selfless, Megan said to me, "Why don't you shower first?" I showered, then joined Sarah-Marie in Rachel's living room while Megan showered. Feeling awkward in my running clothes and a towel wrapped around my hair, I listened as Rachel talked about small-town life and her coffee shop. After Megan finished, Sarah-Marie showered, and then we all talked for quite some time about small-town life.

My discomfort disappeared as I soaked in Rachel's kindness to three complete strangers—one of the few kindnesses we had experienced in a long time. It refreshed us in a much deeper way than a shower ever could. To Rachel, opening her home to us for a few hours did not seem to be a big deal, but our hearts were overwhelmed. As we headed back to our van for the night, I felt re-energized by her simple act of kindness and ready to face what lay ahead.

3

THE UNKNOWN

Curtains of houses opened and closed quickly as people sneaked peeks at the 1989 Ford Econoline van invading their otherwise quiet Kansas town. We laughed about the quirks of the small town, Alton, where we had parked our van for the night. The same white car made six or seven passes to investigate the strangers parked on the otherwise empty street. We made ourselves comfortable under the suspicious looks of many eyes and a few pesky mosquitoes and flies, but no other disturbance. We merely closed our curtains and left the residents to worry on their own.

The next morning, we awoke to a still street before heading to a nearby forest preserve to enjoy breakfast in seclusion. We ate while Atticus begged each of us to play fetch with him. When we finished eating, Sarah-Marie dropped me off while Megan worked at the Hideout.

Two hours and thirteen miles of running passed with only my thoughts for company. The monotony of Kansas scenery—field after field after field—seemed to amplify my loneliness. Hour after hour, day after day, and week after week of running was difficult for my extrovert personality.

As I tried to push away loneliness, I was relieved to see Sarah-

Marie and Megan approaching in our van to pick me up for lunch. After a meal and a quick nap, I felt ready to start my second run. As the van drove away, I was left with only the repetitive sound of my footsteps for company. I again felt alone, but I pushed the emotions aside and simply let my mind drift as several miles passed.

Honk! Honk! I recognized the horn as ours and turned to see Sarah-Marie pull over next to me. Megan hopped out with her usual cheerfulness and said she was going to run with me.

"Your company is just what I needed, Megs," I said through my controlled but still heavy breathing.

"I'm so glad to." Running these few miles was a way for her to take care of me. Her love and care were the balm my lonely heart needed. As she ran beside me, my loneliness lessened. God had sent her at just the right time to ease my ever-growing need for company.

After a few more minutes of running, Megan looked over at me and asked, "Where do you use the restroom?"

"Uh, if there's a tree, behind it, or in a tall field, but that ditch will work for privacy," I said pointing to the side of the road.

I kept running until Megan rejoined me. From then on, we chatted effortlessly about the scenery and the silliness of living in a van, which made me forget my miles and, more importantly, the loneliness.

At the end of the run, I glanced ahead. "Megs, look! Sunflowers!" I stared with open-mouthed joy as the golden petals stood in lovely, yellow contrast to the fields of wheat and corn I had seen for so many weeks.

"Just what I prayed for," I said. As I spoke, the flowers bent ever so gently in the slight breeze. God was taking care of me, even when the road was hard and lonely.

I admired the flowers and Megan took a picture of me in front of them, then I called Sarah-Marie to let her know we were done running. A few minutes later, she pulled up in the red van. When I attempted to walk to the van, my muscles felt tight and sore, and my body stiff and robotic. I opened the van door and eased into the back seat.

"You need to stretch out," Sarah-Marie said. "You can't run fifteen to twenty miles a day and not take care of yourself."

"I'm so exhausted from running, I don't have the energy!"

"What hurts the worst?"

"My calves. They're so tight. They feel like they're in knots."

"Let me rub them out," Sarah-Marie offered.

"Okay." I lay down on my stomach so she could rub them out. She began pushing her hands over my calf muscles almost like she was kneading bread. "Ouch!" I said. "This hurts so bad!"

"It'll be so good for you," Sarah-Marie said, persisting despite my flinching.

"Oh!" I groaned, trying not to jerk away.

"A few more minutes, and you'll feel so much better. Make sure you drink a bunch of water when I'm done. It will help with soreness."

"Oka-a-a-y," I moaned through clenched teeth.

When Sarah-Marie finished rubbing out my calves, we all went to sleep in the back of our van.

I awoke the next morning to the van moving while Megan and I were still attempting to sleep in the bed in the back. It was Thursday, our Sabbath, so I closed my eyes and fell asleep once more. The back doors opened slowly, waking me yet again. There stood Sarah-Marie, her hands full of pastries and coffee from Carousel Bakery.

She spread out the treats like a feast on our bed. Megan and I admired all the beautiful pastries. As we ate in the back of the van, I scanned the street where we were parked. The sunlight warmed my arms as we huddled in sleeping bags in the back of the van. Strangers peered at us as we ate, but we ignored their curious stares. Circled up against the morning chill, our fingers clasped Styrofoam cups of coffee, and we nibbled our treats.

The next day I reached Hill City, marking six weeks and roughly three-hundred miles since I left my parents' house. I was exhausted from ascending the many hills my body was not accustomed to. Just ahead, I spied yet another hill. *I can't do it. I'm just too tired. And lonely. And it's so hard.* I wanted to stop and rest, but I prodded myself. *Come on, Anna, just a few more steps and you can quit forever.* With that false yet effective encouragement, I started up the hill, though my strength and courage were faltering.

Out of nowhere, I heard, "Go, Anna, go!" Megan's overly excited, girlish voice called to me. I looked up. She, Sarah-Marie, and Atticus stood on the side of the road at the top of the hill. Atticus barked and yipped excitedly too. Once again God had answered a prayer I had not fully articulated.

"You got this, Annie," Sarah-Marie yelled, as if it was the most important run of my life.

"Come on, Anna. You're doing great!" Megan hopped up and down, waving her phone in the air and blaring some of my favorite music to cheer me on.

Tears welled in my eyes as the steps up the hill somehow became effortless and light. My heart warmed and my pace increased. I felt like a champion.

My run finished, I added up my miles in my running log and said, "Guys, I hit almost one hundred miles this week. I've done almost twenty every day."

"Wow, Annie!" Sarah-Marie said. "That's pretty impressive considering Kansas is only four hundred miles across! Keep it up." I smiled, delighted to make her proud.

Since my run was finished, Sarah-Marie lay down for a nap in the back while Megan drove, and I rode in the passenger seat.

"God has really blessed this week," I said to Megan. "You mind if we pray and thank Him?"

"Sure," Megan replied.

"Dear God, I want to thank you for your blessings this—"
Sirens blared behind us. I glanced back. A police officer wanted us
to stop.

Megan pulled over and said, "Oh no! We're going to get in so
much trouble. Sarah-Marie is sleeping in the back with no seatbelt,
I have an Illinois license with a Kansas vehicle, and the van isn't
even ours."

"I don't know what to do." My stomach sunk in fear as I dug
for the registration papers in our cluttered glove box.

Megan rolled down the window as the officer approached.
When he reached the front window, he said, "You know you've
been swerving all over the road? I'm going to need to see your
license and registration." His serious tone scared me.

"I'm so sorry," Megan said, as I fumbled through the glove box.
Finally, I found the registration, and Megan handed it to him. My
heart pounded as he took the documents back to his car.

"Oh no, oh no, oh no," Megan muttered. "Do you think we'll
get a ticket?"

"I don't know."

After a few minutes, the officer returned and said, "I'm going
to let you off with a warning this time, but make sure you stay in
your lane in the future."

When the officer was out of earshot, a stressed laugh slipped
out of Megan's mouth before she said, "Well, that was scary. I'm so
glad we didn't get a ticket."

"Yeah, for real, but we really do need to get this van fixed.
Wow! I'm so thankful we don't have to pay a fine."

Back on the road, we headed toward a restaurant. In the parking
lot, Sarah-Marie and I started to get out of the van, but Megan
stared at her phone. After a moment, she looked up and said,

"Guys! The Assemblies of God Church of Colby is getting us a hotel for three nights, starting tonight." She turned to me and finished with few happy bounces. "And they're letting us set up a table in the back of their church on Sunday to share about our mission. They said they'll announce us from the pulpit."

"No way! A hotel? How amazing. And we can talk about our mission. This is so exciting," I said.

We grabbed dinner and took it straight to the hotel. As we walked in, I felt overwhelmed by luxury as the cool air hit my face and the aroma of freshly baked cookies filled my nose. Megan checked us into our room. Without even showering, I jumped into the white sheets face first and lay there for a while as my sore, exhausted muscles relaxed.

After some time, I sat up to see if anyone was going to use the shower. Sarah-Marie was using the Wi-Fi to work on her articles, and Megan was emailing people on her computer, trying to coordinate future hosts and churches.

The shower is all mine. In the bathroom, I cranked the handle in the hot direction and happily watched steam fog the mirror. After my shower, I finally felt free from the grime of running and living in the van. Clean and dressed, I went to the hallway outside of my room to FaceTime James. Due to my exhaustion, our conversation was short but happy. After hanging up, I went back in the room, crawled into bed, and covered myself in the luxurious blankets. I stared at the ceiling in utter delight until fatigue shut my eyes.

The next morning, I awoke and grabbed my makeup. Excited to have a large mirror, I sat on the bathroom sink and got ready. Sarah-Marie and Megan were soon dressed too, so we headed to the hotel lobby for the complimentary breakfast. I went straight for the waffle maker, cooked my waffles, and mounded whipped cream on them, grinning ear-to-ear. I turned to the hotel staff member with a huge smile and said, "This is the best breakfast I've ever had."

The worker laughed at my childlike delight.

When Sarah-Marie, Megan, and I arrived at the church, we set up our trifold information board and some of our materials. My heart raced as I soaked in the joy that a church cared enough about the pro-life movement to let us stand in the back and talk to people about the importance of protecting the preborn.

"So, what are you doing?" a man asked.

"Well, I'm running across America to protect the preborn. I run anywhere from ten to twenty miles a day. I run because every person deserves a right to life, even the preborn. If we don't stand for them, then who will?"

"Do you have hosts? Or where do you stay?"

"We sometimes have hosts, like your church is putting us up in a hotel tonight, but mostly, we live in our van as we travel."

"Do you all run? Or is it just you?"

"I'm the only runner, but my teammate Sarah-Marie writes incredible pro-life articles and operates our website. And my other teammate, Megan, coordinates all the details. I want to speak anywhere that will open its doors—whether that's schools, churches, youth groups, Bible studies, or any other venue."

"Do you run every step or just parts?"

"I run every step. I haven't missed a single step from my parents' house all the way to just past Hill City. I never want to miss a step, so I pick out major landmarks to remind me where I stopped. I even GPS track my running so it's all logged."

"Wow! What do your parents think?"

"They're happy we've set out to do what God has called us to do. They've always lived lives of faith, so when God called us to live by faith, they encouraged us to go."

"You're doing all of this to protect the preborn? How old are you?" the man said.

"Yes. Every bit of the hardship is worth it to protect them, but it's also quite the adventure! And I'm twenty-two."

Many people talked with us, asking us similar questions. As people learned about our mission, some donated to help us keep going. After we had talked with everyone who came to see us, we packed up our materials and headed back to our hotel.

Once there, Megan sat on the edge of the bed and counted the money. "Eighty dollars!"

"God is still providing," I said. "These eighty dollars will bring us closer to the West Coast."

"All we can do is keep going until the money runs out, and so far, God is keeping the money coming," Sarah-Marie said.

The next day I began another two-part run along Highway 24, and I was nearing the end of Kansas. The first days of September taunted me with the promise of cooler fall weather, but the days remained hot. The miles of my first run passed quickly, and after lunch, I was ready to run again.

An hour into my second run, the sun began setting. The light of the huge round orb was blinding as I ran directly into its powerful light. I kept my eyes down to avoid its brightness and squinted. Mindlessly, I asked God for sunglasses, not even organizing my fragmented thoughts into a prayer. I continued down the Kansas highway as the sun painted the sky with reds and oranges, making the Kansas grasses glow.

As my mind wandered, my eyes spotted something black on the roadside. I stooped to pick up the object. A pair of sunglasses in perfect condition. I put them on—an exact fit for my face! I was dumbfounded at the goodness and provision of God. My heart filled with warmth. *He is taking care of me.*

After my run, Megan gave me a heads-up on our finances. We had only what was left of the money given to us at the launch of our Project and the recent church donation—about four hundred dollars. That money would fuel our 1989 van, feed us, feed our dog, and cover other basic necessities. But we also needed to replace our van's tires, and we were hesitant about spending the last of our money.

Sarah-Marie called Dad and tapped the Speaker icon on the phone. After a few rings, he answered with a cheerful "Hello."

"Hey, Dad," Sarah-Marie said. "You're on speaker with Megan, Anna, and me. We want your advice on whether we should replace our tires now or wait."

"They were pretty bad when you left here, and I thought they needed to be changed right away."

"They're bald, splitting, and warping," Sarah-Marie added.

"Dad," I interrupted, "We're calling because we only have about four hundred dollars left, and I don't want to spend the last of our money on tires and then have to come home because we're out of money."

"Well, Sweetie," my dad began with his characteristic gentleness, "the tires are so bad that they are dangerous. I don't want you getting in an accident. I think it's better to be safe and trust God will provide to keep you going after the money is spent."

We talked for a little longer. Megan, my dad, and Sarah-Marie agreed about the tires. Frustration burned inside my chest. We hung up the phone with my dad to take a vote on the tires, but first I said, "Guys, if we spend the money and then have to go home, what was the point?"

"That we'll be safe," Sarah-Marie said in a way that made it seem like replacing the tires was the obvious decision. "Why don't we go ahead and vote?"

I looked at Megan to see if she had any thoughts, but she didn't say anything, clearly wanting to avoid conflict. I could feel my anger rising. We voted, and I wasn't surprised when it was a two-to-one vote to get the tires replaced.

I lifted up a silent prayer. *My faith is in you, God, but this seems too hard. We won't be able to buy food or gas after we buy tires. All we've done and suffered and lived through will be for nothing, and we'll just have to go home.*

4
MIDWESTERN FRIENDSHIP

We handed the last of our money to the mechanic. I crossed my arms and bit my tongue, trying my best not to show my anger, but still a sigh escaped my lips. The mechanics made quick work of replacing our worn-out tires, but the sight of new tires did not encourage me.

"Oh wonderful!" Sarah-Marie said.

"Yeah, but now what do we do?" I uncrossed my arms with a frustrated wave.

"Mr. and Mrs. Beck left this morning to meet up with us," Megan said.

The Becks were on our board and had given us lots of advice before Project If Life began. "They're incredibly kind," I said, "and don't get me wrong—I am excited to see them. But I can't wrap my mind around telling them we're out of money."

"They'll have good advice, Annie. Don't worry. They'll know what to do," Sarah-Marie added.

"Okay, I won't." I tried to put finances out of my mind and focus on the Becks' arrival.

"Get in your run today, and then they'll be here." Megan said, with an even tone, clearly trying to ease the tension.

We arrived at my start spot, and I hopped out. After a few

miles, my knees ached as my feet pounded the pavement. The medium-length grass on the side of the road looked soft, so I moved off the hard surface. I ran in the grass for quite some time, enjoying the change.

My mind drifted between thinking and praying. As I prayed, the Lord seemed to tell me to run on the road again. I shifted from the grass to the pavement. Suddenly, a harsh rattling noise came from the grass beside me. I jumped back and stood still, trying to locate the source of the sound.

Again, a threatening rattle, rattle, rattle came from the grass. I jumped back once more, realizing I had almost stepped on a rattlesnake. I scanned the grass but couldn't see the snake, so I backed up slowly until I felt safe, then began running again along the roadside.

Several paces later, I saw the remains of a rattlesnake that had been hit by someone's car. A few more steps brought me to another large dead snake in the road. Throughout the remainder of my run, I saw dead rattlesnakes on the road. I hadn't even known Kansas had rattlesnakes, yet God had protected me from being bitten.

After my run, we again discussed our lack of money. Toward the end of the conversation, Megan reminded us, "Well, the Becks are meeting us for dinner tonight. They've had so much wisdom before, let's see what they have to say about our finances."

We all agreed and headed to an Italian restaurant called Gambino's. As we pulled in, we spied Mr. and Mrs. Beck's friendly faces. We hopped out and hugged them.

"We can't believe you drove all this way to see us," I said as we entered the restaurant and took our seats.

"We are happy to come," said Mrs. Beck, "and so excited to hear about your journey."

I jumped into a few stories, forgetting our finances and eager to share God's provision. "God literally provides for us in the most miraculous ways. A stranger gave me twenty dollars while I was running down the highway, a police officer stopped and gave me water to keep me going, and all the servers at a diner gave us their tips for the day when they heard about our mission for the preborn."

"How amazing!" Mrs. Beck said.

We ate pizza and continued to talk about our journey. As we finished our dinner, Mr. Beck said in his deep, kind voice, "We're so glad to hear that God is taking care of you. How are you doing financially?" His directness comforted us.

"We're out of money," Megan said. "We spent the last of it on tires for our van, and we're afraid we'll have to go home."

"We've been trusting God this whole time, but this is pretty scary," I added.

"We're proud of you," Mr. Beck said, "and we think you should keep going, trusting that God will continue to provide." He handed me a check for three hundred dollars. "We hope this helps keep you on the road."

"And here's a little something just for you guys," Mrs. Beck chimed in. She handed us a twenty-dollar bill. "Spend it on ice cream. Treat yourself!"

"Thank you for advising us and believing in us," Sarah-Marie said. "It's been so encouraging to have you believe in us from the beginning."

"Yes, thank you," I said, "your visit is the encouragement we needed."

Our meal ended, and we each hugged Mr. and Mrs. Beck goodbye. They had devoted their whole lives to serving God and leading people. We were sad to see them leave, but their confidence in us gave us courage.

After our meeting with the Becks, I ran for several days until we were close to Bird City. Bird City wasn't along Highway 24, but it was close enough for us to commute to and from my run spots.

When we arrived at St. John's, a tall, dark-haired man introduced himself as Pastor Jim Gleason. He showed us to an apartment in the church where we could stay. The apartment consisted of two remodeled Sunday school rooms joined by a door. One room had been turned into a kitchen and living room area, and the other was a bedroom and bathroom.

"I hope you all feel welcome. Please make yourselves and your dog at home here. Come and go as you need."

"We appreciate your hospitality, Pastor Jim. You know, before we left, we spent a whole month calling churches all across Kansas asking for places to stay. You were the only person who called me back," I said.

"It means so much to us," Megan added.

"I'm glad to be of help. I hope all who are in need will feel welcome here." The kindness in Pastor Jim's voice made our weariness disappear.

The apartment was a haven of rest. We had Wi-Fi, a shower, beds, a couch, a stove, a fridge, a toilet, and so many other things we used to consider necessities. Our cross-country trek had taught us they were privileges. When we finished unpacking, we heard a quiet knock on the door. We answered, and to our surprise, a stranger stood there, smiling shyly with eyes focused on the floor.

"Hi ... uh ... I'm Loren White, a church member here and ... uh, well ... I'm also an independent mechanic. And I was curious ... uh ... if anything on your van needs to work better." He attempted to make eye contact as he spoke, but his glance was brief before his gaze returned to the floor. He held his arms close to his body, his hands tucked deeply into his pockets.

"Something's terribly wrong with the steering," Megan said. "No matter how hard we try, we can't keep our van in the lanes very well."

"I can take a look at it and try to fix it." He handed her a piece of paper. "Here's my address. You can drive your van over and drop it off at my house," he said quietly, still looking down.

"Thank you! That would be amazing. Can we come by in about an hour?" Megan asked.

"Sure."

An hour passed, and we headed over to the address the man had given us. A lady with a big smile stood outside the house, her arms full of yellow Dollar General bags.

"I made you dinner, and here are some groceries for you," she said when we got out of the van.

"Thank you so much," I said, as we each took some of the bags.

Mr. White came out to work on our van. We had only talked with his wife a few minutes when he walked back over to us.

"It's all fixed, and, uh, no charge, of course. Easy fix, just tightened the steering belt," he said.

"Oh, thank you!" I clasped my hands beneath my chin as I spoke. "No more swerving across the highway."

"And no more cops." Megan whispered with a giggle.

After we ate dinner at the Whites' home, we headed back to the church. Each of us got the comfort of space to unwind throughout the day: Megan played one of the church's pianos, Sarah-Marie holed up in a Sunday school room to write, and I rested and talked on the phone with James in the air-conditioned apartment.

We stayed at the church's apartment for several peaceful days before my mom and dad arrived for a visit. They pulled up in their SUV, and we happily hugged them, delighted to have their company. After the rush of excitement had passed, I was surprised when the back door to the SUV opened, and out stepped Nick, my younger brother and college training partner.

"What are you doing here?" I asked while hugging him.

Nick laughed, his blue eyes twinkling. "I came to join your team and run with you." Nick, only a year younger than I was, had short, crisply cut blond hair. I consider him one of the greatest athletes and outdoorsmen I know. He is determined, loyal, and far more than my brother. We are extremely close. His joining our team brought me immediate comfort: if Nick was by my side, I could do anything.

A couple days passed, and Sunday arrived. Pastor Jim gave us each a few minutes to share about our role on the team. I sat on my hands to keep them from shaking and repeatedly attempted to stop folding and unfolding my speech notes. We each spoke for a couple minutes, marking the first speeches we'd given to an audience other than my launch speech. I looked down at the floor as I sat in the pew. *Almost a whole state has passed, and I've only spoken once. I thought Kansas would have been so much more hospitable and open to our message. I wonder if speaking will really be a part of Project If Life at all, or if it will mostly be running.*

I was brought back to attention by Pastor Jim's words: "I would like to take up a love offering for this team to help keep them on the road."

Baskets were passed up and down the rows, and with each pass, my discouragement decreased. After the service ended, Pastor Jim presented us with a check for four hundred dollars—the exact amount we had spent in faith on our tires. God clearly was in this project, and His provision required faith, but He never left us without provision.

After church, my parents prayed for us and our success. As I processed their departure, I was flooded with renewed appreciation for them. I had always loved them deeply, but seeing them entrusting us to God's care and what He had called us to do deepened my admiration for them. The run helped me understand that so much of the person I had become was rooted in their steadfast faith and dedication to God. After they finished praying for us, they got in their SUV. Tears welled up in my eyes as we waved and watched them drive away.

That evening we were invited to dinner at the Kelners' home. They lived in a quaint old farmhouse. Mrs. Kelner had prepared a feast of homemade potluck-like food. We served ourselves, eating leisurely around a long family table and enjoying casual conversation.

Toward the end of dinner, Mrs. Kelner asked, "You wanna play some Chicken Foot?"

"Play what?" I asked while discreetly smirking and glancing between Nick and Megan to see if they had ever heard of the game.

"Chicken Foot," Mr. Kelner explained. "It's kinda like Mexican Train, 'cept we're makin' connections of dominoes that look like chicken feet. Yuh make a connection, then yuh gotta cluck loud as yuh can—like a chicken."

The game sounded both terrifying and humiliating. After a couple quick rounds, I finally scored. "Yuh gotta cluck!" Mrs. Kelner said.

I looked up and forced a barely audible cluck out of my mouth.

"Boo! Boo! Boo!" was the unanimous response. "Cluck again," they demanded.

I swallowed and looked around the table about my fellow game players—a grin plastered on every face. "Cluck," I said, only a little louder, but with as much animation as I could muster.

The game continued. Each score was followed by a "Cluck! Cluck! Cluck!"—every one different and always followed by loud laughter. As the rounds passed, I chuckled along with everyone else. An urge to score again so I could cluck again bubbled inside me. When I scored again, I clucked almost as wildly and ridiculously as our hosts had done. My teammates also clucked outrageously, all of us laughing at ourselves and one another.

"Well, wasn' that a nice treat?" Mrs. Kelner said. "We're sad to see that the game has ended."

"It has been so nice, but we'd better be getting to bed because we have an early start in the morning," Megan answered.

"You're welcome back anytime. 'N if yuh need anything, just

let us know!" Mr. Kelner said with a warmth common to Midwesterners.

Outside, they loaded our van with bags of homegrown vegetables. Our hearts full and happy, we looked for a place to spend the night since our stay at the Bird City church was over. We weren't sure what to do for sleeping arrangements since we had a fourth person, and our bed barely slept three.

Nick simply unrolled his sleeping bag on the ground next to the van and went to sleep.

I stared at his sleeping arrangement, unable to fathom sleeping so exposed and unprotected, but he saw this was the only option and did what he had to do to make things work.

Nick's company extinguished my burning loneliness during runs, but more than that, he trained me. Meticulous, disciplined, and consistent, he put all his gifts to work. He introduced new warm-ups and required new stretches to ease the ever-increasing strain on my body.

Nick became not only my trainer but also my protector, which freed Megan and Sarah-Marie to be more productive since they no longer had to check on me every single mile. Nick was exactly what the team needed.

Several days later, we reached Goodland, our last stop in Kansas. Megan had arranged for us to stay with a couple, Mike and Roberta Bretz.

Mike was a gentle, tall man with a sense of humor. Roberta was wide-eyed, had a slim build, and perfect posture. She spent most of her nursing career working for the Red Cross doing emergency relief. We learned all about her travels at their kitchen table as we ate a pot roast dinner with carrots and potatoes.

In Eastern Colorado in mid-September 2016, my younger brother, Nick, introduced rope stretches and many other exercises to help my body be able to maintain distance running.

"This is the best food I've ever had." Eyes wide with delight, I helped myself to a second large portion—as much as my stomach could hold. Roberta smiled as I ladled seconds onto my plate.

After dinner, my team and I excused ourselves for bed. I showered, slept well in a comfy bed, and awoke energized for another run.

We were close to the Colorado-Kansas border that morning. Several miles passed, then rising from the horizon before us was a dense grove of pine trees, which looked misplaced among the fields. As we approached the thicket of trees, my heart leapt with joy. A beautiful sign made of dark wood logs read Welcome to Colorful Colorado. Nick and I ran straight up to the sign and hugged the large, wooden support posts.

"We made it! We made it! Four hundred miles all the way across Kansas without missing a single step," I shouted as I alternately hugged Nick and the posts supporting the sign. The smile on his face told me how proud he was. I couldn't believe it: I had run all the way across Kansas.

I sat next to the Kansas-Colorado border sign, my breathing still somewhat labored, but calming. I put my head in my hands and thanked God. I was humbled that He had brought me to this point. He had supplied our needs from the launch to this first milestone—even when I doubted Him, even when I feared.

5

FROM PLAINS TO PASSES

I was nervous as I continued to run.

Ahead of me were the Rocky Mountains, and, as a girl from the Kansas plains, I feared intense mountain running and the rise in elevation that was bringing me to them. The landscape of Eastern Colorado was similar to that of Kansas—flat and full of fields—with one main difference: an ever-increasing incline so subtle, it was almost imperceptible. Would my body be capable of carrying me across those towering mountains?

On our way to the Rockies, we spent several nights in various places—a church's pews, a gas-station parking lot, and a rest stop. We hadn't showered in days, so we were relieved to discover a lake in Flagler, Colorado, where we planned to swim and bathe.

We pulled off the highway, following our GPS as it led us down a long, winding gravel road. All our excitement for swimming and bathing vanished in a moment. The lake was dry. I stared in disappointed disbelief at what appeared to have been a beautiful boating and picnic area at one point in time but was now dried up, except for a little mud pond in the middle. It was almost eerie pulling up to an old boat ramp that led to acres of dried lakebed ringed by long, yellow grasses.

Our van chugged around the lake loop while we looked for a

spot to camp. We came upon a shelter that looked ancient, its peeling paint revealing extensive rust. The shelter was secluded and had a pleasant view of the former lake. I knew it would make a nice temporary home, so we set up camp. As we set up our tent, Sarah-Marie let Atticus off leash to roam free since there was no one around. He found his way to the muddiest part of the only water left in the lake and rolled in the mud. He came back smelling of putrefied water.

Outdoors, we didn't mind Atticus's stench or mud; we allowed him to run wild and free because he spent so much time in his crate. He found a stick and tried to get each of us to play an unending game of fetch. The only takers were Megan and Sarah-Marie.

After camp was set, we explored the area. Nick, an avid outdoorsman, was quick to find some edible food—prickly pear cactus. He called to me, "You wanna try?" His face lit up with his small, signature smile that he could never hide when he was really pleased by something.

A half-smile filled my face as I sat down beside him in the thick, long grasses. He wore his usual black handkerchief around his neck, a gray-and-red flannel shirt, and well-worn blue jeans. I watched him skin the cactus fruit with dexterity—the knife quickly removing the peel as he gently pulled it toward his thumb. A smile creased his face, his dark blond hair was goldened by excessive sunshine, and his blue eyes glimmered with the joy of being outdoors.

He reclined on one arm as he skinned the cactus, then handed some to me. "Here you go." I bit into its sweetness. My body absorbed the warmth of the September sun, while I relished the wilderness treat. Time seemed slow as we relaxed.

"Oh man!" I said after a few more bites. "I have thorns in my lip and tongue."

I walked back to the van, grabbed my eyebrow tweezers, and plucked the thorns from my mouth, using the side mirror of our van. Sarah-Marie and Megan chuckled at my predicament.

Darkness set in quickly. As we unpacked our tent, Nick pulled out our Coleman stove—a gift from my parents when we first set out. He opened it, and we cooked a meal of rice, beans, and spices that we dumped into a pot by the light of a lantern. The night had become unexpectedly cold and windy, and we shivered as we huddled around the minimal heat the small, two-burner stove provided. As Nick added various spices, he sprinkled the pepper with a heavy hand, and then left the mixture to boil while the spices married. After a while, he carefully ladled the rice goulash onto our blue tin plates. The delicious aroma filled my nose as the steam warmed my cold face. As I ate, the extra pepper burned in my throat in a way that almost felt like warmth in my body.

The starless evening became colder. We tightened our hoodies around our heads as protection against the brutal winds the plains are famous for. We could hardly hear each other, but I felt a deep sense of freedom in the vastness of the lonely prairie. We enjoyed the cool night air and the open sky as Nick's fingers attempted to pluck his guitar, despite the stiffening cold.

"Nick, are you ready to run?"

"Actually, I think I'm going to rest today to let my body adjust to the mileage better."

"Okay." I turned to Megan. "Would you take me out running today? I can run with Atticus."

"Sure."

Megan loaded Atticus into his crate, and we headed out in our van. I had gotten a late start that day and was eager to run. As we were driving, a horrible smell wafted forward.

"What is that awful smell?" Megan rolled down the driver's window.

"I think it's Atticus. I-I-I . . ." I gagged from the overwhelming stench. "I think he had diarrhea," I managed to croak as I tried to lower the passenger window. But it wouldn't budge.

Megan and I covered our noses and mouths with our shirts to help us not gag. Our faces contorted with disgust as we tried to inhale air through our covered mouths.

"What do we do? We have no water to wash him." Megan said.

"No kidding. And we certainly can't leave him that way." I scanned our surroundings as we drove along I-70 to my running spot. "Look, there's a farmhouse. Let's knock and see if they'll let us use their hose."

We pulled up, unloaded Atticus, and approached the front door. We knocked but received no answer other than several loud barks from seemingly large dogs. We waited, unsure if anyone would answer.

After a few moments, the door slowly opened revealing a kind-faced woman with styled blonde hair and a warm Midwestern smile. "What can I do for yah?" she said.

I held Atticus back by his collar from the other dogs while Megan explained the situation. "Our dog got diarrhea all over himself while we were driving. We are traveling and have no source of water to wash our dog. Is there any way we can use your hose?"

The lady studied Atticus and smiled. "You're welcome to use my hose." She gestured to the side of the house, smiled once more, and then shut the door.

We walked over to the side of her house and turned on the hose. We held Atticus tightly by the collar as the cold water washed over him. He was a nasty mess. As we struggled to wash him, the side door opened, and the lady came out with a bucket of warm, soapy water and towels.

"I'm Susan." She bent down to help us wash our smelly dog. We introduced ourselves to her as the three of us worked as a team —one holding Atticus, one soaping him, and one thoroughly rinsing him.

"Thank you so much for your extravagant kindness," I said. "It was so nice to have met you."

After many thanks, we loaded up Atticus and headed to my

run spot on a frontage road to I-70, because Highway 24 had converged with the interstate. Due to the late start and unplanned dog wash, I decided not to run with Atticus. Once we reached my run spot, I hopped out and Megan drove the van up the road a mile to wait for me.

Within minutes, I felt the sting of a mosquito bite and then another. After only a few more paces, I was swarmed. I picked up my pace, but the mosquitoes were not deterred as they continued to feast on my bare arms and legs. I ran faster on the frontage road as I flailed my arms to swat mosquitoes, smacking my hands up and down my arms and legs. My pace became unsustainable, but I knew to stop was to be bitten all over. Finally I called Megan, while still attempting to kill mosquitoes.

She answered with a casual "Hey! What's—"

"Megs! Pick me up now!" I hung up the phone and picked up my pace even more until the van came into view. My wait was extremely short. Breathlessly swatting myself, I hopped into the van. Megan's eyes were wide with curiosity.

"The mosquitoes are eating me alive!" I gasped for air and attempted to swat any remaining mosquitoes that might have made it inside. Covered in sweat and spotted with blood, I inspected my limbs for any remaining pests.

"I ran as fast as I could, but they were still biting me. Look!" I gestured at the window. "They're still waiting for me." The mosquitoes flew against the window, attempting to get to me. From the safety of the van, Megan and I watched the swarm. "They don't look like they're going to go away. I've only run about two miles but being eaten alive isn't worth it. Let's go back to camp."

"Okay." Megan shook her head and laughed.

When we returned to the campsite, Sarah-Marie approached us. "Could someone help me wash my hair with my Nalgene water bottle?"

"Of course," Megan said.

"Oh help me too, please!" I half begged.

Megan took the Nalgene and poured part of it over Sarah-Marie's head. She gasped with shock as the icy water gushed over her head. She then lathered her hair before Megan rinsed it as best as she could with the remaining water in the bottle. Megan then helped me through the same process, but she did not want to attempt to wash her thick, long hair with just a water bottle. Finally feeling clean, I crawled into my sleeping bag for the night.

The commute to the reservoir was soon too long, so we lived in our van again until we reached Limon, Colorado. Entering the town, we took in a glorious sight—the mountains! The plains ended abruptly, and the toothy, towering Rockies rose from the flatlands at what seemed to be a ninety-degree angle.

I had crossed five hundred miles of the great plains of the United States and had finally reached the Rocky Mountains that the subtle incline had long been hinting were coming. The fields spread wide and long with windmills branching off in every direction, their arms turning in massive circles. One thought replayed constantly in my mind as I crept through the foothills: the Rockies will bring a whole new sense of adventure with their challenges, beauty, and seclusion, but can my body run them?

As we crossed through the final foothills, Bill and Linda Wisener and their children, Nathan and Alisha, welcomed us into their home. Their kindness was amplified because it had been so long since we had been in a home. The shelter, food, and encouragement were therapeutic, making us forget the many long nights without beds, a roof over our heads, or the simple kindness of another person.

Many arduous miles lay ahead, and I did all I could to not fear them. I prayed for strength, for relief from fear, and for courage.

6
LIVING IN THE FOOTHILLS

I grabbed a Nespresso with cream and a slice of chocolate chip pumpkin bread before heading up to my room. The team and I had been on the road three months, living mostly in our van.

I had run almost all the way to Colorado Springs—over one hundred fifty miles into Colorado.

We were taking a week-long break at my Aunt Audrey's home in Loveland, Colorado, a few hours north of where I had been running. Her home was a lovely lodge seated on the side of a mountain with ten-foot windows sculpted to take in the mountain views.

My own room! What a rare luxury.

I reveled in the comfort of the sheets, the softness of the bed, but most of all, the privacy from my teammates. The first night I journaled and read my Bible for a while before FaceTiming James. He answered with a huge smile.

"I got your letters." I said, holding them so he could see. "They had a little trouble getting here but thank you so much for sending them. And they smell so good!"

I held them to my nose and breathed in the warm, woodsy scent of the cologne he had sprayed generously on each one.

James laughed, clearly delighted to make me so happy. "I'm so glad you got them. I've really miss you. I so wish I weren't in school, so I could come and see you."

"Me too," I sighed.

Our stay at my Aunt Audrey and Uncle Steve's home was paradise.

I slept in as late as I wanted without having to worry about someone next to me, then I descended the wide split-log staircase into the spacious kitchen.

Awaiting me each morning was chocolate chip pumpkin bread, Greek yogurt, fresh fruit, and a dozen choices of Nespresso pods for espresso.

The five-star resort ambiance continued throughout the day and into the evening. My aunt prepared a gourmet dinner each night—everything from chicken with capers to a roast followed by an incredible dessert of apple pie or fruit and Nutella-filled crepes.

We swapped stories with Aunt Audrey, Uncle Steve, and Cousin Kaleb, laughing about the crazy things that had happened during our trip.

The break and rest were much needed, but the visit also had hidden blessings.

Uncle Steve was an avid mountaineer. Climbing a different 14,000-foot mountain each year was one of his goals. He pulled out several topographical maps to help me route through the mountains.

Pointing to the northern route on a map, I said, "We were thinking about taking Interstate 70 through northern Colorado."

"You could, but if you take Highway 50 through southern Colorado, the elevation of the passes may be lower." Looking at the maximum elevation of each pass, he added, "And you would avoid being on an interstate. Looks like the highest elevation you'd face would be 11,312 feet at Monarch Pass."

"That's still pretty high." I paused and forced a smile. "But I'm glad that the elevation will be lower than the passes along I-70."

From Left to Right: Megan, Nick, Sarah-Marie, and Anna. We visited Estes Park in late September while staying at my Aunt Audrey's home in Loveland, Colorado.

After a lot of rest, good company, and much-needed advice, the team and I said a reluctant goodbye. As we headed back to our route, we needed a place to spend the night, so we drove up the mountains near Denver and parked at a pull-off along the roadside.

As we settled in, I realized I had to use the restroom. Every restroom we found was closed, so we chose some thick trees next to a country club. Megan told me she had to go too, so we headed toward the trees on a steep hill. We climbed until we were deep enough in the trees to be hidden from the road. Pulling up my pants, I hooked a cedar branch, breaking a bunch of needles off. "Aw, Megs," I said, "I got tons of pine needles in my underwear."

Megan burst out laughing. "I'm sorry!"

"It's okay." Her laughter eased my annoyance and I laughed too. It was funny, but it was also painfully uncomfortable.

We drove back to the pull-off that sat high above Denver. We sat for a while and stared down at the city, almost entranced as the city lights twinkled a thousand ways. The darkness made it difficult to tell exactly where we were parked, but we were close to the highway, and the hum of traffic lulled me to sleep quickly.

When we awoke the next morning, we discovered we had camped next to some woods with a rushing stream. We ate pancakes prepared on our Coleman stove, then each of us grabbed books, journals, and Bibles and headed down to the side of the stream. I sat in the lovely pine-needle carpeted dirt and propped my journal and Bible open on my knees. The sun warmed my skin and the stream's gurgles and murmurs relaxed me.

Suddenly, a woman's voice yelled from the other side of the stream. "Get off my property! Don't you know you're trespassing?" She scowled and waved her arms at us. "Move your van and get out of here now!"

Her harsh words and menacing gestures made me feel like I wasn't even human—just a stray dog being chased from someone's property.

We packed up and left.

Later that day, we stopped at Front Range Baptist Church, pastored by Jeff Redlin. Megan had coordinated a presentation there, and I was eager to share about the pro-life movement with the high school students. But when I stared at the room full of high schoolers, my legs felt weak and my mouth dry as my hands trembled.

"Life in the womb is an incredible miracle that God has planned. Each person has a unique DNA from the moment of conception that is distinct from the mom and dad. At just eighteen days, a baby's heart starts beating, before the mom knows she's pregnant." I held up a twelve-week fetal model measuring just over two inches. "At twelve weeks, a baby can already hiccup, move around, kick, and stretch. All its organs, bones, and muscles in place. Isn't that amazing?"

I continued. "Life in the womb is a beautiful miracle, and something to celebrate, but in our country it is legal to kill these innocent children. Abortion violently and intentionally takes the life of an innocent child every single time." I chose my words carefully, knowing that someone in the room may have had an abortion.

After my speech, we headed back to Colorado Springs where we had several meetings lined up. Our first meeting was with Carrie Gordon Earll from Focus on the Family. She led us to a room, where we sat around a long conference table.

"Tell me about your ministry," she said.

"Our goal is to educate and activate people into the pro-life movement." I felt proud of our ministry as I explained our mission to a Focus on the Family staff member. The organization had been a part of my life for as long as I could remember—my parents had read several books published by Focus on the Family, and my siblings and I had listened to *Adventures in Odyssey* every night before bed when we were children.

The team and I talked with Mrs. Earll about God's provision and our hope to end abortion. Mrs. Earll was motherly, wise, and kind when she spoke, "We need to be patient as we work to end abortion. There will be a lot of steps, but I know we can succeed."

She concluded our meeting with prayer, which encouraged and strengthened me.

At our next event, we prayed outside a Planned Parenthood clinic with a group called 40 Days for Life. We prayed in silence for an hour. Some drivers blared their horns and screamed profanities as they passed. The wind blew steadily, and the moment felt somber as we begged God to protect the preborn lives that Planned Parenthood intended to take that day.

When we finished praying, a man who had been praying with the group approached us. "I'm a volunteer for the local 40 Days for Life group, Joel Patchen, and I run my own pro-life ministry called Anna's Choice."

We introduced ourselves and told him about our journey.

"Your team is welcome to stay with my wife and me if you need a place," he said.

"That would be an answer to prayer!" Megan replied.

Joel's home was large and welcoming. Once we were settled in, we discussed our work to defend the preborn.

"Let me show you the books I've written," Joel said as he pulled them out. "Oh, and this one's a devotional." Sarah-Marie, Megan, and I flipped through them eagerly.

"You wrote all these?" Sarah-Marie asked. "This is amazing."

"I love the work you're doing." Sarah-Marie said. "I wish people understood the importance of fighting for the equality of the preborn. It is the greatest human rights violation of our time, and yet people won't talk about it."

"Yeah, if people actually knew what an abortion is, they would be horrified and immediately become pro-life. Once people are educated on the beauty of life in the womb, their hearts and minds change. That's why I speak every chance I get. I want everyone to know how wrong abortion is and what they can do to end it," I said with a warm, passionate tone.

We spent hours talking and looking at the pro-life books Joel had written and discussing the importance of the pro-life movement.

While staying with Joel and his wife, Megan arranged a meeting with Save the Storks, one of our favorite pro-life organizations. Their mission is to partner with women to help them choose life and have the resources to do so. One of my favorite aspects of their ministry is their Stork Buses—mobile medical units used to perform ultrasounds to show the humanity of the preborn.

We drove to their offices where we met with a team member named Abigail Saunders. She listened as we talked about our ministry and then told us about their ministry.

"Do you want to see a stork bus?" she asked.

"Yes, please!" Sarah-Marie said. She had been following Save the Storks for a long time and was a big fan.

Abigail brought us outside to see a Stork Bus.

"Wow!" Each team member echoed my amazement, stunned by the bus's immaculate, beautiful, and practical setup.

Abigail looked pleased. "The units enable pregnancy centers to give free pregnancy tests and free ultrasounds. We also help women through unplanned pregnancies." As she spoke, she handed us some flyers, and we marveled at how attractive and professional they were.

"I love your work," Sarah-Marie said. "It's beautifully done, inspiring, and really makes a huge difference in creating a culture that values life. It's amazing that women in need can come to you for free pregnancy tests, ultrasounds, and STI testing."

"Thank you. We partner with pregnancy centers so they can bring their Stork Buses to the front steps of the abortion clinics. That way women in crisis pregnancies can see that they actually have options and support no matter their circumstances."

Before we left, Abigail let us pick out t-shirts and stickers. They were all so lovely, which made it hard to choose. I felt so honored to represent such an amazing organization.

After our visit to Save the Storks, we headed back to Colorado Springs to my run spot. As Nick and I ran along the highway, cars whizzed past at what should have been alarming speeds, but my mind was distracted. I had so many miles to run before I reached California. "One more mile," I told myself, "and you can quit forever. Think about that—never having to run another step." To my surprise, the encouragement worked, and a mile passed. Realizing the importance of focusing on one mile at a time, I repeated this encouragement again and again.

We ran through Colorado Springs faster than I expected, but the city seemed to cling to us as we commuted from there to my run route on Highway 50 for several weeks. Walmart parking lots became our nightly and hospitable home: a bathroom available all night long, the safety of industrial floodlights, and a place to buy food.

One night Nick and I laid out our mats for our workout.

"Tonight is arm night, Anna," he said as he handed me two ten-pound weights.

"Oh good. I love arm day!" And I did—core or leg day was much harder. As we worked out, other people in the parking lot stared at us, but that didn't faze me. Van-life felt normal.

Our workout was hard, but just what I needed.

Seeing that we were finished, Megan called from the back of the van, "Are you guys ready for dinner?"

"Yep, I'm starved!" I said. "It's so nice to be done exercising for the day, and I love Walmart meals."

We headed into Walmart and purchased a five-dollar rotisserie chicken along with an assortment of sides. We feasted in the back of our van off paper plates and enjoyed one another's conversation and company.

Dinner ended, and we laid out our sleeping bags before grabbing our toiletry bags and heading into the Walmart bathroom. Sarah-Marie, Megan, and I brushed our teeth, washed our faces, used the restroom, and cleaned ourselves with baby wipes for bed. It had been a week since our last shower, and we felt it. As I looked in the mirror, I saw my skin was darkened with caked-on dirt, my forehead, neck, and arms had a coat of dried salty-sweat, and my hair was full of grease. I smelled horrible, and I hoped no one else could smell me.

Back in the parking lot, Sarah-Marie looked at Megan and me and said, "My hair is so greasy. I need to wash it."

"Me too," I sighed. "I feel so gross, and my hair is literally clumped with oil."

"Let's use our Nalgene water bottles again to wash our hair," she said.

"Definitely!" We moved our van to the back of the parking lot for some privacy. Sarah-Marie went first. Once I had finished her hair, she and Megan helped me with mine. Once done, I felt so refreshed. My hair was squeaky clean and oil-free; my face was no longer stiff with dried sweat.

We moved our van back to the front of the parking lot, loaded Atticus into his crate, and crawled into our sleeping bags. Nick set his up on the roof for the night, feeling safer there than on the ground since we were in a populated area.

As we fell asleep, the smell of marijuana filled the air as open-doored vans around us emitted smoke. The scent usually disgusted me, but the odor's presence each evening was beginning to feel normal.

A few nights later, we decided to spend the night in a park instead of a Walmart parking lot. We set out Atticus's crate and laid a blanket inside. He curled up contentedly as we covered his crate with a tarp for extra warmth and to keep him dry from possible rain. Nick set his sleeping bag on the ground next to Atticus' crate.

We felt uncomfortable as people in nearby homes stared at us—four young adults clearly living in a van. We did our best to ignore their scrutiny and continued our routine. We grabbed our toothbrushes, toothpaste, and our Nalgene water bottles for rinsing. A few paces from the van, we brushed our teeth and rinsed before going to bed for the night. Once settled, I fell asleep almost instantly.

Morning came unexpectedly early: an abrupt rapping on our back van window. I sat up and opened the van door. The door was hardly open when screams from an older lady with a thick New Zealand accent rattled me. "How could you leave your dog in the rain all night?" Her eyes blazed with fury as her arms made wide, angry gestures.

"He has a tarp over him to keep him dry and a blanket to keep him warm." I said, exhausted and somewhat confused.

She kept screaming as if I had not spoken, her voice rising in intensity with each more impassioned point. "How incredibly irresponsible! What if I put you outside to sleep in the rain?"

I looked at her, still startled and groggy. "My younger brother slept outside in the cold rain on the ground without a fur coat, a large crate, or a tarp."

She continued screaming again as if she hadn't heard a word of my answer. "This is unacceptable! This is abusive! How could you be so cruel to a helpless animal?" Her gray hair bobbed as her rage spilled over.

"We're not from here. We're just passing through and then moving on," I said, hoping to cool her volcanic temper. But she continued to rant, so I stopped responding and merely waited for her to finish.

She concluded with a calmer though still threatening tone as if trying to control herself. "I come here every day to walk, and I will call the police if I ever see you here again." Then she stormed off.

Her rage had awakened everyone in the van. Nick sat in the front passenger seat in his sleeping bag. He turned around with his hair sticking up and his eyes only partly open. "She yelled at me first, but I quickly realized she wasn't there to have a discussion. She just wanted to yell, so I shut the door, hoping she wouldn't wake you guys. That's when she went around and knocked on your door to scream at you too." Nick's eyes looked puffy, and he yawned as he finished explaining, "I told her I slept outside too. I only crawled in the van fifteen minutes ago to get out of the rain since Atticus has our only tarp."

I looked out in the direction the woman had taken and received another glare from the one who had failed to see the true plight that surrounded her: people who had no homes, no showers, little money, no beds, and dwindling courage. She had missed what should have struck her heart. She took up the cause of our dog, while there were four people who needed much and had little.

If she had offered kind words, they would have helped fuel us to continue our journey for the preborn. This snare grabs many people. Satan sets up causes before people that seem deeply noble (and aren't bad), but they miss the bigger picture. Just as that woman cared more for one dog than four humans, so many are distracted by other causes and miss the millions killed by abortion every year.

"Let's get some good coffee somewhere," Sarah-Marie said, pulling me from my thoughts and trying to ease the stress of the morning. She considered coffee a cure-all, and I agreed with her.

Megan searched for coffee shops on her phone and said, "There's one called Agia Sophia. "Want to try it?"

"Sure." Nick started up the van engine and pulled out of the park. Megan directed him until we reached the shop. We pulled into the gravel parking lot of an old stone building with green awnings over the front windows. The place was decorated in a homey way and reflected the extraordinary beauty and charm of the Russian Orthodox faith.

I ordered a large mocha in a handmade mug along with a Greek panini. I followed a flight of stairs and found a perfect nook on a snuggly couch. Eager to be alone, I pulled out my Bible and began to read. Sarah-Marie, Nick, and Megan each found their own rooms and spaces to read and journal. The barista brought my mocha and panini, and I was soon lost in the bliss of relaxation.

Agia Sophia seemed like it couldn't get any better, and then it did. We found out that they played live Irish music on Wednesday nights. Our family listened to Irish music during our weekly Sunday brunches, so we decided to return on Wednesday to enjoy the music.

Little did we know the fear we would face after our next visit.

7

JOY, THEN TERROR

I rish music filled the air as Megan, Nick, and I sipped our delicious coffee. I held a mug of hot mocha in my hands and gently nodded my head to the rhythms. The old building throbbed with the lively music as people played flutes, violins, accordions, and bagpipes without sheet music. With every note, the joyful music took me deep into sweet memories of being home with my family—all of us together, enjoying our Sunday brunches.

While we relaxed and enjoyed the music at Agia Sophia, Sarah-Marie was in the van gasping for breath. She was so sick she thought she might die there alone.

When Nick, Megan, and I returned to the van, Sarah-Marie was lying in the back of the van.

"Do you feel okay?" Megan asked.

"Now I do. I was having trouble breathing, but it's fine now," Sarah-Marie responded, her voice weak and whispery.

"You look pale and exhausted," Megan said.

"Yeah. A few moments ago, I didn't know if my lungs would open back up and I'd be able to breathe again, but I'll be okay, really" Sarah-Marie said firmly, her raised eyebrows making it clear she wanted to be done with the conversation.

I went to sleep wondering if she would be okay but not

knowing what more I or any of the other team members could do for her.

A few days passed, and Sarah-Marie had no other breathing attacks. We asked how she was feeling and breathing, but every time she said, "I'm fine." We all settled back into our routine until Megan insisted on driving several hours out of our way to see her friend Grace from first grade. Megan never asked for anything, so we all agreed to go see her friend.

We drove the several hours to our meeting spot, Subway. As we walked in, I felt a bit shy about meeting a stranger, which caused me to gulp a couple of times. I tried to ignore my nervousness and slid into a booth. We waited a while, then the door opened and there stood one of my closest college friends, Allison Isola.

"No way! No way!" I jumped up from the booth, ran to Alli, and hugged her so tight she nearly lost her balance. "How is this possible? You're not Grace."

"I wanted to surprise you!" she said.

"How did you even make this possible?" I studied Alli's and Megan's faces.

"We've been planning for weeks," Megan said. "She's going to stay with us for several days."

It was late, so we headed to a hotel a church had purchased for us. We figured out sleeping arrangements and slept comfortably.

In the morning, Alli asked, "Do you guys want to get pedicures? My treat."

"We'd love to!" I said. "What a luxury." Nick and Sarah-Marie decided to remain at the hotel while Alli, Megan, and I went to get pedicures.

Our day was full of laughs and reminiscing from our college days—a much-needed break from our life on the road. That evening, we entered the Paint Mines Interpretive Park, which featured all sorts of sandy white, yellow, and red rock formations and tunnels.

After a full day of climbing, hiking, and exploring, we headed back to our van. After supper, we set water on the stove to boil for hot cocoa and set out our sleeping bags to enjoy the starlit sky. We girls sipped our hot cocoa as Nick lightly strummed his guitar. Undimmed by city lights, the bright stars shone like twinkling Midwestern fireflies, and I saw shooting stars shoot across the sky. The Milky Way spread across the darkness like a brilliant tapestry.

"There are so many shooting stars tonight," I said staring up at the sky.

"Really?" Alli said. Her eyes widened with excitement. "I've never seen one before."

"Keep watching, and I'm sure you'll see one."

When another shooting star crossed the sky, Alli gasped, "Oh wow! I saw that one." With childlike joy, she searched for another one.

"Make a wish," I said, then laughed.

We spent several more packed days of getting in my runs and spending time with Alli before we took her to the airport. Alli had brought so much joy and love to our team. We all felt refreshed, especially me.

The sun set as we headed to our run spot. Nick and I almost never ran at night for safety reasons, but this night was an exception to make up for lost time. After we were dropped off at the road, we both placed lights on each arm, a headlamp on our heads, and flashing lights on our CamelBaks. The traffic was heavy, and we wanted to be visible.

The night seemed to be especially dark—there were no streetlamps, no visible moon, and even the stars seemed hidden. Something about the cool, ominous night air made us run faster and without conversation.

As we ran in the darkness, a huge, black truck aggressively swerved over onto the shoulder ahead of us, stopped, then quickly reversed toward us. Nick and I stopped dead in our tracks, and I put my arm over my eyes to shield them from the truck's blinding rear lights.

The truck continued to back up until we were even with the passenger window. Two large, muscular men in their late forties with shaved heads and tattoos locked eyes with me but said nothing.

As if by instinct, I took two steps toward the truck and launched into why we were running across America. "Hi. We're running across America for the-the-the—" I trailed off as I saw a terrifying expression in their eyes, as if they were going to kidnap me. My stomach dropped with fear, and my body trembled. They continued to stare at me in silence as I stood frozen in fear.

Nick defensively stepped between me and the truck, breaking my eye contact with the men. Their eyes shifted toward him, their expressions haughty and threatening. Nick returned their gaze as if a silent, intense battle was raging between them. The stare-down continued. My heart pounded so loud it echoed in my ears.

Finally, and unexpectedly, they sped away.

We ran for a while before Nick turned to me and asked through pursed lips and clenched teeth, "Why did you run up to the truck?"

"I ... I ... I just thought they were like anyone else asking about our mission and why we were out running."

To my horror, I saw the same black truck approaching us from the opposite direction. It was clear they meant to stop just ahead of us on the road, but we were saved by enough vehicles going westbound that they couldn't pull over. Nick looked at me but said nothing.

My heart throbbed in my ears once more and sweat poured down my forehead, but I kept running, terrified the men would come back and take me. Nick's whole body was tense. I could sense he was thinking the same thing.

I tried to brush aside my terror. "Maybe they were only turning around?"

Nick shrugged as we ran. Deep down, I knew that wasn't true.

With each step, I shook my arms from my shoulders down to my hands repeatedly trying to loosen myself from the grip of fear, but even as I did, the truck made another slow pass. But again, several cars forced the truck driver to keep moving.

The truck went out of sight yet again, and my body began to feel immovable, almost as if each limb was an unbearable weight and impossible to propel forward. It was the same petrifying fear that overcame me when I was almost taken in Pensacola.

Nick and I decided to take a snack break under the shelter of a small tree about two hundred feet from the road. We shut off our lights, ran to the tree, and hunkered down. From our position under the tree, we could see the road, but no one on the road could see us. Between labored breaths, I took small bites of a granola bar and swallowed before taking in another needed gasp of air.

After only a few moments, the truck drove by slowly. As soon as it was out of sight, Nick jumped up and broke off a large, dead tree branch, determined to put up a fight if they returned to harm us.

He sat next to me and said, "Let's wait here and see if they pass again. If they don't, we can keep running."

We waited, but no truck appeared.

Still, we waited.

After a long while, Nick said, "I think they're gone. Let's keep running."

We turned on our lights and began to run again. Nick carried his branch. Only a few steps in, Nick saw a two-foot copper pole about an inch in diameter on the ground. It was hollow and light, yet sturdy and strong. He dropped his branch and carried the pole.

For a while, no cars passed us, but then a steady stream of cars appeared and passed us going eastbound—the opposite way we were going. I watched the cars pass, fearful of the black truck's reappearance.

Then I saw it. Just ahead of us in a pull-off on the opposite side of the road sat the black truck.

The truck's floodlights shone brightly, and its engine rumbled loudly. The driver was ready to pull out, but a long line of cars made that impossible. Nick ran a bit stiffly, and I could tell he had seen them. He quickened his pace. I followed suit.

We continued to run, taking advantage of the traffic, until the truck was out of sight. Without slowing down, Nick instructed me with an even tone, "Turn off all your lights."

We shut off our lights, and I hid mine in my CamelBak. He then led the way off the road about two hundred feet until we reached a barbed-wire fence that ran parallel with the highway.

Nick turned to me and said gruffly, "Hop the fence." I put my foot on the rail, and he boosted me over. My leg scraped the barbed wire, and blood flowed down my shin. On the other side, I trembled as I waited for Nick to climb over. When I met his gaze, his expression was stern.

He wasn't coming.

"Anna, you hunker down here and don't make a noise. If the truck comes by again, run. Don't look back. Just run as far and as fast as you can." The intensity of his tone scared me.

I choked back sobs.

"I will die before I let them get to you." His voice was taut. He then turned around and started walking back to the side of the road. Once he reached the shoulder, he turned on all his lights and waited for the truck's return, the copper rod in his hand.

My body still shook, but somehow reason returned. I took off my CamelBak and pulled out my phone. I dialed Megan. As the phone rang, I glanced over my shoulder and saw Nick next to the side of the road, his lights flashing. The phone rang several long moments before Megan picked up.

"Megs! Pick us up. Pick us up now!" In as few words as I could, I described where we were.

I shoved my phone back in my pack as quickly as I could to hide its light. In the dark, I shakily sang Psalm 91—the one that had helped me through my bad dreams now calmed me in a real-life nightmare. In a half-cry, half-whisper I repeated, "I will not fear the terror of the night, nor the arrow that flies at noonday. I will not fear the arrow of the night." Over and over I repeated, "I will not fear. Oh, God. I will not fear." My whole body trembled. "I will not fear. I will not fear. I will not fear" (NIV).

As I waited, I focused on Nick's silhouette. Terrible images of him taking on the men filled my mind. A large vehicle headed toward Nick.

In an instant, I recognized it: Megan had come. I scrambled over the fence, and we rushed to the van and hopped in. I was too shocked and breathless to tell her what had happened. Nick didn't volunteer an explanation either. He was pouring sweat and still stiff as he set down his copper rod in the van and turned off his lights once more.

My body trembled as I fumbled for my seatbelt. I tried to click it into place but missed. I sniffed in tears that had made their way into my nose and finally clicked the seatbelt into place. I closed my eyes and leaned back against the headrest of my seat.

I will not fear the terror of the night, nor the arrow that flies at noonday. I breathed in and then out slowly calming myself. *Your rod and your staff, they comfort me.* God, thank you for your protection. Now please bring your comfort. I need it now.

8

THE MOUNTAINS

"I'm gonna call an ambulance!" I yelled to Megan. "I don't know how long she'll be able to breathe!"

"No!" Sarah-Marie gasped, then continued her spastic attempts to inhale. "I'm fine" was barely distinguishable.

Sarah-Marie lay in the bed of our van. Her breathing became more strained, and her chest rose quickly, though with difficulty.

"Megs, Nick, what do you think?" I said.

"I don't know," said Megan.

"I'm fine," Sarah-Marie gasped again.

We waited, stressed and unsure if we should listen to her as she struggled for air. Ten minutes passed before her breathing became calmer, but still strained.

Finally, her breaths returned to a normal rhythm. "See?" she whispered, her voice wispy. "I really am fine."

Though the attack had passed, I was terrified of another one. She had told us about her first one when she stayed at the van instead of listening to the Irish music at the coffee shop, but none of us had thought it was as severe as what we had just witnessed.

"How many breathing attacks have you had?" I asked.

She glared at us, clearly not wanting to talk about it. "Several, but I'm fine now."

"Are you, though?" Megan asked.

"What if an attack happens and we're somewhere secluded, and it's worse than this one?" My harsh tone was edged with fear.

"There won't be a doctor or help as we get further from the city," Megan said. The words came out slowly, her voice thick with emotion. Her eyebrows knit closer, showing it pained her to go against her non-confrontational nature.

After some deliberation, we agreed Sarah-Marie should go home in a rental car along with Atticus so he would not have to live in a van anymore. The goodbye was bitter. She had been with us through it all: the homelessness, the hardship, and the hurt. Although we all felt her absence, Megan felt it most, as Sarah-Marie was her coffee shop and work companion. We were now a team of three, and Sarah-Marie's role of running the website and writing articles and blogs would be impossible to fill.

I battled many emotions as we drove to Walmart that night. Did we do the right thing? Will Sarah-Marie be okay driving home alone?

We spoke little to each other as we pulled into the parking lot and drove around trying to find the darkest place to sleep, away from other vehicles. We worked out, then grabbed our toiletries bags and went inside Walmart to use the restroom and brush our teeth. Shoulders slumped, Megan and I entered the women's restroom. We both brushed our teeth and Megan stared at the floor, her eyebrows still knit with sadness.

While we were brushing our teeth, a woman and her about six-year-old son walked by to the bathroom stalls.

He looked at Megan and me. "Mommy, why are they brushing their teeth?"

My stomach dropped with embarrassment, and I wrapped my free arm around my torso, as if to make myself smaller, or to disappear. I looked at my hair that was so greasy it stayed back in its French braid with a disheveled ease. *I look homeless, and I bet they can tell I haven't showered.* I stared at myself in the mirror; I just was not in a good enough mood to handle an insult, even if it was from a six-year-old.

She raised her eyebrows, widened her eyes, and scoldingly said to him, "Don't you brush your teeth?"

Her response brought warmth to my heart as she protected us from scrutiny of a life we knew wasn't normal or pretty.

In Walmart, we grabbed groceries as well as six bottles of pepper spray. Looking at me and Megan, Nick said, "You each need to carry one at all times, and we'll use the other ones to practice with."

As we settled in for the night, Nick set up his bed in the van for the first time. As he positioned his sleeping bag to my left on the passenger's side, he said, "What if we sleep opposite each other so there's more room? I could sleep with my head by your feet, Anna."

"Good idea," Megan said. She placed her sleeping bag opposite mine on the driver's side of the bed. I placed my brownish-red sleeping bag between them and snuggled into it.

I wasn't aware any time had passed before someone rapped loudly on the back of our van. Terrified, Nick and I sat up. It was 6:00 a.m. I moved the striped bath towel that we used as a curtain and saw two police cars had blocked us in. One police officer was outside our door. Nick opened the back van door, and we both leaned out.

"You must move your van. People are no longer allowed to sleep in Walmart parking lots," the officer said through tight lips.

"Really?" Nick said, trying to stifle a yawn. "We're sorry. We thought they let people camp overnight in them."

"Used to be allowed, but people have begun to live in them indefinitely, so some Walmarts changed what they allow."

Nick and I apologized, then he climbed out of the open van door. I followed behind him. We walked to the front of the van, waited for the officers to unblock our van, then climbed in the front. We moved enough stuff from the front two seats to squeeze into the driver seat and passenger seat. Megan lay in the back, half asleep. Nick drove to another parking lot, where we went back to sleep for a few hours.

Before breakfast, we rearranged the luggage that filled our seats back to the bed. Nick set the stove on the end of our bed to cook. Soon we were enjoying Kodiak pancakes with chocolate chips and homemade peach syrup. Our strong percolator coffee cut the sweetness of the pancakes.

After breakfast, we set out to take care of several errands. Nick asked, "Could we buy a bike today? I hurt my knee on that forty-mile run we did in college. It was fine for a while, but now it's hurting again."

"Of course," I said. Megan nodded. Nick never complained, so for him to say something about pain meant it was serious. We went to Dick's Sporting Goods and found a suitable bike—somewhere between a road bike and a mountain bike.

"I think I'll have to alternate between running and biking from now on to help my knee," he said to me.

Our next errand was mail pickup. We had asked people to send mail to a nearby post office. That day we received an unexpected gift package from our friend, Lisa Drake, who had supplied running clothes throughout our journey. Inside the box we found ear warmers, long-sleeved running jackets along with running leggings, gloves, and socks—exactly what we needed since fall and winter were fast approaching.

Days of running passed, and the terrain became even steeper. Tough hills made my heart pound, and the ever-growing elevation and October weather made my lungs pant for air. Prairie dogs darted in and out of their holes all over the desert landscape, and scrubby, green brush as well as cacti dotted the contoured desert land.

We were surrounded by mountains and felt like true athletes braving the Rockies. We ran through Cañon City and beyond it. One day, Nick pedaled his bike ahead of me. We had left all buildings behind us—nothing lay ahead but Highway 50 and the mountains.

After ten tough miles, my legs burned and my limbs felt heavy. Nick seemed to be slowing as his legs struggled to propel his bike forward. The terrain had shortened our initial goal, and I felt bad calling Megan away from her work early, especially since she had Wi-Fi and cell service at the coffee shop where she was working in Cañon City. She was always extremely productive—scheduling churches for me to speak at and possible places for us to stay as well as balancing finances and tracking gas and food receipts.

When I stopped my Runkeeeeper GPS, I realized I had no way to let Megan know we were done. "No cell signal," I told Nick.

"We'll have to hitchhike back," he said. "Might be an hour or two before she comes looking for us."

"Let's run up to the pull-off ahead so cars will have an easier time picking us up. We might have to wait a while, but it should still be quicker than waiting for Megan."

At the pull-off, we put our thumbs up in the air. We were surprised when a black truck pulled up alongside us. The driver rolled down his window and asked, "Are you heading to Cañon City? I'm headed that way."

Nick loaded his bike on the back, and we both got in the cab. The driver was a large-built, balding man in his mid-thirties with a bushy, brown beard.

"How did you end up so far from Cañon City with only one bike?"

"I biked as she ran," Nick said.

"Wow! That sure's a long way." He chuckled, his eyes wide with animation.

After we explained the reason for our journey, the man did most of the talking for the remainder of the drive—mostly about growing marijuana and hating litter.

He dropped us off along Highway 50 back in Cañon City.

"Oh no, Nick, we are still a couple miles from the coffee shop."

"Really?" Nick looked around at the semi-familiar scenery. "Oh, yeah, I guess you're right. How about you stand on the back of my bike, and we can ride together?" Nick said.

I laughed nervously. "How about I pedal, and you do the balancing?"

He hopped on the back, and we rode all the way back to Megan, looking like a two-man circus and laughing hysterically most of the way.

The next day was Sunday, so we went to a local church, Calvary. The church family was kind and knew my boyfriend James' family well. They took care of us in so many ways—giving us food, money, and kindness. Pastor McDonald invited us to eat with him at any restaurant we chose, but he understood when we told him we were exhausted and needed to rest.

We grabbed coffee and donuts and headed to a graveyard. On our trip across America, we discovered that people don't bother you at a graveyard no matter how odd you look, maybe because they think you're grieving. I found a shady spot for our large sleeping bag. A warm breeze flitted through the graveyard, making the trees sway in a gentle rhythm.

We enjoyed our treats in the warm, fall weather, then I lay down to rest. I was deep asleep in a matter of moments. When I awoke, I took in the stillness of the graveyard; the only noise was the gentle rustling of the deep, green grass between the tombstones. The dappled sunlight hitting the stones and grass was beautiful.

We van-camped that night and awoke the next day determined to run hard. I would turn twenty-three the next day, and we planned to take a few days off to celebrate. As we ran, the mountains felt like great walls closing us in on two sides as they towered over us. When we had run fifteen miles, we stopped along the side of Highway 50—proud, breathless, and weary.

Megan picked us up, and we decided to spend the night at a pull-off next to the highway. We found one that looked semi-private and large, so we pulled over next to a large boulder. The Arkansas River wound along Highway 50 where we parked. A steep, rocky bank led down to the water, and we clambered down the bank, keeping low to the ground for balance until we made it to the water. One dip of my toes convinced me that the rushing water was too cold for a pleasant swim, so I contented myself with wading.

Nick, however, was going under and coming up for air over and over in the rushing water before I had waded past my ankles.

"Really, Anna? You're not going to swim?" he asked with teeth chattering and half a smile, trying to make the frigid water look enticing. Then addressing both Megan and me, he said, "You get used to it so fast, and it's so refreshing. Don't be wimps." He looked back at me. "Come on, you're running across America, and you won't go for a swim?"

He begged until finally Megan and I went in together. The strong current made it difficult to keep our balance. My body broke out in goosebumps as I waded into the rushing water until it was just above my waist. I crossed my arms for warmth and prepared to go under, knowing Nick would never be satisfied until I did.

After several deep breaths to get up the courage to plunge myself below the surface, I dropped into the painfully cold water. The forceful current almost took me with it as I pushed myself upward toward the surface. My lungs gasped for air, as if the wind had been knocked out of me. Megan was in a similar state as we soggily made our way back to shore. Meanwhile, Nick was still blissfully bobbing in and out of the water, pleased we had joined him.

When evening came, the temperature dropped, so we set up our Coleman stove and made hot soup out of the assortment of items stored in our food tubs. With our pot sitting over our Coleman's crackling blue flame, we poured in a mixture of instant rice, canned chicken, and lots of pepper for its pseudo warmth.

We ate in the back of our van, huddled with blankets around our shoulders. As we spooned the last bits of hot soup into our hungry, cold bodies, we started a pot of hot water to enjoy apple cider. Sipping the hot cider, we soon felt warm enough to again become adventurous. We remembered a boulder protruding from the Arkansas River and made our way to it. Water ran on either side of it, but it was still close enough to shore for us to crawl onto it.

"Let's have a fire and coffee up there," Nick said with his usual enthusiasm to build a fire.

We grabbed our sleeping bags and scrambled onto the boulder to enjoy the scenery. The top of the rock was flat and spacious enough for us to lie down. Nick built a small fire on the rock, and with a few trips, we managed to bring pots with water for hot cocoa and a percolator for coffee. Once the water boiled for the hot cocoa and coffee, we poured ourselves some and huddled together to read aloud. We took turns reading *A Tale of Two Cities* on Megan's Kindle. The sun had set and darkness settled over us.

We were so deep in a canyon that I felt like we were in a bowl. As the darkness around us deepened, the mountains became black, their triangular tops contrasting with the lighter, gray sky. One by one, the stars came out. Every so often Nick pointed out a specific planet, star, or constellation for us to admire. The crackling of the fire and the rushing river below lullabied us as we sipped our steaming drinks. Steam rose from our hot mugs and warmed our faces as we sipped, read, and sat in awe of our Creator.

9

A CELEBRATION

A shrill alarm broke the peacefulness of the mountains. It was way too early to be waking up, but Megan and Nick emerged from their sleeping bags and crawled to the front of the van. I figured they wanted to surprise me for my birthday, so I went back to sleep.

I was vaguely aware we had been driving for a while when the van stopped. I didn't know it yet, but they had driven back to Colorado Springs for a day full of birthday surprises.

I sat up and stretched as they came around the back of the van. Nick opened the rear doors and blindfolded me with his black handkerchief. We all laughed as I tried to get my bearings from a small strip of light at the bottom of the blindfold. They each took one of my arms and led me through a seemingly small parking lot.

When they removed my blindfold, my heart warmed. I stood in front of Agia Sophia. Nick and Megan ordered me a large mocha with whipped cream. They smiled as Megan handed me a gift—a large, handcrafted mug with Agia Sophia written on it.

When the barista gave me my mocha in my new mug, I wrapped both my hands around it and headed up the old stairs to find a cozy nook. Unable to keep from smiling, I sat down to enjoy my drink. When I looked up again, Megan stood before me with a dozen pink roses.

"They're from James!" said Megan.

"Oh, thank you, Megs!" I said, hugging her. "How on earth did you coordinate this?"

Holding and smelling the fragrant blossoms, I called James over FaceTime to thank him.

He answered with a beaming smile, his dark green eyes twinkling. "Happy Birthday! I see you got your flowers."

"They're beautiful! I feel so special. Thank you." As we talked, I took in his sweet, boyish smile and his clear delight at a plan well-executed.

As we left Agia Sophia, Megan and Nick asked me if I was ready for my next surprise. They had booked a hotel.

When we entered the lobby, there stood Sarah-Marie and my mom, Jeanne. "What are you guys doing here?" I said as I hugged my mom.

"We drove here for your birthday," Sarah-Marie said.

I then hugged Sarah-Marie. "Thank you so much for taking over a nine-hour drive to come and see me! I feel so loved."

We continued talking as we checked in and headed to our hotel room.

"We were planning to order pizza for dinner and watch a movie. Does that sound fun?" asked Nick, always eager to please and make a celebration personal and special.

"Sounds perfect."

Megan called a local pizza place while Nick searched the channels for a movie to watch. We found one and enjoyed it until the pizza arrived. I could not believe how much work everyone had done to make me feel loved.

When the movie ended, Sarah-Marie said, "Mom and I have some stuff in the car we need to grab. We'll be right back." They returned shortly and I heard the door unlock. They were loaded down with a dozen or more gifts wrapped in red paper and a homemade, four-layer birthday cake with chocolate icing.

My eyes brimmed with tears. "I feel so special. Thank you for all the time and thoughtfulness that went into this." I smiled even bigger as I looked at the cake, still beautiful even though a little disheveled from its long road trip. Every bite of my mom's cake made me feel like I was back at home.

The next day, Mom and Sarah-Marie left in their rental vehicle. Sarah-Marie still needed to see a doctor, and although it was terrible to say goodbye a second time, we had to.

I watched them drive away and thought of the steep mountains, the deep winter, and the extreme elevation that lay ahead. I ran my hands part way through my hair. *I'm gonna need your strength to face this, God. I don't know how I can do this.*

10

THE DREADED PASS

Nick and I were deep into the mountains as I ran and he cycled.

A few miles into the run, Nick spotted a campsite called Salida East Wildlife.

"I wanna check that out and see if we can camp there," he said.

"Looks like an RV spot. Think it's worth your time?"

"How about you keep running, and I'll meet you when I'm done looking at it?"

"Fine with me," I said over my shoulder as we parted ways.

Nick soon caught up with me. He stood as he aggressively pedaled toward me, his face beaming. "I found the perfect spot along the river!" He paused to breathe, and his smile broadened. "Could we be done running and get the spot before someone else does?"

"Sure." I stopped my Runkeeper GPS and headed back to the RV site.

Nick had found a space to the right of where all the RVs were parked. Megan met us there, and we followed Nick as he led us on a trail past some trees down the steep riverbank. Along the shore was a sandy spot—almost beach-like. A large green section with grasses looked as if they had recently been the bed of a deer herd.

Another ten feet back, a bare dirt patch was so conveniently tucked into a grove of small deciduous trees that it looked intentionally constructed, but it wasn't.

Nick made quick work of building a ring out of river rocks for our fire while Megan and I set up the tent. After the sleeping bags were neatly laid inside the tent, all three of us gathered wood. Since we cooked our meals on the fire, we needed what most people would consider an excessive amount of wood—a stack about three feet high and four feet wide.

Nick built the fire as Megan and I prepared the dinner. Soon a fire was roaring with a soup mix in one pot and in the other, pine needles and water for pine needle tea. "This will help with your vitamin C," Nick said crouching next to the fire as he dumped more needles into the pot.

We sat around the large fire on logs and sipped our tea. The Arkansas River rushed only a few feet from our fire, and the mountains formed a jagged backdrop jutting into the sky. The evening sun was still warm as it sank.

As the temperature fell, we bundled up in our warm clothes, made hot cocoa, and read more of A Tale of Two Cities. The stars sparkled in the chilly night air. I suddenly sensed an oncoming bout of diarrhea. I rushed barefoot from our cozy fire to some woods along the river, but before I had made it to the woods, I soiled my clothes. I was a freezing, horrible mess, and I had no way to clean myself. I stood in the woods shivering and bent over in pain as my stomach twisted and turned, too embarrassed to return to camp. After a few moments of deliberation, I returned to our site.

I walked up to Megan and whispered, "I got really sick and soiled my clothes. I don't know what to do. I'm such a mess."

"I'm so sorry that happened," she said, placing her hand on my shoulder. "Let me get you some baby wipes and fresh clothes. Everything will be okay. Don't worry."

I went back to the woods where I cleaned up and changed, but

I still felt ill as I walked back to our camp, my dirty clothes wadded in my hand.

"I don't know what to do with my nasty clothes," I said to Megan with a sigh.

Megan extended her hand for my clothes and said, "Just rest. I'll take care of these." With that, she took my soiled clothes, walked down to the rushing river, bent over, and washed them in the chilly water. I watched for a minute as she labored and wondered if I had ever seen such humility.

I crawled into the tent and fell asleep before the fire died and awoke the next morning to smoking ash. Nick relit the fire, and I mixed batter for chocolate chip pancakes. Bacon sizzled over a wooden arch, a pot of buttery fruit syrup bubbled on the coals, and coffee percolated. We savored the unique flavor that campfire cooking added to our breakfast.

After we cleaned and set aside our blue tin plates, Nick waded across the river. Once across, he began free climbing the mountain across the river—no surprise to us since he had been eyeing it since we got there.

While he climbed, Megan and I waded out into the river to wash our hair. I shivered as we let down our hair—Megs from her messy bun and mine from my French braid. We wet our hair in the chilly water, lathered it with shampoo, and then dunked trying to get it clean. Even though the icy water took my breath away, I felt refreshed and clean, especially after my sickness.

The sun was strong and warm despite it being the end of October in the Rockies. We got out of the water, I built the fire back up, and then Megan and I watched Nick continue to climb the mountain across the river. He became a dark speck against the mountain face —so hard to see that we lost sight of him from time to time. We reclined on the sandy beach warming ourselves and taking in the peacefulness of the bright sun, rushing river, and crackling fire.

The campsite was exactly to our liking, so we used it as a base for a while. After only a few days of running, we made it to Salida,

Colorado, but we returned to our campsite each night. The temperatures were steadily dropping into the upper twenties at night as November loomed. We lingered longer next to the fire and bundled up in layers to keep warm.

After a few more days of running, we left that campsite for the last time. Megan dropped Nick and me off for our run at the base of Monarch Pass.

I had dreaded reaching this pass ever since my uncle had mentioned its high elevation. As I gazed ahead, I was not sure I could meet this challenge.

Our starting point was a rural driveway at the base of a hill just before the pass. The weather was cold and brisk. Large ranches with grazing horses lay in the lowlands. The day's goal was daunting—a twenty-mile ascent with about nine miles of it at a six percent grade.

I stood there trying to get myself to take the first step, but I couldn't get my legs to go or my brain to click into my running zone. Nick must have seen the fear on my face. As he looked at me, fresh, hot tears burned in my eyes. *How could I do this run?*

"God will be your strength," he said, then placed his strong hands on my shoulders. "Give Anna strength, God, and enable us to do what you have called us to do."

His prayer restored my resolve. I started my Runkeeper GPS and took the first steps of the challenge I had feared for weeks.

As we ran, horse ranches gave way to mountainsides thickly covered in pines on one side and sheer rock faces on the other. Cars zipped past us as we ran on the shoulder of the winding road. Up and up we went, from one crest to another even higher than the last. We passed signs saying the summit was close, but it seemed much farther away than was manageable.

The pines grew taller and thinner as we neared the pass. To our left was a dilapidated mining area, its buildings in shambles. Miles passed. On we ran until we spied a long, winding set of switchbacks carved into the mountainside. They ascended left, then right—up and up. My legs flexed and relaxed in an ongoing alternating pattern. My lungs repeated their breathing pattern as the air continued to thin. Step after step after step.

I wanted to quit. I stopped and checked my GPS. I had covered 13.80 difficult miles. I looked at Nick. "I can't. I just can't go on," I said, thinking he would want to push me farther.

"You did good today. Let's call it."

I was shocked but grateful.

When we resumed the next day, my stomach fluttered. Six or so miles lay between the summit and us—the steepest portion of the ascent. To get past the mental fear of the run, I decided to run only as far as I felt I could and then be done for the day, no matter how much or little ground we had covered. Another version of my mental game of one mile more.

I was focused and determined. All I had to do was run one more mile.

The temperature was in the upper thirties. A steady rain blurred the scenery around me, making everything seem gray. I wore a purple, long-sleeved running sweatshirt, black leggings, and black ear warmers. Slowly but surely, we ascended the switchbacks. As we gained elevation, the temperature dropped to the mid-thirties. On we climbed, as the switchbacks turned to miles behind us.

My lungs ached. My legs burned. Icy raindrops stung my eyes and bare skin. The pelting rain turned to sleet, then to snow. A layer of slushy ice formed on my clothes and hair.

On we went.

Just one more switchback, just one more mile.

Nick was a few paces ahead of me as usual, but the gap grew larger as my discouragement mounted. I stopped, convinced I could run no more. "I ... I can't," I stammered, overcome with shame. Not only was I facing an intense physical battle, but a spiritual one was raging as well. *I'm so weak. I can't keep going. How could I have ever thought I could run across America?* Each lie that entered my mind added more weight to my weary legs.

Nick yelled over his shoulder articulating each word, "Yes, you can!" His directness snapped me back to reality.

Yes. I can do this.

My legs felt limp with exhaustion, but I lifted them and kept running. *You don't have to even run one more switchback, merely a few more steps and then a few more.* Every step was a laborious triumph.

I rounded the corner of a switchback and ahead was a sign marking the top of Monarch Pass. Only a few more steps. The sun was breaking through the clouds and driving the cold rain and sleet away. My muscles engaged with a drive I didn't know was in me, and I stood up straighter, allowing my legs to stride out longer. My pace increased until I was in stride with Nick, and we crossed the finish line of Monarch Pass. We hugged breathlessly, my legs shaking and muddy from the ascent—11,312 feet, the toughest and highest elevation of the entire journey.

I looked back over where we had run, and my eyes widened as my mouth fell open. A rainbow arched beautifully over the wet, green mountainside.

A rainbow. The symbol of God's faithfulness and God's promise to bring us through every trial. In that moment of aching legs and lungs and all my shameful, human weakness, I reflected on the goodness of the God who had brought me this far—from the plains of Kansas to the heights of Colorado.

He truly was the God of faithfulness. The God who provided strength, finances, and resources. He would enable me to do whatever He called me to, and I never needed to worry. All I had to do was trust in Him.

Many people think God only performed miracles in biblical times. Maybe their lives are so comfortable they don't need the miraculous hand of God and therefore never see His miracles. But maybe God wants us to take risks, to venture into the uncomfortable and the seemingly impossible so that the only way to carry on is to wait for His miracles.

On October 25, 2016, Nick and I stood at the top of Monarch Pass at 11,312 feet in Gunnison, Colorado (and according to my Runkeeper GPS, gaining 2,772 feet of elevation the first day and 2,284 feet of elevation the second day). We had just finished running to the top of the pass, the highest elevation of the entire run across America.

Nick and I celebrated our accomplishment with Megan at a gift shop there on the summit. It was packed with knick-knacks, t-shirts, and other collectables, but what caught our attention was the sign in the back of the store advertising hot coffee and fudge.

We ordered fudge and coffee and sat down at one of the few tables. We laughed and smiled, relishing the fudge as the coffee restored warmth to our shivering bodies and mobility to our numb hands.

Evening came, and we didn't want to take our van all the way back down the mountain only to ascend it the next day, so we drove partway down the mountain from where we had come and found a pull-off on the shoulder near the summit.

Thick, green pines surrounded us on all sides, and we felt alone on the majestic mountainside. We parked and rearranged the luggage for bedtime. The weather was cold, so we poured several soup cans and instant rice into our pot. Once the soup was ready, we shut the van doors and wrapped up in our sleeping bags and blankets, holding our steaming bowls tightly. I could hardly wait for the soup to cool so I could devour it.

The weather remained cold, but we had not thought about how much colder it would be at such high elevation. After we finished dinner, Megan and I hopped out of the van to wash dishes. We pulled out our plastic collapsible five-gallon water container, filled a pot with water, and began scrubbing our dishes with a sponge and dish soap. Our hands became red and stiff with cold, until we could barely move our fingers.

When we were all settled for bed, we layered up to prepare for what we expected to be a miserably cold night. We put on multiple pairs of wool socks, leggings with sweats on top, long-sleeved shirts with sweaters over them, and then our coats, neck warmers, and hats. Once we were as layered as we could be, we curled deep inside of our sleeping bags.

I had only needed my sleeping bag for warmth up until then, but I pulled out a big brown blanket to add another layer inside my sleeping bag—a gift from James I was extremely grateful for. I pulled my sleeping bag around me as tight as I could and shivered. A few hours later, I woke up cold and hoped morning would come soon.

When morning arrived, we woke up, rearranged our van, and ate. Once we finished breakfast, Nick and I did our warm-up routine, and then Megan drove us to the top of Monarch Pass. I was ready for an easy, all-downhill run.

Nick and I seemed to fly effortlessly down the mountainside. But the steady, steep winding downhill made my joints ache with every pound on the steeply angled pavement. Semis on the ascent chugged past us, but the ones descending flew past on the winding turns. The wind that pummeled our bodies as the trucks sped past us made it difficult to maintain our balance.

We had hoped for high mileage that day, but the pounding from the steep six percent downgrade made us wish we could end the day's run with each painful step. Eventually, the ground leveled. We had run ten miles and arrived at a log building that was both a small gas station and a convenience store called the Tomichi Creek Trading Post. Nick and I were both hungry, so we decided to grab a snack.

I opened my pack and pulled out some money. "Aw man, Nick, I only have two dollars."

"Let's see if we can afford something. I kind of doubt it."

Inside, we looked for any food we could afford. "The ice cream bars are under two dollars," he said. "I don't see much else."

We approached the register to purchase our single ice cream bar to share. At the counter, a kind-faced lady with gray hair and a sweet smile asked, "What brings you here today?"

I smiled, delighted by the opportunity to share about our run and said, "We are running across America for the pro-life movement."

"How far did you run today?" she asked.

"About ten miles," I responded.

"With all that running, why on earth are you buying so little food?"

"It's all the money I had in my pack." My eyes dropped to the floor as hunger bit at my sides.

She gave us a big, sweet smile again and said, "Follow me."

She led us to the restaurant portion of the store. Many signs and deer head mounts covered the walls. We didn't have time to say anything before she instructed us, "Sit down here. I'm taking care of your lunch today."

She disappeared into what must have been the kitchen. Soon the aroma of burgers and fries wafted from the kitchen.

After a short wait, a waitress brought out a massive burger and fries for us to split.

"She gave you her lunch for the day," the waitress said.

11
HOSTS OF THE MOUNTAINS

M y feet hardly left the ground as each mile was covered. My eyes occasionally scanned the horizon in hopes of a friendly face but found none as we entered our next town, Gunnison.

The terrain leveled out as we passed lovely horse pastures with large, gently sloped hills on either side. But another set of snowcapped mountains lay ahead. The late October temperatures hovered in the fifties during the day and dipped into the twenties at night. For several days, we camped out and cooked over an open fire.

We had not showered in ten days. My hair was pasted back with oil, my nails were full of dirt, my feet and ankles were brown with earth, and my smell was unbearable. Thankfully, Front Range Baptist Church opened their doors for us to sleep inside.

"You must be exhausted from your journey." The pastor took in our unkept appearance with a gracious smile. He leaned forward as he spoke, his eyebrows lifted with sincere empathy. "You must need showers. Here are some passes to our local gym; there will be showers there."

"Oh thank you." Megan reached out for them quickly, as if holding the passes would make us cleaner.

"And go ahead and pick out several gift cards from these." The pastor set several restaurant gifts cards on the table. Megan grabbed a few of our favorites as he added, "You can also share your ministry on Sunday."

After meeting with him, we headed to the gym to shower before returning to the church for bed. The next morning in their worship service, I shared about our run across America. "I must say it's been tough living in a van with two other people and rarely showering after so much running, but I love getting to tell people about the importance of defending the weak. God calls us to defend the weak and the needy, and I can't think of any group more weak or more needy than the preborn. Every day, thousands of children are killed. We must do something. Will you use your strengths to defend these children?

"There are so many ways you can get involved. First is pray. Pray for an end to abortion. Pray for God to protect His children. Pray for mothers and fathers who are facing an unplanned pregnancy, even today. Next is politically. Email your representatives and tell them you want them to protect our children. Also, always vote pro-life first. There is no greater human rights violation than the slaughter of the preborn; therefore there is nothing that should be more important on the ballot than ending abortion. And lastly, get involved on the local level at a pregnancy center. They are literally on the front lines of this battle. Every single day, women come into their centers who are deciding whether to take the life of their child. Pregnancy centers need you to come alongside them whether that is with a donation, web design, lawn care, janitorial, or more. Let them know your gifts, and they will help you get plugged in. Join me and Project If Life as we rise up against the evil that is abortion and work to end the killing of our innocent children."

I walked off the stage as the congregation clapped loudly. My hand was shaking as I carried my unused speech notes to the back of the church. Immediately, people formed a line to ask questions and find out how they could get involved locally.

We spent the next several nights in a church member's Airbnb for free and then several more at pull-offs along the highway.

Our route through the Gunnison area wound along the side of a gorgeous lake and ended abruptly with a dam that blocked the water from a deep, jagged multi-colored canyon. We then ascended into the mountains beyond. As days and runs passed, the terrain changed: winding up and up, then dropping again deep into the valleys.

One day as we ran, we came upon a sign that read Cimarron Welcomes You. Just beyond the sign sat an old Sinclair gas station surrounded by junk cars. As we passed the cars and scrap metal, an orange cat skittered in front of us and disappeared in the rusty, eclectic ruin around us. In the gas station, we grabbed snacks, then walked back outside and sat in the dirt, chatting and enjoying our treats.

"Do you want to be done for today?" Nick asked.

"We've done ten miles, so I'm happy with that, but I also feel really good. What if we go a few more miles?"

"Sounds good to me." Nick stood and stretched a bit, trying to loosen his stiffening muscles. "But we'd better get going because it's getting dark."

We ran a while before coming across a sign that announced Cerro Summit, 4 Miles. Signs about summits usually discouraged me, so Nick looked over at me, assessing how I felt about a huge hill.

"I've got this one. I feel really good!"

We put our heads down and kept running. A light rain fell as we persevered uphill mile after mile. Up and up we went. Mud covered our shoes and streaked our calves. The sun set as we pressed toward the summit. I felt strong as my muscles propelled me up the hill.

Nick suddenly stopped at a guardrail to stretch, clearly trying to relieve pain from his knee injury. "I'm fine. Let's keep going," he said.

I knew better than to argue with Nick about injury, so on we ran. Finally, up ahead we saw the headlights of our two-toned van. Its rumbling engine was barely audible through the sound of the rain. Next to the van a sign read Cerro Summit.

We were weary, soggy, and cold but elated as we climbed into the warm van.

"Wow! Good work, guys." Megan's eyes were wide with encouragement.

Hearing her congratulations, I sat up taller as we drove to find a pull-off for the night.

A few more days of van-living passed before we reached the next town, Montrose. A good-sized town, it spread out in a flat area surrounded by mountains. When Megan picked us up at the end of our run, she was sitting on the edge of the driver's seat and her thumb was thumping the steering wheel energetically.

"I found a place for us to stay. It's a church called Victory Baptist. The pastor said we could stay in the Sunday school rooms, and"—she paused for dramatic effect before looking at me and then back over her shoulder to Nick—"they have showers. Plus, you're speaking in their church on Sunday, Anna!"

"Wow, Megs! That's so impressive. I don't know how you manage so many details and coordinate so many things with hardly any cell signal and working from the van." I patted her arm.

"I already met with the pastor, and he gave me the access code, so we can go there now."

We arrived at the church and looked for the best rooms to stay in, then took turns using the church shower. The room I chose was a brightly decorated child's Sunday school room full of child-sized tables. I set out my toiletries on the small tables, arranged my bags, and made up my sleeping bag for the evening. I stepped back to admire my handiwork.

I knelt at one of the child-sized tables to write James a letter. I told him how much I admired him. I signed the letter, then sprayed it with my peony-scented perfume. I folded the letter, placed it in an envelope, and crawled into my sleeping bag.

On Sunday morning, all kinds of people walked through the halls—the church's early birds. I was groggy and embarrassed as people passed by the classroom window and looked in at me in my crumpled running clothes with my untamed, morning hair. Megan and Nick sneaked into my room through their adjoining doors.

"I woke up to people looking in my window." Nick put his hands to his eyes, rubbed them, then ran his fingers through his wild hair.

"I didn't expect people to be here so early. I would have definitely set an alarm." Megan was wrestling her mound of dark hair out of the messy bun she had slept in.

"Let's see if we can get ready before anyone else peers in on us." With a sarcastic smirk, I patted my poofy French braid flatter.

Knock, knock, knock. The three of us turned toward the door as a tall man with a full-toothed smile entered the room. I discreetly wiped sleep dust out of my eyes and ran my tongue over my unbrushed teeth as Megan continued to tug and rip her hair tie out of her hair. Nick stood motionless and stared through narrowed eyes with slightly pursed lips.

"I'm Pastor Welch," the man said, another smile creasing his whole face. His hearty welcome suggested that he was unphased by our early-morning appearance. "I'm glad you're here!" He was a tall, large-built man with a neat, short haircut and no facial hair. He had a dimpled chin and a smile so large and kind it seemed his whole face smiled while he talked.

"Thank you," said Megan. "This is Anna, our runner and speaker for Project If Life, and this is Nick, her brother and trainer."

"Nice to meet you." I said in a high-pitched tone, trying to hide some of Nick's unconcealed frustration. Nick shook Pastor Jim's hand as well and managed a polite half-smile.

"Well, I'm off to get ready for the service." Pastor Jim excused himself to leave and walked away almost bouncing with each step.

Once he left, the three of us scrambled to clean up the rooms, then get ready before any more church members arrived. Megan and I went to the women's restroom and started curling our hair. Our hair was partly curled, our toiletries were spread across the counter, and we were still wearing our athletic clothes when some older church ladies entered the restroom. They were talking as they entered but paused their conversation and stared at us.

"Uh, hi." One of my hands held a curling iron and the other hand gave a small wave. "Sorry for taking over the bathroom." A quiet chuckle escaped my mouth as I shrugged. The ladies smiled back at me in response, used the restroom, and left.

"Well, that was awkward," Megan said, giggling after the ladies had left.

"No kidding! I wouldn't feel as weird if I weren't about to go speak." We both laughed as I applied mascara with an open mouth. "At least they'll know we're genuinely living on the road!"

After getting ready, we headed to the front of the church auditorium. I felt many eyes on us as we took our seats close to the stage. I sat up straight with my speech notes in my hands. I folded and unfolded my speech notes as my hands shook. I sat on them to still the extra energy trying to escape. The few minutes before my introduction dragged by.

"And now a young woman who is literally running across America to end abortion will share for a few minutes. Anna." Pastor Jim gestured toward me. Everyone's eyes again turned toward me. I stood and forced my legs to stop shaking and walked up on stage.

I stepped behind the podium, which gave me a buffer from the audience's uninterrupted gaze. My words came out quicker than I wanted them to: "I'd like to share a story from the Holocasut that was originally told to pro-life activist Penny Lea." I paused, knowing I was speaking too fast and found the oldest person in the audience and tried to speak slowly enough for him to hear every word.

I lived in Germany during the Nazi holocaust. I considered myself a Christian. I attended church since I was a small boy. We had heard the stories of what was happening to the Jews, but like most people today in this country, we tried to distance ourselves from the reality of what was really taking place. What could anyone do to stop it?

A railroad track ran behind our small church, and each Sunday morning we would hear the whistle from a distance and then the clacking of the wheels moving over the track. We became disturbed when one Sunday we noticed cries coming from the train as it passed by. We grimly realized that the train was carrying Jews. They were like cattle in those cars!

Week after week that train whistle would blow. We would dread to hear the sound of those old wheels because we knew that the Jews would begin to cry out to us as they passed our church. It was so terribly disturbing! We could do nothing to help these poor miserable people, yet their screams tormented us. We knew exactly at what time that whistle would blow, and we decided the only way to keep from being so disturbed by the cries was to start singing our hymns. By the time that train came rumbling past the church yard, we were singing at the top of our voices. If some of the screams reached our ears, we'd just sing a little louder until we could hear them no more.

Years have passed and no one talks about it much anymore, but I still hear that train whistle in my sleep. I can still hear them crying out for help. God forgive all of us who called ourselves Christians yet did nothing to intervene.[1]

---

[1] Sing a Little Louder," Penny Lea Ministries, accessed 15 August 2022, https://www.pennylea.com/sing-a-little-louder.

My voice strained with emotion as I studied the church members' faces. "When we hear stories like this, we are horrified. We know that during the Holocaust six million Jews lost their lives. When we hear a number like six million, we're overwhelmed and enraged, and we should be! But did you know that America has a Holocaust of its own? Sixty million children have lost their lives to abortion in the United States alone."

I could hardly articulate the number as I spoke. "That is over three thousand children a day, or one child who will die every thirty seconds in America alone, even as I speak. Someday abortion will end, and we will all look back on this part of history with horror at what our nation allowed. Stand with these children in their hour of need. Defend the weak and the needy. Hear their desperate cries. I beg you, do not be the church that sings louder."

After the speech, I headed to the back of the church and was met by a large line of people waiting to talk with us. As they talked to us, they donated. Every donation meant we could go a little further.

The pastor introduced us to his wife, Paula, who had big, expressive eyes and gray hair neatly pulled back in a small bun. She smiled after almost every word she spoke. "It's so neat to hear about your journey. Where are you staying while in Montrose?" she asked.

"In the Sunday school rooms," Megan said. "We're so grateful to have rooms to ourselves. The lack of privacy and space is tough when we stay in our van."

Mrs. Welch's big smile turned to a frown. She turned to Pastor Jim and said, "J-i-i-i-m! How could you let them sleep on the floor when we have beds?"

With a sheepish chuckle, he shrugged his shoulders, then replied, "Well, Paula, I'd never met them."

Mrs. Welch turned to us and said, "You can stay with us."

That evening we joined them for supper. As we sat down over a giant pot of piping hot elk-meat chili and homemade cornbread, we fell in love with the Welches. Their kindness, humor, godliness, and authenticity were evident in every word and action, and sweetened by their childlike love for each other.

After dinner, we stood to help clear dishes, but Mrs. Welch shook her head and said, "Oh no, no, no. You must be so tired. Let me show you to your rooms." She walked toward a bedroom and motioned for Megan and me to follow her. "This will be your room," she said. It was a large, perfectly neat room with a queen-sized bed. We moved in our belongings and felt right at home.

"You're welcome to spend as much time or as little time in here as you'd like. Make yourself at home, and don't feel shy about anything." Turning to Nick, she said in a sweet, almost teasing way, "You must need your own space after being with those girls all the time." She then led Nick down to their basement where he would have his own room and bathroom.

When morning came, Megan and I lingered in our rooms unsure what to do. "Do you think they'd mind if I make breakfast? I don't know where they are, and I don't want them to walk in and I'm cooking, ya know?"

"Yeah. Let's just at least go out to the kitchen and see if they're up."

We walked through their living room just as Nick was emerging from the basement. The three of us rounded the corner into the kitchen together and there stood Mrs. Welch with an apron crisply tied around her waist, her hair pulled into a loose, neat bun, a spatula in hand, and an ear-to-ear smile on her face. "What can I make ya?" she asked. "I make made-to-order breakfasts, and I love doin' it!" Her voice was shrill with excitement. "Take a seat, and I'll make ya whatever ya like! And there's hot coffee and fresh orange juice too."

We gave her our orders, and she cooked us each a breakfast feast as quickly and skillfully as a well-trained chef. She had three potatoes hashed and frying, toast browning, pancakes cooking, bacon sizzling, and three styles of eggs on the stove while she flitted around the kitchen telling stories about cooking. Her joyful hospitality made for wonderful company, and we spent most of the morning with her.

After breakfast, Megan said to me, "This town is so welcoming to the pro-life message. I have two news interviews and several speaking engagements already lined up. Two of the churches are giving you their whole service to present."

"Oh wow!" I paused. "That's a lot of speaking. I don't know if I'm ready for that."

Mrs. Welch chimed in, "Well, you feel free to stay here as long as ya need so you can prepare."

We stayed longer than we thought we would so I could work on speeches and interviews. With such a comfortable place to stay, the genuine hospitality of the Welches, and much-needed Wi-Fi access, I spent the next couple days completely absorbed in writing my speeches.

The first interview was with the *Montrose Mirror*. Nick, Megan, and I sat in a library room as the young journalist asked me questions. I did my best to answer and act professional but sat on my hands to hide my nervousness. The second interview with the *Montrose Daily Press* went more smoothly, and I sat up straight with a smile as I told my team about it. Over the next couple days, I spoke at a Bible study, a young girl's group, and a church called Solid Rock Ministries.

After speaking at Solid Rock Ministries, the pastor and his wife, Dave and Kate Tabor, approached us. "We so appreciated your talk about the preborn. Thank you for taking the time to come and share with us. We'd just love it if you would join us at our house for dinner."

"That sounds great." Megan pulled out her planner to write down the details.

We joined the Tabors for dinner, along with their daughter and son-in-law, Geoff and Megan Illa. The table was set with handcrafted candles and lovely plates, and enticing steam rose from pans of chicken and rice.

Conversation flowed effortlessly. Their complete faith and trust in God were shown in every part of their conversation and lives, and the joy of the Lord flowed out of them as they shared stories of missions, church ministry, and God's miraculous hand.

After dinner, they prayed with us, donated to our mission, and encouraged us before we headed back to the Welches for the night.

The next day we visited a pregnancy center called Life Choices to see if we could be a blessing to them in any way. We walked in and were greeted by some of the staff.

"Hi, I'm Anita Daly, and this is Gi-Gi, Andrea, and Linda. We run Life Choices, and we're eager to give you a tour."

"It's a pleasure to meet you." I shook each of their hands.

"Come this way." Anita motioned for us to follow her. We entered a medium-sized room. "This is our ultrasound machine. When women come in, we let them listen to their baby's heartbeat and show them their ultrasounds. Many women who watch their babies squirming and jumping on the screen end up choosing life."

"Wow!" I ran my hand over the leather seat where women received the ultrasounds and wondered how many humans had been saved by that machine.

"Now come this way." Anita led the way to another room. In it were rows and rows of baby clothes, maternity clothes, shelves neatly lined with packs of diapers, cribs, car seats, baby toys, books, informational packets, and more. "This is our Baby Boutique, where we keep all the donated items for mothers and their babies."

My finger traced over a pair of baby socks only a couple inches long. A tiny blue bow adorned the ankle. I picked up the socks, ran the soft material between my fingers, and held them up. "It's amazing to think that the baby who will wear these socks would have lost his life to abortion if you guys didn't live your lives to protect the preborn."

"It's amazing to see God work through our center." Anita

117

paused and her eyebrows drew together seriously. "A lot of people call us 'fake clinics' and say we are 'pro-birthers,' but the truth is we help women know their actual options with parenting and adoption. We equip them to be able to parent with counseling, resources, and the knowledge that they are not alone."

I set down the socks and looked around the room stuffed with resources, then back at the smiling faces of the workers. "I'm so impressed at the work you do. Every single day you put yourselves on the front lines to defend children who will otherwise be killed, and you assist mothers who are afraid, ashamed, and alone. It's impressive, and we would love to help. Is there any way we can?"

"Well, actually," Anita looked at the other staff women. Each one nodded at her and then smiled at me. "We love what you're doing to spread the pro-life message, so we have a gift for you."

Anita and Gi-Gi each grabbed an end of a large tub and with strained arms, carried it toward us. Nick took off the lid and revealed neatly organized rows of canned beef, peaches, beans, fresh fruit, and oatmeal.

"We thought this would help you in the upcoming wilderness of Utah and Arizona." Gi-Gi gestured toward the food. "A lot of the food is canned by hand."

"Oh wow! Thank you so much." I exchanged excited glances with Nick and Megan, then we hugged each lady before heading back to the Welches for the evening.

We had entered Montrose feeling alone, and God had met us through the hands, homes, and hearts of so many people. With each city I ran through, each home we stayed in, and each church I spoke at, I was learning the goodness of leaning on God. He had a plan—all I had to do was be willing to follow it.

12
WINTER'S ARRIVAL

The colder weather made my breath and Nick's white against the mountain landscape.

Run days went well as we progressed through the remainder of Colorado. We conquered mile after mile as November weather arrived. I regularly wore leggings, long sleeves, and ear warmers, but overall God kept the weather bearable. After many miles, we neared the beautiful San Juan Range.

Tucked in a valley by those mountains was the home of a Swiss-American family, the Zauggs—a blond-haired couple. One son, Jonathan, still lived with them. The house looked like it had been moved straight from Switzerland with its high ceilings and Swiss-style decorations. The Zauggs gave us a warm, energetic welcome and handed each of us a Lindor chocolate when we walked into their home.

We stayed with this family while we ran through Ridgway, a rustic town surrounded by open fields that sat at the bases of giant, snowcapped mountains. One day as we ran, a herd of cattle crossed the road ahead of us. With the road blocked, Nick and I sat down for a snack to watch the cattle drive progress. The cows moved together almost like a wave as men on horseback skillfully directed the herd to their next pasture.

On Sunday, we attended a nearby church, where Megan had scheduled a presentation. The service started in a typical manner, then the pastor said, "Today we have a team who is running to protect preborn babies. We are proud to have strong women who stand for other women," placing emphasis on the word *women*. "They are running across America to stand against abortion. Megan, Anna, please stand."

Megan and I stood, a bit confused about why the pastor hadn't asked Nick to stand. The church seemed tense. Only a couple people clapped or even looked at us as the rest of the congregation stared forward. I smiled shyly before Megan and I sat down.

After the service, we headed to the back where we had set up our board and our fliers. We greeted people on their way out as we had in other churches, but person after person walked past me, acting as if I was not there. Their iciness should have deterred me, but I assumed they needed me to say something first.

"Hi," I said loudly to an older lady walking by me. "Would you like a flyer?" I smiled as I held out our team's flyer.

She met my eyes with a glare. Her jaw seemed clenched as she pushed back my flyer and said, "I'll never agree with anything you're doing."

I stepped back, stunned. The church continued to empty, and people still passed by our table and averted their eyes. We packed up our display and left confused as to why we had even been invited.

A few hours later, we drove to Ouray, Colorado, so I could speak at the evening service of Ouray Calvary Community Church. I walked in and was immediately surrounded by people asking me questions about our journey and about the pro-life movement. Again I sat in the front row of the church and felt the congregation looking at me, but this time my hands shook less. I stood as my name was announced from the pulpit, and I scanned the crowd as I began my speech. I again found the oldest person and did my best to speak to him so he could hear every word I spoke. I kept the audience's attention as I spoke.

Every day, we lose thousands of children to abortion. These children need us to speak for them because they cannot speak for themselves. If we don't defend them, who will? Think how horrified future generations will be when they realize what we allowed in our lifetime in one of the wealthiest, most prosperous nations of all time.

Sometimes in history, what is wrong is gruesome and obvious, and sometimes it's hidden and secret. Abortion is perplexing because it's both. It's heinously wrong: images of tiny children ripped apart leave me feeling sick. The knowledge of what happens is readily available and easily accessible, yet no one speaks of it. Abortions occur every day in almost every city. People know the horrible fate of these perfectly formed innocents, yet it goes unacknowledged. To bring it up in conversation is to pick a fight. To talk of these children is, some say, the equivalent of oppressing women. The topic is too raw, too painful, too ... taboo.

So on Americans go with their lives, driving by abortion facilities where unspeakable horrors occur daily. On Americans talk, but conversations never lead to the details of this gruesome fate of our children. On Americans shop, passing these gray buildings without a second thought as women bring their children to be killed. Evil has an odd way of making itself obvious to the historian and yet unseeable to the people living it.

As I scanned the congregation, I wanted to say, "Wake up, America! See the fate of these children next door. Hear the cries of the women in desperation and the children heading to their slaughter. See what is right in front you."

When I concluded, I saw many tears, encouraging me that I was conveying how pressing standing against abortion is. Again, a line formed near our display after the service, and I shared in more detail about our cross-country journey.

After we left the Zauggs' home, we slept at pull-offs along the highway. The mountains rolled into canyons, and the elevation gradually decreased. Our route had taken us close to the town of Norwood, and we had already run ten miles when we came to a hill called Norwood Hill. We later learned it was infamously steep, but we had never heard of it. The cold weather gnawed at me with each miserable burst of wind leaving my bare skin red and raw, feeling tight—almost like a burn—but I kept running, assuming the terrain was no more difficult than any other ground Nick and I had covered.

We ran on the right shoulder of the road as close to the guardrail as we could. On the other side of the rail was a sheer drop off, and the wind whipped and nipped at us from the depths below. Up and up we ran, pushing forward on the icy, snow-covered road, slowly leaving more and more of the hill behind us. The cold pierced my clothes, and I felt its chill in my bones. Cars crept passed us as we ran on the narrow shoulder. Eventually, as we neared the top, the sun peeked over the road with blinding brilliance but no warmth.

At the top of Norwood Hill, the scenery changed drastically, and my heart warmed as open, golden fields whispered a reminiscence of the Kansas Plains I grew up in. We ran with the goal of fourteen miles that day and ended in a stranger's driveway. The temperature dropped as the sun sank behind distant mountains.

"I have no cell phone service to call Megan, so I guess we have to wait. I'm so cold," I said, wrapping my arms tightly around my torso and hunching a little.

The sky grew darker, and the temperature dropped even lower. My muscles tightened.

"Let's skip stretching and just try to keep warm," Nick said. We sat behind some small, scrubby bushes to block the cold.

The wind was whipping, and I trembled as it chilled my body, damp with sweat. Nick shivered too as he wrapped his arms around himself to keep warm. We hunkered even lower. I had no idea how long we would have to wait.

"Nick, I'm just so cold!" I half shouted above the biting wind.

"Hunker down lower. Megan should be here soon." We crouched lower as the sun set faded into the gray that comes just before nightfall. I ducked my face into my gloved hands to avoid the relentless wind. My body shook violently. Just before the last lingering light vanished, a car pulled into the long driveway where we waited. It stopped next to us, and I expected the driver to ask why we were trespassing. A lady with gray hair rolled down her window and gave us a puzzled look.

Before we offered an explanation, she asked, "Do I know you?" She studied our faces. "I know you from somewhere. I just can't place where."

"No," I said. "We're actually both from Kansas."

She seemed unconvinced. After another moment, she exclaimed, "I'm your next host, Mrs. Oliver! I'm supposed to host you starting tomorrow night. I knew I'd seen you before! I have your flyer." After a short pause, she said, "Where are you staying tonight?"

Shivering, I said, "At a pull-off in our van in the bed in the back."

"No, no, no, that won't do. That won't do at all. You can stay with my husband and me. You can't stay in this miserable cold. It's seventeen degrees out. Please, come inside and get warm."

We were shivering too much to refuse, so I said, "That would be so wonderful. Thank you! But we have to wait for our teammate to find us, and then we'll come in."

As we waited, my body shook. *How will I ever stop shivering?*

A short while later, Megan arrived and we entered Mrs. Oliver's home. The scent of homemade chicken noodle soup filled our noses as we crossed the threshold. We were weary, hungry, and cold as she directed us to the couch.

"Dinner will be ready shortly," she said.

"Thank you!" I said, still shivering.

Mrs. Oliver bustled about making us feel at home. Soon we were wrapped snuggly in heated blankets and sipping piping hot chocolate with mini marshmallows. Under the blanket, my body still shook convulsively. I felt literally chilled to the bone, and I kept wondering how either Nick or I could have possibly gotten warm if we had slept in the van that night.

When it was dinnertime, I took my place at the table. I hugged my arms tight around me as my body continued to tremble.

Mrs. Oliver served the soup, and I tried to pace myself as I ladled spoonful after spoonful of the medicinal soup into my shaking body. As the soup warmed me, I reflected on the marvelous, providential hand of God.

God had brought us to our next host's home at the right time. We could have ended our run a thousand other places and never met Mrs. Oliver that night. She could have come home from work before we got to her driveway or just after Megan had picked us up. But, no, God knew we needed a home that night. We had suffered through many cold nights, but we knew, and God knew, this night was different, and He provided. His goodness in caring for us, His children, is truly awe-inspiring.

Once dinner was over, I took a hot shower and crawled into bed. I snuggled deep under the sheets and blankets and pulled them tight around me. A few minutes later, a smile spread across my face. I finally felt warm.

We stayed with the Olivers a few days. I spoke in their church and at a public school where I was allowed to speak to whoever wanted to come during their lunch break. A few kids came along with a couple female teachers. Although the students did not say much, one teacher wept and thanked me for my presentation.

After my speech at the school, the team grabbed lunch at a nearby diner, then Nick and I started running. We didn't make it far—only eight steep, rainy miles—before we stopped for the day.

We found a pull-off under a huge pine tree to spend the night, but the rain did not let up.

As the cold rain pelted our van, we opened the back doors to let out the fumes as we cooked on our Coleman stove. The wind drove the rain into the back of the van, soaking our bed.

"All our supplies are getting soaked. What should we do?" I pulled one door shut as I spoke to Nick.

"Our large blue tarp might work." Nick dug in our supply bins under our bed for the large tarp, pulled it out, and we both worked to drape it over the open door. I shivered in my soaked clothes as we worked. The rain caught the tarp and smacked it loudly against the van and the doors.

We mixed together a stew of home-canned beef (from the pregnancy center), canned veggies, and the usual extra pepper for warmth. We set a pot of warm water on the second burner for hot cocoa so we would not have to keep the doors open longer. The stew pot steamed as the rain dripped into it, despite the tarp's protection. The savory aroma made my stomach rumble. After our meal boiled awhile, we removed the tarp and shut the van's doors.

My wet clothes stuck to my skin, and shivers ran up and down my arms and legs as I ladled out the stew. Although we were cold, the sound of the rain pelting our van was lovely. We held our bowls close to our bodies as we spooned the stew into our mouths. With each mouthful, warmth spread down my throat and into my body. After a second portion of stew, we pulled out our mugs for hot cocoa.

We had finished *A Tale of Two Cities*, so Megan pulled out our next read, *Treasure Island*. We took turns reading aloud to the sound of the rain and drinking steaming hot cocoa with mounds of whipped cream.

The next day, ten miles passed with relative ease as I ran and Nick biked. This was my last run before Thanksgiving, so I was determined to run hard. Although the terrain was difficult, we ran with our shoulders back and our heads high while driving our knees high to increase our strides.

When we got to the van, Megan sat in the driver's seat, attempting to work without any cell phone reception. Her hair was swept up in a curly, messy bun, and she wore her thick-rimmed black glasses. A pile of color-coded receipts sat in her lap. She was using her phone for work because her laptop had broken.

She rolled down the window so we could talk to her. "You've made it so far already!" she said, her face radiant with characteristic joy.

"Thanks! We feel great today. We're planning to make it to the top of the next hill." I pointed to the incline ahead that disappeared out of site. "We'll meet you at the top of it, if that's okay with you."

She looked at me in an odd way and paused as if unsure of her answer, then said, "Okay. That's fine with me," with a reserve that confused me.

After a little distance, I saw a sign that read Slick Rock Hill and realized what had caused Megan to react so weird. We had reached an extremely difficult hill after running ten miles. As my feet ascended the hill, I set my mind to conquer. I can do this, I determined, as I had many times before. Run one more mile. Just one more.

After much difficulty, I saw the first mile marker. I set my pace firmer and told myself, "This is it: the last mile I ever have to run." I pushed the difficulty of the miles I had already run behind me and ignored all that lay ahead except one mile more.

When we reached that goal, my legs felt tired, but light. I had achieved something great: another mile to save the lives of the innocent. Once we crossed the finish line of that important mile, I reset my mind over and over as the miles passed. I looked over at Nick, his calves taut with the strain of pumping his heavy bike up the hill.

I am not envious of his bike right now. All I had to propel up that hill was myself.

My mind soon became numb to the fact I was even running—a phenomenon most distance runners understand. My mind pushed my body up an almost unbearably difficult hill without me being fully aware I was still running. After much perseverance, we reached the top of the hill. I felt proud as we stretched out.

We arrived at my cousin John's apartment in Durango for Thanksgiving after dark. John was in his mid-twenties and could make anyone laugh. We chatted with him awhile before Nick, Megan, and I went to sleep on the floor in his living room area.

As we drank coffee the next morning, we dreamed up the perfect Thanksgiving feast. Since we were not limited by a two-burner cook stove, we wanted a grand meal. We each picked a dish or two we wanted to make, then shopped for groceries.

I was in charge of the turkey. I had never made one, but I was confident because my mom was a master at making the most tender poultry—her technique involved a towel saturated with butter. The more butter the better, I thought, and poured an excessive amount over the bird.

As I placed the turkey in the oven, butter sloshed out of the disposable pan and into the bottom of the oven. After a few minutes, smoke poured from the oven and the shrill ring of the smoke alarm disturbed the entire apartment complex. The alarm continued to go on and off throughout the evening as the butter boiled. Despite the obnoxious smoke alarm, the turkey and the rest of the meal were a success.

13
SHELTER

We shivered as we entered the door. Winter was becoming harsh, and hosts were becoming a necessity.

We had reached our next host, Pastor Greg Liming of Dove Creek, Colorado, a town on the Colorado-Utah border. A recent widower with two affectionate dogs, he was a medium-sized, gray-haired man with expressive eyes and a bright, energetic voice.

As we chatted with him, his pitch rose and his eyes widened as he asked, "Do you like coffee? I have an espresso maker, and I love making cappuccinos."

"Yes, we do. A lot, actually," Nick responded in an overly eager voice. He then added in a more regulated gruff fashion, "It's been a while since we had a good cup of coffee."

"Good to hear." Our host smiled as he tamped espresso. "When we're done having cappuccinos, I'll show you to the small apartment I have out back where you'll be staying. Another couple will stay in it after you leave or else you could stay longer." Pastor Liming frothed milk and conversed happily with us over the loud humming of the steam wand.

He handed each of us a medium-size mug. I sipped the foamy

cappuccino and found it to be delightfully strong and hot. "Who is the couple coming in after us?"

"Oh, some people I found living in the woods where I like to hike." He knelt and placed some kindling in his fireplace and lit it as he spoke. "The old camper they had just wouldn't do with our winter temperatures regularly getting down below the teens, and we get lots of snow. They wouldn't have survived the winter." The fire ignited, and he placed some sticks and then logs on the flames.

He took a seat in a recliner, sipped his cappuccino, and patted one of his dogs as I prodded more. "So you found a couple you didn't know and invited them to live with you?"

"Yes, they had nowhere else to go." His voice was flat and matter-of-fact.

"That's so kind." Megan's eyes peered over the mug she cupped tightly in her hands. "It's not very often people do things like that."

"God just seems to bring people across my path who are in need." Pastor Liming paused with a contented smile on his face. A few minutes passed as we sat in contented reverie. My eyelids fluttered as the fire crackled but quickly opened when Pastor Liming sat up. "Oh my, I've lost track of time. It's late and you must run in morning."

"Thank you for the cappuccinos. It's been a long time since we've had such good coffee," Nick said.

Pastor Liming led the three of us to the small apartment behind his home.

"What a perfect evening." Megan rubbed her hands together to warm her hands in the cold outside air.

"I'm glad you enjoyed it. Now here's the apartment." He twisted the handle and pushed open the door. He let us all enter ahead of him so we could get out of the cold. He followed us in and then continued, "There's no kitchen, but you're welcome to come to my house and do all the cooking you need. Please let me know if I can do anything for you to make you more comfortable."

"Thank you," we each said.

Pastor Liming smiled and raised his shoulders simultaneously, then said goodnight in a sing-song way before leaving.

Once the door was shut, I looked at Nick and Megan with disbelief. "Wow! I felt right at home, as if we've known him forever."

"Yeah." Megan said through a happy yawn as she heaped her hair in a messy bun for bed. "And he really is the gospel in action —taking in those in need."

When Sunday arrived, the pastor entrusted me with the whole church service. Afterward, the church members were extremely excited about Project If Life. One man told me he had recorded my speech and would air it on the radio several times. Several other church members asked to join my team for lunch to hear more about our ministry.

Pastor Liming suggested a nearby diner, and soon my team and I were seated at a table crowded with church members. Our orders of burgers and fries were set before us, and the whole table was alive with questions.

"How do you stay sane while living with two other people in a van?" A lady asked as she looked at me and shoved a large ketchup-smothered fry in her mouth.

"Lots of organization, and owning only a little stuff, I guess. For instance, I have a gym bag of running clothes, one skirt, a couple nice shirts, and a small backpack with my laptop, journal, and Bible."

Her mouth gaped. "And you can live with that little stuff?"

"Yep. Megan and Nick are packed in the same way. The main thing I own are running shoes. I alternate between several pairs to help my joints."

"It's funny," Megan chimed in, "It seems like Anna is always looking for another system of organization to make the van more livable. She creates a place for every item like our Nalgene water bottles, our flannels, where our sleeping bags go, where our gym bags go, and so on. It makes it much more doable." I looked down and hid a smile by biting into my burger as she spoke.

The conversation drifted as we explained van-life until the waitress brought the checks. Pastor Liming made a small motion to her before she had any time to speak. He whispered something and handed her his card. A minute later, she was back with a receipt. He turned to the side and signed it and quickly handed it back to her before anyone could protest.

In the evening at Pastor Liming's house, we sat around his living room once more. Each of us had a brownie in one hand and a foamy cappuccino in the other. The fire once again crackled as we relaxed in the warm home. A dog cuddled between me and Megan, while harsh winter winds whipped against the house.

"Do you have any more stories of people in need crossing your path?" Megan asked leaning forward a bit on the couch where she sat.

"A few days before you arrived, I found a sixteen-year-old boy along the highway heading west. I pulled over and asked him if everything was okay, and he told me he'd run away from his family back in Chicago. We got a meal together and talked about his family, and I was able to convince him to return home to his family. So I got him a bus ticket, and he went back." His gaze moved toward a piano in a room joined to the living room. "Could I play some piano music for you?"

"We'd love that." Megan answered.

I reclined further on the couch, coffee in one hand and the other absent-mindedly stroking the dog. Again my eyes closed as peaceful improv piano music and the popping of the fire lulled me to sleep.

"It's late and tomorrow I have work. And you need your strength to run." Pastor Liming looked over at Nick and me.

I yawned as Megan asked, "Sermon prep?"

"No, my church is small, so I work a full-time remote job to support myself."

I lifted my eyebrows. *Literally every part of his life is living the gospel.* Aloud, I said, "Thank you for yet another perfect evening." We headed to the apartment to sleep.

First thing the next morning, we received a medium-sized narrow package addressed to Megan from a friend of mine, Logan Taylor.

Megan sat down on the couch and tore open the brown cardboard packaging. "A laptop! No way! How did he even know I needed one?"

I sat down beside her to get a closer look. "Logan messaged me to see if there was anything we needed or anything he could pray for. It was a long shot, but I told him your laptop had broken, and he offered his!"

"My life just got so much easier." She set it up exactly to her liking.

"I knew even a broken laptop couldn't deter you, but I'm glad your job will be so much easier."

A short time later, Megan dropped Nick and me off for our run. The weather was a chilling twenty-one degrees. The biting west wind hit us almost head on as we ran. We were layered with ear warmers, leggings, and long-sleeved sweatshirts. It was almost December, and the temperatures had been steadily dropping, but the terrain was mostly flat and easy as our legs carried us past Dove Creek and onward to the Utah border.

Snow fell and the wind picked it up and whipped it in my face, stinging any bare skin and making my eyes water with hot, burning tears. Nick and I lowered our heads to keep the snow from our faces and eyes. We had covered just over thirteen miles when we saw a giant billboard with a picture of the Delicate Arch and Welcome to UTAH across it in large white font. Staring at the sign, I momentarily forgot the frigid temperatures and the snow. I hugged Nick and gaped at the sign as the snow pelted my face. We had done it. We had run across Colorado!

On November 29, 2016, Nick and I finally reached the Utah border after running in freezing temperatures and snow.

We were chilled but happy when we made it back to Pastor Liming's home. He greeted us with another offer of cappuccinos, piano music, a fire, and conversation. The more we talked with him, the more Pastor Liming proved to be the gospel in action: taking care of the orphans, the widows, and the homeless—all with deep, genuine love. We were proud to know him and honored to receive his hospitality.

The next day I spoke to a group of elementary school students. Their eyes were wide as they studied me nervously. I stood behind a podium and started a long speech I had prepared to share with them.

Only a few words in, I saw several kids fidget and look from side to side. I took a breath, set down my notes, and walked right up in front of them.

"You wanna know something amazing?" I spoke in a sing-song way with a higher pitch. The children's fidgeting stopped, and all eyes were back on me as they nodded eagerly.

"I'm going to tell you about what babies are like when they are in their mommy's tummy." I patted my abdomen. "Are any of your mommies pregnant?" Several hands went up. "Have any of you seen a pregnant mom?" I smiled and nodded as many more hands rose.

I grabbed a box of fetal models and spoke slowly. "I'm going to show you exactly what the babies look like before they're born." I held up a seven-week fetal model.

"Awwwww" came from the audience.

"This little baby's features—his eyes, nose, mouth, and ears are becoming defined. He even has arm and leg buds." I pulled out a 12-week model. "Look at this precious, fully formed baby! Can you believe that at just over two inches, he already can open and close his hands into fists, and those little hands have itsy-bitsy fingernails? Those are some pretty tiny fingernails, aren't they?" The children laughed and leaned forward to see the model better.

I pulled out a sixteen-week fetal model just under five inches and weighing about 4 ounces. I held it up. Again the kids leaned forward and murmured their admiration for the baby. "This baby can already suck its thumb, yawn, stretch, and make faces." I stuck my tongue out and the kids erupted in laughter.

I set down the fetal model as I concluded, "There are people who want to hurt these precious children." The kids' faces frowned. "We must protect them, right?"

"Yes" and "Mhm" came from the little mouths.

"I have a way you can help." I held up a quart jar with a hole in the lid. "If you have any change, go ahead and drop it in this jar. I'm going to leave it with Pastor Liming, and after a few weeks, he is going to give it all to the pregnancy center here. They work to protect little babies."

After my speech, Megan dropped Nick and me off at our run spot late in the afternoon, so she did not even bother to find a place to work because she knew we would not run far.

"Oh no! I forgot my leggings at the house," I said. *How could I overlook such an obvious necessity?* I added out loud, "I'll just do my best without them."

After only five miles, my legs were bright red and stinging with intense pain. I called Megan to pick us up so I could warm up in the van. She arrived, and I hopped in the passenger seat. I rubbed my legs energetically, trying to warm them as hot air gushed from the van's vents.

Nick said, "Come on, Anna, we only did five miles. We can't stop yet."

"My legs are burning! It's too cold."

"Come on, just one more mile?" he prodded.

Out the front window, the sunset painted the sky orange and pink, signaling even lower temperatures. "Okay." I sighed. "Let me at least cover my legs with our flannel shirts to keep them warmer."

I wrapped all three of our flannel shirts around my waist, attempting to protect my legs against the gnawing cold. When I opened the door, the wind whipped in, immediately chilling me. I forced myself out, and Nick and I started running again.

We ran in a weird mood of misery and, somehow, the giggles. The flannel shirts whipped against my burning skin, and the buttons stung as they hit me. We ran about another mile—almost six for the day.

Back at Pastor Liming's home, we slept well.

The following day was our last day with Pastor Liming. He was concerned about our route through Utah and Arizona, so he invited his friend, Bob, over to help us with routing. An avid outdoorsman, Bob gave us wise counsel on which roads to take, depending on whether we ran through Utah or Arizona. He and Pastor Liming also advised us to buy tire chains—the roads ahead could be treacherously icy.

Before we said goodbye, Pastor Liming wanted to show us a nearby canyon overlook. The canyon's dark walls contrasted with the fresh fallen snow all around us as we hiked and admired the scenery.

"I love taking hikes in nature. It shows me the goodness of God." He looked from the ground to the trees covered in snow. "One of my favorite parts of God is that His mercies are new every morning. No matter what has happened the day before or in our past, His mercies are new each time we wake."

I looked at the pure snow around me and breathed in deeply, as if inhaling God's new mercies for me. "I love that knowledge."

"Oh, look over here!" Pastor Liming almost skipped as he took a few steps toward where he was pointing. These are bobcat prints." We circled around the prints.

"They're so big," Megan said with a slight shudder.

We hiked until we reached an overlook. The sun's brightness was amplified by the snow, casting a surreal glow over everything. Pastor Liming pointed out landmarks: "That is Abajo Peak, that one there is Ute Mountain." Megan, Nick, and I got closer to better follow the path of his finger. "That one is Lasalles." He pointed again. "That one is Laplatas, and those over there are the San Juan Mountains."

As we hiked back down, I eyed the snow around me. Before I could stop myself, I had formed and thrown several huge, wet snowballs that found their mark on Megan, Nick, and Pastor Liming. Snowballs soon whizzed from every direction—every hiker for himself. We then formed teams—Megan and me versus Pastor Liming and Nick. We all erupted in deep, aching gut-laughter. I could hardly form a snowball because I was laughing so hard.

When the hike ended, we headed back to Pastor Liming's house for the last time. We stood in his driveway, and a heavy sadness shrouded my heart. Nick's face was drawn downward, and his normally erect posture slightly sloped forward. The usual bounce in Megan's walk was flattened. We were exchanging beds, warmth, and the perfect company for van-life and loneliness.

Our host frothed us one last round of cappuccinos. We sipped them as he gave us a stack of firewood, a large water container, oil for our van, and dry food for camping. He understood the harsh, barren wilderness that lay ahead of us much better than we did.

14

THE WARNING

"You'll die! I don't know what you read on your internet back East, but this is still the wild, wild west," warned Pastor Bart with gravelly seriousness.

As Pastor Bart spoke, I shifted uneasily in the chair Megan and I shared. Nick sat in the only other one available. The tall, large-framed man in his early sixties sat across from us at his desk. A cowboy hat covered most of his black hair, and his penetrating eyes spoke of dangers unimaginable.

He had given us permission to stay in the Sunday school rooms of the small church he pastored in Blanding, Utah. When he discovered we planned to run through the Navajo Reservation in Arizona, he drawled, "You can't cross the reservation. You kids got a lot to learn, m'kay? There's a lot of stuff that goes on, m'kay?"

He leaned across his desk. "I keep my gun and a hundred rounds in *this* office. So, you know, you kids don't need to be running this segment." He waved his finger at us. "You get to Flag [Flagstaff, Arizona] where you're safe. And when you get to Flag, I *need* to know you're in Flag."

His voice almost cracked with earnestness. "I need to know. There's things happening where it's gonna get wild. I've said it over and over and over again, and I'll say it again— this is not a

139

game over here." He paused as his gaze went from Nick to me to Megan without a blink.

"You've listened to what you can see on the internet and what people have told you from back East," He gestured sideways with his thumb. "And what you've been able to gather as you got closer, but we live out here, m'kay? I have rounds that will go through metal. Trust me—I will use them." He poked his finger on the table with each word.

"If I head down to the reservation, I have enough ammunition to start a small war." He squinted his eyes and asked, "What do you kids got? If you kids have a gun down in there"—he pointed toward our van parked outside the building—"you're had. They'll take and confiscate the gun, throw you in jail, and throw the key away." He wagged his head as he continued, "And you can't call Momma and you can't call Daddy and say, 'Come and get me out of jail.'"

Nick leaned forward and interrupted. His voice was gruff with frustration. "What if we don't run through the reservation, and we run through Utah instead? Would that be safe?"

We had proposed an alternate route through Utah several times, but Pastor Bart didn't think anything would be safe other than driving to Flagstaff. Weather was too bad in Utah, he said.

"So your ultimate concern with us going through Utah is the weather?" Nick asked.

"Well it's weather, it's a lot of things," Pastor Bart said. "Weather just . . . it just compounds everything. Number one, you're picking the wrong time of year to try to come through here. 'Kay?"

"We were looking at kinda going west and zigzagging down through Utah," I said. "We were using a paper map and routing it through the towns in southern Utah and then dropping down to go through Vegas. Would that be practical?"

"No." He clipped the word. "It's a long way, and it's not good weather. I say your best bet is to drop down and get to Flag, and you're okay. Best way is to drop down, get up, and get out. It's hot during the summer. Gets above a hundred and can be dangerous." His slow, serious monologue was almost impossible to interrupt or direct.

"But it's winter," I said.

"Just get to Flag. 'Kay? You run after Flag. If you wanna get hurt, if you wanna say, 'we don't need the advice,' go whichever way you want. But let me tell you, somethin' is gonna happen." He pronounced each word slowly.

Pastor Bart was so deeply concerned about our safety and the dangers of the reservation that we decided to rethink routing options. We headed to a gas station to pick up coffee and chocolate to fuel our decision-making session. When we returned to the church, we carried in our sleeping bags as well as our coffee and treats.

The large Sunday school room's cinder-block walls were yellowed with age, and the floor was a brownish-white laminate. We laid out our sleeping bags and pillows on the floor, then set out our paper maps on the large tables in the middle of the room.

We highlighted the route through Utah as well as the route through the reservation in Arizona. We had received so much conflicting advice, but we wanted to make the decision that night so we could continue running. We studied the maps for hours as we sipped coffee, discussed, researched, and prayed.

The next morning we rose early, packed our belongings, and left before Pastor Bart's church service began. Megan called Pastor Weaver—the father of a college friend, Katie—who had lived on the reservation.

"Hi, Pastor Weaver. I was calling about the Navajo Reservation. Katie told me you guys used to be missionaries there. Could you give us some advice about running through there?"

"Yes, we were missionaries there, and we loved it," he said.

"The people are so kind and wonderful. We were so sad to leave when we did."

"We've been warned about the dangers of crossing the reservation, especially at night. What do you think?"

"I think you'd be fine. I wish I could come and travel with you until you finished, but I have my own church here in Pennsylvania to pastor," he said.

"Thank you," said Megan. "Your advice means so much to us."

We spent several days at a standstill, weighing the advice. After much rest and prayer, we agreed the best route would be through southern Utah and not through the reservation. Although the route zigzagged between canyons and lakes, we still thought it would be best. God had brought us this far completely on faith and we trusted Him, even though Pastor Bart had made us nervous about what lay ahead.

Decision made, we drove to where I had left off running at the western edge of Blanding. The van began to make terrible noises—a thudding sound came from the front wheels. We had no idea what to do, so we called Pastor Liming, and he recommended we call Schafer's Auto. As Megan talked with someone at the auto shop, the thudding increased. My stomach churned. *How could we afford repairs?* Nick pulled off the road.

"Hi, this is Schafer's Auto. What can I do for you?" the owner, Mr. Schafer said.

"Hi! Our van is making terrible noises, like a thudding sound, and we're scared to keep driving it." Megan said. "We're only a few miles from your shop, but we just pulled over."

"I'll come and meet you in my truck," he said.

In a few minutes, a truck pulled up and a friendly looking older gentleman with grayish-white hair and a gray mustache stepped out. "I'm Mr. Schafer. Let me see what I can do."

He started up the van and pulled it onto the road. The thudding noise began again, so he handed his keys to Nick. "Go ahead and drive my truck right behind me as I drive your van. I'll try to make it to the shop without having to tow your vehicle."

Megan and I rode with Mr. Schaffer. The van made the same awful noise, but he just drove slowly. When we arrived at the shop, he pulled the van right into his garage, and some of his mechanics immediately started working.

The shop was large and dark with parts and tools piled everywhere. Nick, Megan, and I walked into the garage and stood motionless, unsure where to go. The van was our home, and with it being worked on, we had nowhere to go.

Mr. Schafer noted our discomfort and said, "Feel free to make yourselves at home in my office."

"Thank you." We followed him into a cluttered yet welcoming room and sat in the mismatched chairs. We chatted with Mr. Schafer as he came in and out of his office over the next several hours. As time passed, my anxiety grew about how much work needed to be done and how we would pay for the repairs, but there was nothing we could do but wait.

Our conversation with Mr. Schafer eventually drifted to our pro-life ministry. His eyes lit up as he told us a story. "A friend of my family ended up pregnant. She didn't know what to do, so she went to a pregnancy center for help. They showed her an ultrasound of her baby and told her they would help her through the crisis. The girl ended up keeping her baby because of them. I've always loved the pro-life movement and pregnancy centers because of that."

"Wow!" I said. "What an amazing story."

As I finished my sentence, one of his mechanics came in and said, "The van is all done."

Mr. Schafer turned to his computer to finalize our bill and print it out. My palms sweat with the fear of a high bill. He smiled and handed me the printed copy of the bill.

I took the bill and scanned the paper until I saw the cost line. Zero dollars. His mechanics had done over a thousand dollars' worth of work for free.

"Thank you, thank you, thank you!" we all gushed.

"Oh, don't thank me." he said, then laughed. "Thank the guys. They did the work."

We thanked the mechanics as we left. When we turned to say goodbye, Mr. Schafer handed us a hundred dollars and said, "Keep going and doing what you're doing to protect those little ones!"

When we pulled out of the mechanic shop, Nick said little, but had a small smile as he drove. Megan chatted energetically while sitting on the edge of her seat, and I held the printed receipt in my hand and stared at the balance line. Our van had been repaired, and we were leaving with more money than we went in with. I smiled and smiled, thanking God for His unending goodness and provision.

After Schafer's Auto, we returned to where we left off running in Blanding, ready to head into the wilderness of southern Utah. We knew little of what lay ahead other than that there were a few small towns as well as canyons and lakes and the depths of winter in a desert. We had stored those facts in our heads, but they soon became harsh realities.

We were about to delve into the craziest part of our journey: the wilderness.

15

THE WILDERNESS

"We're almost out of water," I said, assessing our water storage containers.

"We'll have to ration it until we can fill up again at a gas station." Nick shook one container, and I heard the air pocket. "It's too much wear and tear on our old van to take it all the way back to a gas station. We don't want to risk another breakdown."

"And it's a lot of gas," Megan said.

"We need to save as much for drinking and cooking as we can. That means cutting cocoa and coffee and trying to use minimal dishes," Nick said.

Megan and I nodded.

Nick had found a nice spot to camp deep in some cedar woods off a narrow, reddish-dirt road that jutted from Highway 95 just before mile marker ninety-eight. Our van was parked deep enough into the woods to be out of sight of the road, making us feel even more secluded.

Several running days had passed since we left Blanding, and we had not had a chance to refill our numerous water containers. Despite being low on water, we set up our camp to make everything as homey as possible. The cedars were dense and grew in an almost perfect circle around our dirt clearing. Nick gathered stones to make a fire pit, then constructed a lean-to out of our tarp and some branches. Once the fire was going, we set up our tent. I smiled as we arranged everything—it felt so cozy.

We slept well in our tent, although the temperature hovered in the low thirties that night. When morning came, we awoke to celebrate our Thursday Sabbath in the wild. We took the day slow, made breakfast over the fire, and even took off our shoes as the weather rose into the fifties. The dirt felt like soft powder as I walked barefoot around the site. For dinner, we used more home-canned beef to make a hot stew, then we crawled into our tent and read more *Treasure Island* out loud before we went to sleep around sunset.

The night wasn't as restful as we had hoped. An unexpected rain fell—everything, including our sleeping bags, was wet and soggy. In the morning I awoke wet, cold, and tired. Nick and I layered up our running clothes and set off for our run. We ran over twenty miles in the rain, and as we finished, the frigid December rain turned to snow.

Back at the campsite, Nick built a fire despite the rain and snow. We cooked our dinner over the fire and got ready to pass another cold night in our tent. Intense layering would help me make it through the cold night, but I added a thick black coat, a new neck warmer from Pastor Liming, ear warmers, and a wool hat to all the layers I had previously been wearing. The layers made my body stiff as I tried to move, but I was grateful for the much-needed warmth. I curled deep into my sleeping bag, and after a few minutes of shivering, was fast asleep.

I was startled awake by something pressing on my face. Darkness made it impossible to see, but I could tell it was the tent. It had collapsed on us as we slept! I pushed upward. The weight immediately gave way, and I realized snow had caused the tent to collapse. Shivering, I pulled my sleeping bag tight, then cuddled my knees to my chest and my head in tight as I tried to warm up again.

Nick and I woke up at the same time the next morning to several inches of pristine snow coating the ground. After we admired its soft beauty against the rugged wilderness, Nick rebuilt the fire. He knelt down with his small kindling in one hand and some sort of moss as a fire starter in the other hand. As if by magic, a flame appeared.

As Nick labored over making a fire in the snowstorm, I marveled at God's goodness. He had sent snow as our water source, and I filled all our pots. God had provided money, hotels, hosts, and meals, but never something so obviously miraculous as water in the desert—exactly when we were in desperate need.

As I placed the first pots of snow to boil, Megan awoke and joined me. We continued taking our pots and scraping them along the ground to scoop up the snow, careful to avoid the dirt. After we set yet another round of snowmelt on the fire, we tried to dry out our sleeping bags and pillows from the rain and snow of the past couple days.

"If you hang them in the trees," Nick said, "I can build up the fire to help them dry faster."

"Good idea."

Nick continually stoked and fueled the fire to help. Our campsite went from looking cozy and organized to rather chaotic with scraped snow trails along with sleeping bags, blankets, pillows, and pillowcases hung from the twisted, semi-bare cedar trees.

Many hours passed as we melted and stored snow-water. As our bedding dried, we took a short break to have hot tea from the snow-water. The tea water was grayish and bits of ash floated in it, but it was delicious—and most importantly, hot.

"No more rationing." Megan slurped her hot tea.

"No kidding. It's like manna in the desert. Only God could do that!" I cupped my hands tightly around my mug. Nick and Megan smiled in agreement.

After the break, we methodically packed up our campsite, smothered the fire with dirt, and made sure the place looked as if no one had been there. Nick and I did our core workout routine and began running. Hardly a soul passed us on the road. The many cow trails (and yet few cattle) alongside the Utah roads delighted us because they gave our joints a break from all the pounding of running on asphalt.

We felt pressured to run far and fast because we wanted to take a ferry across the upcoming Lake Powell rather than drive around it. If we didn't make the ferry, we would have to wait until the next week or drive several hours north to get to the road on the opposite shore.

We ran ten miles that evening but were still short of the ferry crossing. The next day was another sixteen-mile push to reach the edge of the lake before crossing.

"We're here for the ferry. How do we pay for it?" we asked a lady behind the counter of a building on the dock.

"Oh, I'm sorry. The ferry is not running right now. You'll have to wait until next week, or you can drive around, but that is many hours."

"Thank you," Megan said.

"Well, we don't want to wait a week. I guess we'll have to drive around," I said.

"But it's getting late, and I don't want to drive the canyons in the dark," said Nick. "We'd better park somewhere for the night and drive tomorrow."

We drove back a little way to a hill called Salvation Knoll, named for Mormon settlers who found their way by climbing to the top of it when they were lost. We van-camped at the base of it, made spaghetti, and layered up for the night.

I shook uncontrollably in the biting cold as I curled into my sleeping bag, using my brown blanket from James as another layer. My multiple layers no longer felt insufferably stiff, but comforting. I burrowed deep, trying to capture every bit of heat. I pulled the hooded part of my sleeping bag over me but still couldn't warm my shaking body enough to fall asleep. I pulled the sleeping bag closed and tight over my face, nearly suffocating myself to keep warm, but it was easier to stifle my breathing than to have shivers rack my body. A few minutes passed, and I was almost asleep when I realized I had to use the restroom.

Tears burned my eyes as I thought of facing the cold to use the restroom, but I would not make it through the night otherwise. I forced myself to climb out of my sleeping bag, tugged my running shoes part way over my layered feet, and after a short mental battle, crawled toward the door, apologizing to Nick as I scrambled across his sleeping body to get out. The temperature outside was twenty-three degrees, the wind vicious. The cold whooshed into the van. Megan and Nick drew their sleeping bags tighter.

The snow crunched under my feet as I looked for a place to use the restroom. The wind whipped across my body as I walked hunched down to keep warm. My arms wrapped around my body as I scanned my surroundings. The cold, deep darkness of the desert night scared me. *What if I wander too far and can't find my way back?* I took a few steps and crouched down. *This is miserable.*

I hurried back to the van, kicked the snow off my shoes, and crawled into my sleeping bag again, trying to calm my shivering body. During the night I was vaguely aware that Megan and then a few hours later, Nick, endured the same hardship. The van door opened, the wind brought in more cold, and then the door reopened when someone returned. I longed for the sun to bring morning and warmth.

I awoke in dim daylight; the sun had not crested. The water in my Nalgene water bottle was frozen solid next to my head. Nick crawled forward and used our ice scraper to remove the ice that had formed on the inside of our front windshield.

"Let's have a cookout on top of Salvation Knoll since it's as cold inside the van as outside." Nick clapped his hands together and then blew into them for warmth.

Megan and I agreed. Hiking up the short, winding path, the steep incline and the weight of the cooking supplies we carried made us pant. We made it to the top, spread out our sleeping bag to sit on, and began cooking.

Overlooking the scrubby, snowy desert below, I made homemade syrup, and we ate pancakes and drank our usual strong, hot coffee. Far below our perch, cedar trees were surrounded by snow. The rising sun showcased its reds, oranges, and yellows as we cooked. The brilliance of the snow seemed to make the sun's rays brighter. The silent beauty was surreal, the clinking of our forks on our blue tin plates the only sound. I savored the warmth provided by my hot coffee and the sun.

As we hiked back down, my phone buzzed inside my pocket. We had not had cell service in a week. I dug into my pocket and pulled out my phone. A single text from James had managed to come through—a good morning message telling me he missed me and cared about me. I tried to text him back but did not have enough service to send a reply. My heart ached as I put my phone away and headed back to the van.

We loaded up and drove several hours through canyons until we reached the Bullfrog Marina on the other side of the lake where the ferry would have taken us. We began our run at the water's edge, exactly where we would have ended up had the ferry been running.

About six miles ahead lay the Burr Trail: roughly eighty miles of wilderness road through Bureau of Land Management lands, or public lands. We had been told we would not see anyone on the untamed, wilderness stretch in the winter. We planned to take this wild, partially paved, partially gravel road as a shortcut to save us close to 100 miles of running, but if we had known what hardships lay ahead, we never would have set foot on the Burr Trail.

We covered the six miles from the marina with ease and reached the Burr Trail, a rather flat gravel road that quickly ascended into the hills beyond and out of sight. The land around us was a mixture of reds and whites dotted with sparse, scrubby bushes.

The flat beginning ended abruptly: a huge hill lay before us—one that wound and wound and seemed to never end. We ran up, up, up. Behind us, the giant lake faded as we covered distance. On we ran until we reached a seemingly insurmountable hill.

Nick and I decided to run to the top of what we could see. If there was more difficulty ahead, we would deal with that when we got there. Ever so slowly, one visible hill was conquered. At the foot of another hill, I set my mind to simply run that next bit. Finally, after what felt like forever, we reached the top, and the land leveled out a bit before us.

We quit for the day, stretching and waiting for Megan. When she pulled the van over on the left side of the road, we looked back and saw the lake we had left behind. It looked so small. *How could my legs have carried me to the overlook?* Nick and I had traveled fifteen miles and gained a thousand feet in elevation.

As we prepared dinner and got ready for bed that night, we talked about our plans since Christmas was fast approaching.

"I have a hotel booked for the twenty-fourth through twenty-sixth in northern Utah where there is actually some population," Megan said.

"That means we only have one more run before Christmas break," Nick said.

"Just one more!" I echoed.

16

CHRISTMAS IN THE WILD

The next morning when we awoke, snow fell at a rapid rate.
"If we don't get to better roads, we might be snowed in
here on the trail for Christmas," Nick said.

"We'd better skip our run for today and just try to beat this
storm," I said.

The snow continued fast and heavy. I did not think it would let
up any time soon. We packed the van and hoped to reach some
sort of civilization before we were snowed into the wilderness.
After slow and cautious driving, we arrived at a gas station in
Bullfrog, Utah. The snow accumulation indicated that we would
not make it to our hotel for Christmas.

At the gas station, Nick approached the counter and asked the
cashier, "Do you have any idea if this weather is going to pass?"

"Not a clue, hon," she said.

"Do you think the roads are safe for driving?"

"I sure wish I could tell ya, but I don't know."

Nick returned to our table in the gas station's restaurant. The
snow fell so fast that we knew we would spend Christmas in our
van eating canned goods. We called home and told our parents the
disappointing news, and they said they would pray.

Several hours passed before the cashier called Nick to come

over. "This is a ranger," the lady said pointing to a tall, dark-haired man in casual clothes. "Maybe he can answer your questions."

Nick explained our situation and concluded with "What do you think about us driving north?"

"Well, the snow is coming down really hard," he observed, then paused. "I don't want you to run off the road, but I can offer you an escort for a few hours until we pass the storm. That way I can help you if anything goes wrong."

We headed north in our van as he followed us in his large, black truck. For hours, we drove through beautiful canyons and past looming cliffs. When we stopped in a small town for gas, the roads were much clearer, and the storm was mostly behind us.

We got out to say goodbye to the ranger. "Thank you so much for your help. You were an answer to our prayers," Nick said as he shook the ranger's hand.

"I didn't have much else to do on my day off, so it was my pleasure." The ranger laughed, then got back in his truck and pulled away.

We filled our van with gas, then entered the small grocery store. We picked out sparkling juice, soda, and cookies to celebrate Christmas. We also selected stockings for one another and treats to fill them.

As the cashier rang up our items, we told her about our journey. "Oh, how wonderful!" she said. "I'm pro-life too." She then discounted each item as she scanned it. Her face was illuminated with kindness and love.

We drove until we reached our motel in Hanksville. We camped in our van one last night, but it passed quickly since we were so excited for our Christmas break to begin the next day.

Early the next morning, Megan received a phone call from our friend Roberta Bretz, who had hosted us in Goodland, Kansas. She wanted to pay for all three nights of our hotel stay.

"That was so kind of Roberta and her husband!" I said to Megan.

When Megan presented her ID, the hotel employee said, "A package and a letter are here for you."

"Thank you!" said Megan as she took the package. "It's from Alli!" (Alli had visited us in Colorado).

"How sweet of her!" I reached out for the letter, seeing James's handwriting on the envelope. As we walked back to the room, I tore the seal. The woodsy fragrance of his cologne wafted toward me. In our room, I read the letter, feeling very loved.

I set up our stockings and laid out the gifts in an attempt to make the room feel like Christmas. The stockings, the wrapped presents from Alli, and the snacks made the room cheery and festive.

When I looked up, Megan was talking on the phone, smiling and toying with her hair. "Oh that would be just wonderful." I walked closer to her to ascertain what she was discussing. "Sounds like a plan." She hung up the phone. "Pastor Liming invited us to have a second Christmas with him after our motel stay."

"Really?" Nick asked, sitting up from the bed where he had been reading.

"Yeah! It'll be the Christmas we dreamed of." I swayed as I thought of us having a home again.

On Christmas Eve morning, we learned that every restaurant and store in the town would be closed for Christmas Eve and Christmas—even the hotel restaurant. We had no idea what to do for food, so we planned to order two pizzas—one for Christmas Eve and one for Christmas Day so we wouldn't have to eat canned goods. I called to order the pizza but forgot to order two. I realized my mistake, and I called back to order a second one, but the restaurant was closing soon, and it was too late to order more. That night all three of us shared half of the pizza, so we could have food for the next day. The snacks we had bought helped too.

I awoke Christmas morning determined to make it special. The wilderness had made us feel lonely, and we longed for our families. Spending Christmas away from home was depressing. Nick and Megan were exhausted, but I was ready to celebrate.

I went out to the van, opened the doors, and set up the cook stove to make pancakes for breakfast. I went to our cooler to grab eggs and realized we were out. I went to the front desk and explained our situation, my face flushed as I spoke. One of the workers volunteered to go to her house and get some eggs.

Once I had the eggs, I mixed and then fried the pancakes on one burner and percolated coffee on the other. I laid the pancakes out stacked partially on top of each other in an attempt to make the pancakes look festive and fancy. I walked up the steps balancing all three plates, then ran back through the cold outside air for the percolator and mugs. We turned on classic Christmas music and ate our pancakes leisurely, sitting on our two queen beds.

After the pancakes, we opened stockings. We each pulled out favorite candy bars, bottled sodas and coffees, and snacks. The gifts were wonderful, though simple. After the stockings, we opened the gifts from Alli.

Megan held up a gift addressed to all three of us and unwrapped it.

"Oh, it's Peete's coffee, our favorite, and chocolate! How special," said Megan.

We opened gifts addressed to each of us. Nick smiled as he unwrapped and held up a wool flannel shirt. Megan and I gasped as we pulled out long, beautiful cardigans. We both rushed to the mirror and pulled on our new sweaters.

"I feel so lovely in this." I gripped the ends of the sleeves.

"And so loved." Megan swayed back and forth as she looked in the mirror.

The last gift came in the form of an email from our fiscal sponsors, the McElreaths. We had received an unexpected but perfectly timed grant from the Templeton Foundation.

"Oh guys, this is the perfect Christmas gift. Money when we

are in the desert without hosts or churches to speak at. God has provided again!" I said.

"It is literally perfect timing. This grant means we can easily make it through the next several-hundred-mile stretch without donations," Megan responded.

We finished out the restful day with movies, half a cold pizza, and more snacks. Our stay at the motel ended, so we packed up and drove roughly three hours to Pastor Liming's home.

When we walked into Pastor Liming's house, we were greeted by his two dogs, the smell of his crackling fire, and Pastor Liming's wide eyes and big, kind smile. On the table was a huge honey ham, mashed potatoes, and delicious rolls. We ate, talked, laughed, and shared with him about our latest adventures.

After dinner, Pastor Liming said, "Now this stay, I'm afraid you'll have to sleep on my couches. The couple I found in the woods now live in my guest house. I'm sorry I can't offer you a better place to rest."

"Oh, that's no problem," Megan answered.

"Can I interest you all in some more cappuccinos?" Pastor Liming asked.

"Yes, please," Nick responded. Megan and I nodded in agreement.

As he prepared the coffee, Megan and I made three types of cookies to enjoy throughout the evening. With mugs and plates of treats in hand, we spent much of the evening talking and laughing with Pastor Liming. After many stories, Pastor Liming stood, left the room, and returned with a huge gift. Excitement twinkled in his eyes.

He set the gift before us, and neatly typed on top of it was Wilderness Survival Kit. We opened it and each of us pulled out gift after gift—several varieties of expensive dark chocolates,

Intelligentsia coffee, and many types of quality tea—exactly the comforts we craved on the cold, lonely Utah nights.

"Thank you so much. These are the perfect gifts to help us take on the wilderness winter." I held a bag of coffee in my hands and smelled the dark aroma.

"Yes, thank you," Megan echoed.

"I don't want you to run out, so I have one more gift," Pastor Liming said.

He returned with another tub labeled Wilderness Survival Refill Kit. This was filled with more survival supplies after we had eaten through the others.

Just before we left the next day, our friends Anita and her husband, Cyril, from the pregnancy center back in Montrose, CO, arrived. They had hosted another food drive for our team and had driven about three hours one-way to deliver the items to us in Dove Creek.

Anita and Cyril presented us with a tub filled with more home-canned beef, home-canned peaches, and homemade jelly. We loaded our supplies and said goodbye to Anita, Cyril, and Pastor Liming. I sat in the back seat and waved goodbye. My gaze dropped from them to the back of the van now crowded with tubs of provisions. We should have been alone in that barren, desolate wilderness, but God's people met us— Pastor Liming's hospitality, the ranger escorting us through the storm, the motel clerk providing eggs, Alli's gifts, and the pregnancy center's food drive.

I placed my pillow on the tubs, leaned against them to rest, and fell asleep knowing we were cared for even when we felt alone.

17

HARDSHIP

The axle to the bike was gone.

We were back on the Burr Trail, Nick's knee injury was inflamed, and there was nowhere to purchase another axle. Megan called any number she could find in the closest town, Boulder, Utah, just on the west side of the Burr Trail. When she called a museum, a man named Jake answered. She explained our story and the loss of the axle.

"We don't have an axle," he said, "but my wife, Kate, and I need to head up north this weekend to Salt Lake City to get supplies. We'd be happy to pick one up for you, and you could stay at our house while we're gone." Although we were disappointed about a running delay, the offer of a home was thrilling, especially since it was New Years' weekend.

As we drove the long, tumultuous Burr Trail, our old van's engine rumbled loudly as it sluggishly ascended and descended the hills of the trail, but we made it to Jake and Kate's driveway. Their home was set far off the road and surrounded by farms and small, round-topped mountains.

Jake was a tall, athletic man with dark hair. Kate, also athletic, was kind and extremely hospitable, but a bit more reserved. She baked a homemade pizza, topped with all sorts of colorful, delicious vegetables.

Before they left for Salt Lake City, they asked that we keep their wood-burning fire going and tend to their animals: two dogs, two snakes, four indoor birds, chickens, ducks, pigeons, a peregrine falcon, a hawk, and horses. Caring for that menagerie felt overwhelming, but it was small inconvenience when compared with a free place to stay and their willingness to get an axle for us.

Feeding the falcon was intimidating. With a pair of tongs, Nick grabbed a dead quail and carried it to the shed where the bird was housed, but we could hardly see through the metal-barred window. Nick guided the tongs with the quail through the bars. The falcon launched itself, grabbed the quail, and flew to the opposite corner of the cage in one startling, fluid motion. Feeding the other animals was simple, and a welcome change from our routine.

After the feeding chores, we relaxed and took hikes on their nearby mountains. We celebrated New Year's Eve by heading to the local Mini Mart and buying candy and sparkling juice. We watched a movie on my laptop and stayed up to welcome in the new year while enjoying our treats.

A couple days later, Jake and Kate returned with their supplies and an axle.

"Thank you for the bike axle and for letting us stay," said Megan, "and for trusting us with your place while you were gone."

"Of course," Jake said as if taking in three perfect strangers was normal.

We loaded our van and started the long trek back to our run spot. The ground around us was snowy and icy as we drove back over the Burr Trail. Nick drove cautiously as we traveled through the tree-spotted desert. The ground was a mixture of snow patches and brown earth and rock. Scrubby, tangled cedar trees sat along the roadside, dry and bent from years of surviving in the brutal desert terrain.

We took a sharp turn and hit a large patch of ice. Our van careened out of control as it made a 180-degree turn and slammed into a massive cedar tree. Our necks whipped sideways on impact, and our van lodged in the tree, the passenger side pinned in the branches.

Few vehicles, if any, crossed the Burr Trail during the winter months, so it could be days, or even weeks, before someone found us. We climbed out of the van on the driver's side because the passenger doors were blocked by the tree. The van was angled somewhat sideways on the edge of the road, almost leaning against the cedar.

As Nick walked from the front of the van to the back taking in the damage, he shouted, mostly to himself, "What are we going to do? We're stuck." He ran his hands over his mouth. "We're not going to be able to get the van out!" One hand was buried in his hair while the other hand waved wildly. He continued yelling and stressing.

"Calm down!" I yelled. "Do you think being angry about it is going to get our van unstuck?" I clasped my hands over my head and exhaled slowly. Megan stood near the van motionless and silent, her hands clasped in front of her.

"And you think you're calm, Anna?" he retorted with a glare.

"Yelling and freaking out won't solve anything." I could feel the heat in my face as my temper rose to the point of exasperation, so I walked a few feet away trying to control myself. The shock of the wreck and the fear of freezing to death on the trail clouded my judgment. And Nick's.

I pulled out my phone to confirm what I already knew: no cell service. I rubbed my face in my hands as fear washed over me. I breathed out slowly to calm myself and approached Nick again. Megan still stood perfectly still and tight-lipped.

Nick climbed into the driver seat and put the van in reverse and tapped the gas. The tires spun, mixing dirt and snow into mud that sprayed out from beneath them. He gave it a little more gas; the tires dug in and then spun. He let off the gas, put the van in park, and turned it off before he hopped out.

"We should put gravel behind the tires to give them some traction." I pointed toward the back tires.

"It'll just get shot out like the mud." Nick's eyebrows were raised as he spoke through clenched teeth. He then opened the rear doors of the van and retrieved a saw. He cut a branch that was smashed up against our van. While he sawed, I tried to layer gravel behind the back tires to give them traction on the ice. Nick continued sawing branch after branch until about a third of the tree was bare.

With the branches sawn, dislodged, and removed, we might be able to back our van out of the slanted, icy area where it had crashed. Nick hopped behind the wheel, put the van in reverse, and gave it a little gas. The tires spun, and gravel and dirt shot into the air. The back wheels sank deeper into the now dirty ice-mixture. I placed more small rocks at the back and front of the tire to get traction, but those also spun out and shot into the air.

We tried and failed repeatedly. I wanted to give up, but Nick wasn't prepared to quit.

"Let's try the tire chains. I know we can't put them on the tires but maybe they can give us some traction if we put them behind the tires," he said.

Megan pulled out the chains, and we placed them behind the tires. Nick put the van in reverse, and tried backing up, but the chains were kicked up just like the stones.

I rubbed my filthy hands together to generate some warmth.

We tried again. No luck.

And again, no luck.

Frustration and fear bubbled in my chest.

We tried once more.

Somehow the chains helped the van grip the ground, and it shot backward onto the paved road. We surveyed the damage, but the van seemed fine except for a dent in the passenger side door.

I was so relieved I could have cried but still remained angry. Nick sat forward in the driver seat, posture erect and his hands clenched almost white on the steering wheel. Megan remained still and silent.

We drove a short way down the road to get away from the ice before stopping to put the tire chains on the van. We would not make the same mistake twice. We laid the chains down, drove onto them, and fastened them. There was extra slack in the chains, so we zip-tied the extra chain down. None of us had experience with tire chains, and I was grateful for our quick success.

As we drove, the clank of metal slapping the wheel wells of our van startled me. "That doesn't sound good," I said.

Nick stopped the van. "I can check," Megan said as she hopped out. She came back and said, "One of the zip ties holding the slack of the chain broke. I'll fix it fast."

When she got back in, the clanking stopped. Soon the road switched from smooth, black pavement to brownish-gray gravel. Only a short distance farther, the chains began slapping again. Nick got out this time and replaced the zip ties. It happened repeatedly to the front right tire.

Frustration about the accident created a silent tension in the van. And the slapping chains only increased it.

We drove another mile or so, and again the chains were slapping. I got out, knelt under the front right wheel, and fixed it again.

We drove another quarter mile or so before I realized my phone was missing. My hands immediately went to the pockets of my black coat. Not there. Then I felt beside my legs and under me. Not there. "My phone must have fallen out of my pocket when I was bent over fixing the zip ties," I said.

Nick slowed the van and turned around. We retraced where we had driven and where we thought we had stopped. We looked and looked. No sign of my phone. After another twenty minutes of pacing, arguing, and searching in the cold January air, Nick shouted, "I found it!"

Elated, I jogged over to him. He handed it to me, and my heart dropped: it had been completely destroyed—it was smashed to bits and merely held together by the back. The chained tires had ground my phone into the gravel road.

Back in the van, I held the shattered pieces in my hands. *I have no way to keep track of my mileage. No way to communicate with James or my family. All this because we had to get a bike axle.*

When we reached the run spot, Nick and Megan hopped out to get the bike ready. I waited in the van, but after a few minutes wondered what was taking so long. I climbed out and walked over to Megan and Nick. "What's the holdup?"

"The bike tire was flat, so we put on a new tube, but this second one won't inflate. We're trying another one right now," Megan answered.

"Could I borrow your phone, Megs? Maybe I can get service and call James," I asked.

Megan handed me her phone, and as I walked away, I pulled up James's number. After a little walking, I had enough service, and my call actually went through. He answered, and I broke down crying.

"We lost an axle, and ... and we got in a car wreck." My sobs made it difficult to speak. "And my phone got run over, and the bike still won't work. I feel so-so-so overwhelmed."

"Oh, Anna," he said, his voice soft and soothing. "It will be okay. I'm so sorry it's been so hard. We can get you a new phone, and I'm sure the bike will work okay. I'm so sorry it's been so awful." He reassured me again and again until we said goodbye.

For the first time, I felt love for James. My affection for him had grown slowly but steadily for some time. What I felt now was more than a goofy crush, more than admiring how handsome he was, more than how he made me feel. He loved me, despite the hardships.

I was at my worst—exhausted, un-showered, homeless, unknown, no makeup, worn down by the loneliness. All my surface attractions gone. Yet week after week, even the weeks with no cell signal and no way to communicate, then month after month, even the many months without seeing each other, he continued to treat me with affection, kindness, and love.

James listened when I cried. He sent letters to addresses all across America when I felt alone, he texted even when he knew they wouldn't be delivered, he made me laugh when I was defeated, and he believed in me when few others did. He loved me despite my unwashed, oily French braid, the dirt on my skin so caked that I could scratch it off, and my face haggard from the unending running and spiritual warfare.

He was the only person who knew everything I was feeling—discouraged or encouraged, weary or energized. And I loved him for it. As I reflected on our conversation, I pictured his tall, handsome frame, his crisply cut red hair, and his understanding green eyes.

After my phone call with James, I walked back to Megan and Nick. They had tried a third tube, and then a fourth, but none would inflate.

Through gritted teeth, I said, "I'm going to start running. I'll meet you up the road, Nick."

I needed to get out of there before I lost my temper again. As I ran, I fought back tears. My breathing was stressed at first, but after a few hundred yards, my breathing leveled out and my pace steadied. Despite the hardships, I felt better after a few miles passed.

I had run about three miles when I became concerned that Nick had not come yet. Something must have gone wrong. I turned back and walked for what seemed like forever, though only about forty minutes passed. I was almost back to where I started when Nick came into view.

"We tried five tubes. None of them would inflate," he said.

"Seriously? The trip to Boulder, the van wreck, my phone being trashed, and all the frustration and time we have wasted, and we *still* don't have a working bike?"

"Yeah, I know. It's been awful," answered Nick, his voice was hoarse. His disheveled hair nearly reached his darkened, weary eyes. "Well, you wanna start running?"

"What about your knee? Doesn't it still hurt?" I asked.

"It'll be fine. Let's just have Megan take us to where you finished before you walked back to find me."

Megan soon picked us up. When we arrived at the run spot, Nick and I hopped out of the van and began running, though discouragement slowed my pace. As we ran, I could tell Nick's knee was aching by the stiff way he ran. His face was stoic, but occasionally I noted a well-disguised grimace.

Ahead lay huge rock structures, but for now we covered the flatter gravel road with relative ease. As I looked around, it seemed as if behemoth rocks in hundreds of shades of reds and tans had been pushed out of the ground at an angle and then dotted with little shrubs.

When the flatter, easier miles ended, the road became steep. The rocks I had admired became my foes. Nick and I made it a little way up the steep road but stopped at just over ten miles. We wanted to be well rested before running the switchbacks we had driven through to get to Jake and Kate's home.

We van-camped at a grayish-white canyon near the red-rocked switchbacks. After sunset, the stars glimmered just above the ridge of the rocks. Nick built a fire on the edge of the road that glowed and flickered, illuminating the rock walls around us. We roasted marshmallows until they were perfectly golden for s'mores. We crunched into our hot, melty s'mores and chatted, keeping close to the fire for warmth. The peaceful evening slowly eased the day's frustration.

As we talked, we discovered the canyon echoed.

"Ah-h-h!" I hollered at the rock walls as if telling them of our recent trials. "Ah-h-h, Ah-h-h, Ah-h-h" was the crystal-clear response.

"Ay-y-y-y-ie!" Nick yipped loudly as he tilted his head back. The yell seemed to decompress the tension our last several days had built up in him.

"Hello-o-o!" Megan cupped her hands around her mouth with the shout.

We yelled, yelped, and hollered into the stary night. The canyons played catch with our voices, throwing them from one side to the other, the volume shrinking with each pass and taking our stress with them. We sat in the perfect silence of a windless night far from people, cities, or sounds. Incredibly steep running lay ahead, but I sat contentedly near the fire with hardly a thought of the upcoming hardship. I was learning to rely on God's strength, and I felt it as we relaxed in the deep seclusion of the Burr Trail.

In the morning, we awoke to cold but bearable temperatures. Patches of snow dappled the ground. Nick's knee felt good enough to run, so we started, fearing the upcoming switchbacks. We ran to the base of them and saw what looked like someone had taken a canyon wall and cut steep, 180-degree zigzags. The switchbacks, roughly a mile long, were a 12 percent grade, the steepest grade we had yet encountered.

Up and up the road wound, almost doubling back on itself as it turned. On tiptoe, Nick and I persevered. My lungs burned with each inhalation, and my legs resisted as I pushed them forward. I panted heavily, my mind begging for the road to level out.

I cut in as close as I could to the inside of each turn to shorten the run. Nick was ahead of me by several paces, and the fact his feet had covered the steps ahead gave me courage that I could too. After much perseverance, we reached the last switchback.

Megan was at the top. "Wow! Good job, guys."

We stopped to catch our breath.

On January 3, 2017 Nick and I ran the Burr Trail switchbacks just outside Boulder, Utah. We stood at the top and overlooked much of what we had run so far.

"Could you meet us at the top of the next hill?" Nick said between breaths.

"Sure," Megan said.

The van's engine rumbled and sputtered as she drove out of sight. As we ran, we the snow had gone from being spotty to covering most of the ground around us. After what seemed like hours, I saw the shape of the red van. We reached it, breathless and legs worn, even though we had only run just over six miles.

In the evening we searched for a spot to cook dinner. We found a cozy nook among some cedars. We were above the canyons Nick and I had run that day and back into flatter desert lands. The sky was dark above the trees. We all gathered firewood, and Nick started a fire. The wood was plentiful and dry despite the snow, so it burned easily and quickly.

We knelt on our striped falsa blanket while we cooked to keep our knees out of the snow. The sight of dinner cooking on the coals was lovely: onions browning, ground beef frying, and beans simmering. After dinner, we made tea and read *Treasure Island* aloud next to the warmth of the fire. After a while, we put the book away and soaked up the beauty of the densely growing cedar trees illuminated by the glowing campfire. Behind the trees a starlit sky —our only roof.

As the warmth of the fire and our sleeping bags held the snowy cold at bay, we talked about what was coming up: James was planning to visit us in two days in Las Vegas, and I could hardly talk of anything else. After our run the next day, we would drive to meet James.

In the morning, Nick relit the fire. I placed a pot of water on it for oatmeal, thoughts of James bouncing in my head. When Nick added more wood to the fire around the pot to speed the boiling process, the flames leapt up in bursts as the fire consumed the dry, desert wood.

One flame leapt especially high and caught the cedar branch nearby. Before we could react, the fire leapt again and began to consume the tree branches closest to us. We jumped back from the intense heat. Nick reacted swiftly and grabbed water to douse it. The water roared when it made contact with the flaming tree branches, but it quenched the fire. Instantly, wispy black smoke replaced the once threatening flames.

Our run that day was a relatively easy seven miles with lots of downhill slopes. When we finished, we began the long drive to Las Vegas. We stopped at a gas station in a small town in Utah for the night. As we got ready for bed, Megan emailed a college about our friend Meagan Isola doing a writing internship with us.

Megan composed the email accepting Meagan Isola as an intern. "We look forward to having Meagan Isola intern with us.

Please send the information packet and our office will forward it to us as we are on the road."

I burst out laughing as I said, "Megs, you're typing on your phone in the back of an old van, unshowered and parked in a gas station parking lot. What an organization!"

All three of us laughed so hard our sides hurt.

The laughter soothed the ache the hardships the last few days had caused and helped lift a shadow that had settled over my joy. I knew God refined us by fire, and I felt the pain of that fire in the loneliness, seclusion, strife, and trials we had been through. As I settled in for the night, I thanked God for the much-needed relief from the pain and His uncanny provision during our trials.

18

STUCK

My heart pounded and my whole body felt electrified with energy. I couldn't stop smiling or laughing. In the airport, my eyes darted here and there trying to catch my first glimpse of James. I then saw his red hair and six-foot-two frame walking toward me. He looked so handsome and polished wearing a white jacket, cuffed jeans, and dress boots. I ran to him and hugged him tight. His woodsy cologne filled my nose as I buried my face in his chest.

Five months.

Five months since those arms had wrapped around me. He pushed me back a little and looked into my eyes before he kissed my forehead and hugged me again.

"Let's go on a date!" His goofy, boyish smile spread across his face.

We headed to Caesar's Palace on the famous Las Vegas Strip. We wandered around hand-in-hand, lost in the beauty and the illusion of the resort.

The casino featured columns with giant tan archways, ancient-looking statues, ceiling murals, and mosaic-like floor tile. It was stunning, but the fact that it was all a facade to lure people in to spend their money somehow made it look cheap despite all the glitz. I assumed everyone would be dressed beautifully and be laughing—just like in the movies. But the people seemed zombie-like as they stared at the game screens.

James and I weren't there to gamble, so we enjoyed wandering around and taking in the beautiful sights. After a while James asked, "Are you hungry? There's a fancy steakhouse if you'd like to go."

"I'd love to."

The waiter brought out the menus, and my stomach dropped as I read the prices: steaks were fifty dollars each. James whispered, "Are you okay with splitting?"

"Of course."

"Oh look!" He pointed to the baked macaroni side they offered. "It's your favorite. We have to get that as our side."

"I'd love that."

James held and stroked my hand as we ordered. I grinned at every word James spoke. The waiter smiled at our shy and yet joyful love and catered to us in an extra-attentive, sweet way. The steak steamed as he carried it out from the kitchen, already split in half for us. My mouth watered as I bit into it. I had never tasted a steak that delicious. No wonder the prices were so high. James and I talked and laughed as I sat in disbelief that we were together again.

After dinner, James ordered a ride share that took us to another beautiful casino, the Bellagio. I held his hand tight as we wove in and out of the crowded area around the fountains the Bellagio is famous for. We strolled to the backside of the fountains between the hotel and the water. The chaos of the crowds subsided as people turned to face the water for a show.

Fountains shot up in the air in perfect unison to the music. The water twisted and turned in the air, and colored lights illuminated it as it rose and fell. We leaned against a beautiful stone railing, our arms wrapped around each other, and watched for a long while. So many people bustled around us, but we somehow felt alone.

"Happy One Year, Anna," James said.

All the noise and craziness of Vegas faded as James took my hands, turned me to him, and put his hand on my cheek.

"I love you," he whispered.

He then stooped and kissed my lips for the first time. A million flutters spread through me. His smile filled his whole face, and he couldn't keep from giggling. The rest of the night passed in a blur as we floated around the streets of Las Vegas in a haze of love.

Several wonderful days filled with dates and exploring Las Vegas passed before James and I had to say goodbye. My heart broke when I thought of a return to distance-dating. I didn't know when I would see him again.

When we left the airport, Megan, Nick, and I started the drive back to the Burr Trail from Las Vegas. To give Nick a break, I offered to drive. As I merged onto I-15 heading out of Las Vegas, cars whipped past us at eighty miles an hour. I scooted forward to the edge of the driver seat and gripped the steering wheel tightly with both hands.

Vehicles darted in and out around me as I tried to maintain a safe distance from the cars around us, but I also had to merge aggressively and quickly before other drivers cut me off. To my horror, a terrible thudding noise came from the front of the van. It grew louder with startling intensity. I thought a tire would fly off at any moment.

When I took the next exit, the thudding worsened on the ramp. I tried to slow, but the brakes wouldn't engage. I kept my foot away from the accelerator, hoping we could coast to a stop.

I spied a gas station ahead on the right. "I don't know if the van will stop." I pumped the breaks, but they wouldn't engage. I kept pumping, and after several attempts, they worked well enough for me to make the turn into the gas station's parking lot.

When I pulled into a parking spot, I thought we might hit the bumper and roll over it, but it brought the van to a fairly gentle halt. We got out of our van, sat on the curb, and deliberated what we should do.

"I think we're going to have to get it towed," Megan said. "I'll start looking for a tow and the best-rated auto shop." She pulled out her phone, called for a tow, and soon a truck arrived and took our van to an auto shop.

"We'll look at it as soon as we can, but it will be a while," the worker said.

As we walked out of the shop, I said, "I'm hungry. Hopefully, there is somewhere close since we're going to be walking."

Megan searched again on her phone for food within walking distance. "I found a pizza place!"

As we ate, we discussed our options. Then Megan's phone rang. She answered, talked briefly with the mechanic, then hung up. The look on her face said it was not good news. "The shop is closing for the night, and they haven't looked at our van yet."

"Where are we going to stay?" Nick asked.

"I have no idea," I said.

"Even if we find a place to stay, how will we get there? I'll start looking anyway." Megan began calling hotels. After many calls and searches, she said, "Everything in our price range is booked."

We sat silent a while, slumped in our seats, before Megan straightened and said, "I have an idea: Rembrandt Ramos, from college, texted me this morning saying his parents live here in Las Vegas. Let me reach out to them."

She pulled up their number as she spoke. Nick tapped his fingers, and I could hardly breathe as she chatted with them.

Megan hung up and told us the news: "Rembrandt's parents are willing to have us over, and Mr. Ramos is on his way to get us."

"Oh, thank God," I said. "What a miracle!"

Mr. Ramos arrived soon. He was a short-haired Filipino man with animated eyes. He drove us to his home where we met his wife. Mrs. Ramos was a kind lady with dark hair. She served us a second dinner of *pancit* (a Filipino noodle dish) before showing us to the room we would all share. Nick set his sleeping bag on the floor, and Megan and I shared the only bed. When I closed my eyes to fall asleep, I thanked God for a roof over our heads.

In the morning, Megan called the owner of the auto shop to get an update. When he answered, she tapped the Speaker icon on her phone. "After looking over your van, there's a lot wrong with it. You drove your van on broken axles for so long that the tires cannot be put back on. The bolts crumbled as we took them off. It will be eleven hundred dollars to fix it."

"Hold on," she said to the owner of the shop, then muted the phone to whisper back and forth with Nick and me. We quickly agreed we needed a second opinion. Megan unmuted the phone and put him on speaker. "We decided we want a second opinion, but thank you anyway."

"I will give you a major discount and only charge you nine hundred! The van is so bad that it can't be put back together. We *have* to be the ones to fix it." His voice was intense yet still smooth. "It can't be fixed. You can't drive it away. There is literally no way to put it back together. You *must* have it fixed here."

We all recognized the threatening tone of his response. With an exchange of glances, we knew we could not trust this guy, but on and on he talked, trying every angle of persuasion.

"We'll call back with our decision," Megan said and hung up the phone.

After a short discussion, we decided to call Mr. Schafer for advice—the last mechanic who had worked on our van and who had been so honest and kind.

When Megan called him, he was perplexed that any of those things could be wrong. He offered to call the auto shop and talk with the owner to see if he could make sense of the situation.

When Mr. Schafer called back, he confirmed that the man was

conning us, and we should take our van elsewhere. Megan called the auto shop again. After arguing with the owner, Megan hung up again. He still refused to put the van back together.

Better to confront him in person, we decided, so Megan told him to have the van in one piece when we arrived. We borrowed our hosts' car and drove to the auto shop. When we arrived, the van was still in pieces. The owner walked toward us with a slick smile and again tried to convince us to have it serviced there. He said he would lower the price to $600, but we refused. Realizing he was getting nowhere with Megan, he turned to Nick and said he would do it for $400.

Nick's voice was strained but calm. "Put our van back together, or we will call the police."

The owner still refused. "We can't. It's too broken. You drove it so far that when we took it apart, it crumbled."

"We don't want our van fixed here. Put it back the way we brought it in," Nick's voice deepened with authority.

The mechanic refused again. They continued arguing, the volume of their voices rising almost to a shout. Other customers stared at us.

Then one of the mechanics walked up to his boss. "Boss, you're making us look bad," he murmured. "I'll put it back together."

The owner frowned, shot Nick a glare, then nodded his consent and left.

The mechanic bent down and began to work.

I released my breath with a whoosh of relief when he finished the job.

We had avoided a scam, but we still had to find a new mechanic. In Las Vegas. A city which was living up to its reputation for dishonesty and deceit.

We called our hosts and told them our predicament. They recommended an independent mechanic named Ron.

Ron was a short man with a white comb-over. He wore a button-up shirt with a pointy collar and a pair of blue jeans. He introduced himself as "Mr. Ron." He spoke slowly with an accent I couldn't place. He, his wife, and his numerous yapping Chihuahuas lived in a small house with typical Las Vegas landscaping—colored rocks. We left our van in his driveway and headed back to the Ramoses' house in their car.

That evening the Ramoses invited us to attend their church, Calvary Chapel. Mrs. Ramos energetically scuttled in and out of our room bringing a large stack of clothes as well as perfume and a curling iron. Megan held up an outfit to herself in front of the mirror as I flipped through the large pile.

"There are so many options, it feels like a mall." Megan held up yet another combination.

"No kidding! I don't know how to pick. It's been so long since we've had this many options," I said before I found the perfect outfit. I tried it on and came back into the room.

Megan and I attended the service where our ministry was introduced during the service. We were also flattered by the praise of some girls who had been following our journey online.

Several days passed with no word about our van. I sat at the dinner table in the Ramoses' home working on pro-life content for our website when Mrs. Ramos invited me to go to their Bible study that night. I agreed and Megan and I left to go without Nick since he had started feeling sick.

We arrived, and I sat in a chair with my Bible open, ready to learn about the topic they were studying. A few minutes into the meeting, the leader turned to me and said to everyone, "This young lady is running across America for the pro-life movement. Would you like to share, Anna?"

All eyes turned on me. My palms grew sweaty as I stood to

address the group. I stepped into the middle of the circle, took a deep breath, and began.

"I am running across America to bring attention to the tragedy gripping our country. If you don't rise up and defend the preborn, who will?" As I spoke, I shared about how our country was losing people with unique personalities, gifts, and abilities. As I concluded, I saw eyes turned red, tears streamed down faces, and heads shook with dismay over the horrors of abortion.

After I finished speaking, I shook hands and hugged many people. Toward the end of greeting people, a retired doctor came up to me and said, "I know now what I'm going to do with my spare time. I'm going to volunteer at a pregnancy center."

"That's amazing!" I said, clasping her hand. Her time and advice would be worth so much to a clinic.

When we returned home, Nick was on the floor lying in his sleeping bag on his side, curled tightly in the fetal position. I knelt down beside him and could see he was sweating and shivering. "Nick, are you feeling okay?"

He slightly lifted his head. His eyes were red and underlined by dark circles. "Not really." His voice was weak and dry.

"What's wrong?" I leaned closer to him and placed the back of my hand to his forehead. He was extremely hot. "You have a fever. How long have you had a fever?"

"It came on suddenly just a few minutes ago," he said quietly.

"Is there anything I can get you?"

"No, I'll be fine."

I laid another spare blanket on his shaking frame and climbed into the queen bed where Megan was already lying and fell asleep.

I opened my eyes to daylight. Shivers ran across my whole body, causing me to curl deeper beneath my blankets. Megan must have felt my shivers and sat up with puffy eyes and looked over at me. She pulled my blankets up more over my shoulders. "Are you okay?" she asked.

"Yeah. I must have what Nick has. I'm so achy and tired." A

shiver shook my whole frame forcing me to pause. "And I'm so cold."

A few minutes passed, and Megan returned with steaming cups of tea. "I know being feverish is awful, but I looked up the current weather on the Burr Trail. The temperature has been down in the teens at night. I can't imagine if you guys were on the trail right now with these fevers."

I patted down some blanket from in front of my face. "Not being dramatic, but I don't know if we could have survived. This breakdown is the last thing I hoped for, but God must have known we were going to get sick. I'm so glad for a bed and a home during this sickness."

As we waited for the van to be repaired, Nick and I slowly healed from over a week of high fever. As I went to bed each night, I thanked God for the warm house, the shelter of a home, and the kindness of strangers. Soon we were well, but the van was still not fixed. Megan, Nick, and I met with as many people as we could to set up events and speaking engagements for when we ran through Las Vegas.

Although we used our time productively, we were eager to head back to the Burr Trial to keep running. Megan called Mr. Ron for an update, and he still needed one more day.

Slowly but surely, God was working more good out of our vehicle breakdown: I received an invitation to speak at Pro-life Conference with the Family Research Council, we held a 5K run with Pastor Rich, the youth pastor of Calvary Baptist, spoke at Dr. Dave Ties' church, and I was invited to watch an ultrasound at a pregnancy center.

All the events went well, but I was most thrilled about the ultrasound. I entered the room hesitantly, but the expectant mother gave me a warm, encouraging smile. Still in the first trimester, she didn't look pregnant, so I was surprised when the nurse quickly found the baby's heartbeat. It thudded loud and fast through the speakers. The nurse then began to probe to show the baby on the screen. The screen was black at first, but soon a baby became visible. The small head, torso, and legs were distinguishable first, then I could see the hands moving up by the face and down by the baby's feet. The baby moved up and down and squirmed. The mother giggled with delight at seeing her baby so active. Even at such a young age, the baby was clearly human.

After the ultrasound, Megan followed up with Mr. Ron again. He asked for another day, and we hoped that would be the last delay. The next day we drove the Ramoses' car to pick up our van. Mr. Ron told us it was ready, so we asked how much we owed him.

"Just for the parts," he said with a shrug.

"Thank you, Mr. Ron!" Megan said shaking his hand energetically.

19

COMFORT FOR THE WEARY

W e were back in the wilderness.

Our vehicle breakdown had delayed us three weeks, but we had avoided running on the Burr Trail during the coldest part of the winter, and we knew that even in trials God was working to protect us and provide for us. Our return to the wilderness after being in busy, chaotic Las Vegas was odd, refreshing, and lonely all at the same time.

Dark red rocks were strewn about the landscape as if giants had finished playing catch and left their boulders out. Amid the rocks grew cedar trees with gnarled dead branches jutting from the living ones. The branches were bent, twisted, and tangled, marking the years the trees had battled and won against their desert climate.

Nick and I started running at a huge cattle guard next to some cedar trees where we had stopped so many weeks prior. We felt good as we started to run.

Only a few steps in, I said to Nick, "It's been three weeks, and I think I might be out of shape."

"I doubt it." I looked at Nick with my eyebrows raised hoping for more explanation. He caught my look and continued, "If you're patient, I think you'll see the rest will make you feel refreshed rather than out of shape."

"I sure hope so."

We passed a canyon with a small stream at the bottom. Leafless trees rose near the stream, clearly happy to be mired in the water under the shade of the canyon wall.

In early February 2017, I cooked breakfast over the fire at a pull-off along the Burr Trail in Utah before going for a run with Nick.

The canyon was the perfect camping spot, so we stopped our run at just over seven miles. We followed a long dirt pull-off jutting from the left side of the main road until it came to a giant tree that overlooked the valley-like area and stream we had admired. We waited for Megan to find us, then we hiked down to set up camp close to the stream.

After we erected the tent, the wind picked up, which signaled a brewing storm, so Nick used our small shovel to dig a trench around our tent to catch the rainwater and keep us dry. We made dinner as the weather continued to threaten rain. The sun set, and a huge moon illuminated our campsite. Winds blew between the canyon walls and whipped as we hunkered around the fire. The temperature hovered in the upper thirties, but the wind bit through our layers.

My sleeping bag provided little warmth as the wind continued through the night, whipping our tent cover and smacking it against the tent's dome. I slept poorly with the slapping fabric and howling wind but, thankfully, no rain came.

In the morning, we clambered out of our tent. As we cooked breakfast, a truck drove down the switchbacks and pulled off next to our van. Two rangers hiked down to where we had set up camp.

Why are you camping down here instead of on the pull-off?" one said, his tone stern, as if he were lecturing rebellious teens.

"We wanted more privacy from the road," Nick explained.

The rangers exchanged smirks, then pointed to the secluded land around us. "You need more privacy?" he scoffed. "And why the trench? They're not allowed."

"We were expecting rain. We're sorry. We didn't know they weren't allowed," Nick said.

"Rain? No rain is coming. You need to move your camp, fill the trench, and make it look like you were never here," the same ranger answered.

"Yes sir," we said in unison.

Our respectful response softened their attitudes. We packed up our campsite, and by the time the rangers left, we were talking cordially with them.

After we moved camp, Nick and I started our warm-up routine. I was ready to run and cover ground, but I was not in the mood to waste energy warming up.

Nick called me out on it, so I worked to hide my annoyance and finished the warm-ups.

We started the switchbacks with relative ease. My body felt good. Running with confidence instead of dread was energizing. We reached the top of the switchbacks, and instead of being tired, I was ready for more.

"I can't believe how easy those were."

"I told you you'd feel good after so much rest," Nick replied with a kind, small smile.

Our run that day ended on much flatter terrain, at just under six and a half miles.

I ran eagerly the next day because the end of the trail was near. The miles again passed with ease. As we closed in on Boulder, Utah, deciduous trees grew dense as they replaced the old cedar trees. Nick and I marveled when we saw a man walking his dog. *Could we really be that close to people?* After all the wilderness solitude, I could hardly keep my pace reasonably slow as I longed to be back with people.

On we ran, our strides longer, and our pace quicker as we anticipated the monumental moment of finishing the Burr Trail. We passed a winterized farm, cattle roaming in their fields, and some rock mountains just before we entered Boulder. Only a few more weary steps and there it was: the intersection of Highway 12 and the Burr Trail. Nick and I hugged the signpost, then each other.

We had finished the Burr Trail. The almost nine miles we ran that day could not have felt more rewarding.

We had anticipated the Burr Trail would take about fourteen days, but it had taken forty-nine days. Although we experienced a lot of joy during those weeks, we had also never experienced such dangerous isolation, deep loneliness, intense frustration, lost time, overwhelming trials, and miserable cold.

The following day was our Sabbath, so after van-camping, we went to the Burr Trail Trading Post, a coffee shop at the end of the trail. We ordered bagels and coffee, then relaxed. We occupied ourselves with journaling, reading, writing letters, and decompressing. After many hours of rest, the shop closed, and we headed back to the previous night's campsite.

We ran through Boulder the next day toward the town of Escalante. We sailed past the Burr Trail Trading Post and the Hills and Hollows Mini Mart to the base of a steep road cut into the side of a giant hill. Our bodies felt strong as we climbed the many hills, each step requiring effort but still manageable and exciting.

Eventually, we reached Hogback Ridge, a monstrously large mountain backbone that seemed to rise out of nowhere. The road snaked back and forth over the top of a rocky ridge with sheer drop offs on both sides and no guardrails. Below lay innumerable jagged, multicolored rocks.

I looked down on either side of the ridge, and though I knew I was safe, my stomach dropped at the thought of being blown down into the depths below. Meanwhile, Nick's face radiated with joy as he yipped and yelled, happy to undertake an incredible adventure.

A drastic 14 percent downgrade followed, and we seemed to soar downward as we ran. The harsh wind continued to blow. I felt feel free as we followed the road with its occasional small ascents, which gave our downhill muscles a break. I gulped the clean, crisp air. The winds calmed as we descended into a canyon next to Calf Creek. The red rocks on either side of the road made the route feel narrow, as if only we and the creek could squeeze through.

We camped in our van on a pull-off close to Hogback Ridge. The weather was windy and cold as we rearranged our van for the night. After dinner, we settled in our van, ready for bed.

Knock, knock, knock. Someone pounded on our back door. I jumped. Nick moved aside our striped beach towel curtain to reveal the face of the ranger we had seen on the Burr Trail. Megan and I looked at each other and let out a sigh of relief that it was not a stranger.

When Nick opened the door, the ranger said, "I saw your van as I was driving and recognized it." He smiled. "I wanted to say thank you for being so polite and respectful back on the trail. I've never had anyone say 'yes sir' or be respectful before. Thank you for that."

"Of course," Nick replied. "We understand you deal with people who don't want to obey the law."

"Yeah." The ranger nodded. "Well, I'd better let you get to sleep. I wish you the best. Thanks again. Good night."

Over the next few days, we ran the last few miles from Boulder to the next town on our route, Escalante. A large metal and stone sign reading Escalante welcomed us. The town seemed to have been snatched from the past and brought into the present. Its buildings rose from the street with tall square faces. People lived in old homes and drove slowly. It seemed as if at any moment, cowboys would ride out of the surrounding canyons and stop at the local bar. We explored the town, ate burgers at Nemo's, and restocked our supplies at Griffin Grocer.

Many days had passed since we had stayed with a host, and Megan was happy to have found one, Lella Richards. She was a kind woman with shoulder-length, curly brown hair who loved to tell stories. Her home seemed small when we entered it, but when she showed us our rooms in her basement, it was actually very large.

In my room, I FaceTimed James. My face flushed with joy during our brief conversation. As soon as we ended the call, I took a shower. The hot water turned brown as it washed away the dirt caked on my skin. I rubbed my hands over my dirty feet and my toes; my toenails soon became visible under the layer of dirt covering them. I scrubbed and scratched at the dried earth on my ankles, the thickest dirt on my whole body, until it finally began to release its grip and wash away. I lathered my greasy, tangled hair slowly relieving tension from my whole body as I became clean.

After Nick, Megan, and I showered, Lella invited us into her living room. As soon as we sat on her large, comfy couch, two large dogs approached us. They looked like round sausages with wagging tails. They licked us and slobbered on us affectionately as we took turns patting their soft heads. The evening passed quickly as we chatted with Lella.

Lella invited me to speak at her Bible study, where I shared one of my favorite verses, Psalm 139:13–14:"For you formed my inward parts; you knitted me together in my mother's womb. I praise you, for I am fearfully and wonderfully made. Wonderful are your works; my soul knows it very well" (ESV).

I then explained, "I always quote this verse when I speak because it's the verse that made me pro-life. When I was in the fifth grade, I had a kind-hearted teacher, Mrs. Steinbrink. She shared this verse with our class and made it so obvious to me that God cares about each and every child. God literally knits us together in our mother's womb, giving special care and attention to each detail. He made each of us intentionally with a purpose."

After I finished speaking, an elderly woman with gray hair and a small frame approached me. "I'm Harriet, and I'm just so proud of you."

She took my hand in hers, nodded, and smiled at me in a mysterious sort of way. As she held my hand in what seemed like a simple, affectionate clasp, I felt a wadded bill. Her eyes were full of warmth when she said, "Keep sharing your message."

As she walked away, I opened my hand. In it lay a one-hundred-dollar bill.

On our run the next day, the road went downhill for quite some time after we passed Escalante. A sudden pain shot through my hamstring and grew worse with each step. Fear of injury and inability to finish running across America hit me, but I did not want to stop. I jogged and slightly limped for a few more steps, then stopped. "I know it's only been two miles, but I can't run anymore today, Nick. My hamstring is killing me, and I'm scared running more will worsen the injury."

"That's okay. Let's go back to Lella's and rest."

We relaxed for the rest of the day and evening at Lella's home. Though the day's run was disappointing, the next morning was wonderful: we awoke to delightful smells coming from the kitchen. Lella made us a nutritious breakfast of eggs and hash browns—the perfect breakfast before a run. After we ate, we packed up and said goodbye to Lella.

Over the next several days of running, the terrain changed from canyons to pines, then to white desert rocks. My mileage continued to be low due to my hamstring injury, but when we reached Henriville, my hamstring seemed fine. I kept expecting to feel pain again, but I felt none.

Our run ended, Megan picked us up, and we found a place to park at a pull-off between Escalante and Henriville. The pull-off sat just below a huge rock cliff, an American flag waving on its peak.

The next morning, we were enjoying pancakes and percolator coffee when a car approached us from the direction of Escalante. The car pulled off just beside our van, and Harriet climbed out.

"I knew if I kept driving long enough, eventually I would find you by your big red van," she said with a twinkle in her eye and a toothy smile.

As she spoke, she produced from her pocket an eight-ounce jar containing a light pink substance. She smiled again as she held it out to me and said, "It's Prickly Pear Cactus jelly."

We could tell she had canned it herself. "Wow! Thank you, Harriet. We can't wait to try it," I said. "Nick gave me some of the fruit to try when we were in Eastern Colorado. It was delicious."

"I'm glad," Harriet said. She looked down at my leg. "I've been praying for your injuries to heal."

"Thank you, Harriet. My leg stopped hurting yesterday." I hadn't told anyone besides Megan and Nick about my injuries and wondered how she knew.

She smiled again at me, and I realized that God had answered her prayers and mine by healing me.

We said goodbye to Harriet and continued to cover ground. I ran and Nick biked until we reached the next town, Canonville.

"There's a Sinclair gas station up ahead. Do you want a snack? I'm starved," I asked between breaths.

"Sounds great!" Nick said.

We entered the gas station and looked around for a treat. We settled on ice cream drumsticks and a whole pack of Oreos. We sat at a park across the street, enjoying each other's company as we ate our ice cream.

When we finished our ice cream, I laughed. "Aw man, I'm too full for Oreos!"

Nick laughed too. "Me too." He then strapped the package of cookies to the tray on the back of his bike before saying, "People will think we look so funny running with Oreos strapped to my bike." We both laughed.

"These stops are one of the best parts of running with you. So fun and goofy!" I said, still laughing as I took off running and Nick biking.

As we finished our run, I realized something: the God I served was not a dull God. When I was in high school, I feared that serving God would be boring, and I was sad because I longed for adventure. But as I sat there, on a journey running across America, I knew it was the opposite. Serving God was a wilder adventure than I could have ever dreamed, and it would take me farther than my wandering feet could have ever gone.

I serve a wild God who calls us to the most wild and wonderful adventures.

20
HARSH REALITIES

Orange and white tapered rocks jutted up like spires from the rocks around us. Pine trees grew tall throughout the canyon as if competing with the stones for height. Pristine snow coated the rocks—a perfect contrast to the bright orange rock formations beautifully spread throughout Bryce Canyon National Park.

We wore many layers to keep the freezing February temperatures at bay. When we passed a giant red sign advertising espresso in a Subway window, Nick and I could not resist. We laughed when we entered. Megan was already inside, working.

Nick and I ordered hot lattes, but they tasted bitter and burnt. Disappointed, we still relished the warmth of the cup on our cold hands. Unwilling to return to the cold, we sat at the table long after the heat from our coffee was gone. When I looked up, Megan walked toward me, carrying a dozen red roses.

"James sent them to you for Valentine's Day. We've been trying to coordinate for days, and it finally worked out."

"How on earth?" I asked.

"A little bit of driving and some phone calls," she said.

I took them, smelled them, and hugged Megan, grateful for her sacrifice. Only James could make me feel so special.

We had not showered in a week, so we stopped at an extremely cheap hotel to get clean. Using baby wipes and splashing our faces in rest-stop sinks was no substitute for a hot shower and fresh clothes that didn't smell rancid. Sleeping in a bed was a treat too.

The next morning we stopped at a small store and purchased black curtains and curtain rods for our van to add more privacy. I labored for several hours shortening the curtains to hang between us and over the back window.

That night I attached them to the ceiling, running them from the top of the bed to the bottom and from the roof of the van down to the bed to create small, narrow rooms to sleep and relax in. Not only did the curtains provide much-needed privacy but also more freedom. Megan embraced her night owl tendencies, Nick read with a light as late as he desired, and I went right to sleep in the darkness of my room between them.

Several runs, nights in the van, and cold run days brought us through giant arches, down sparsely traveled roads, and into the lands beyond Bryce Canyon. One evening was especially cold, and we were overjoyed to find a gas station called K. B.'s Express. We entered the gas station hoping only for hot coffee, but we also enjoyed a friendly chat with a female Lithuanian who worked there.

As we explained living in our van, she frowned. "You sleep in your van when it's so cold outside?" We nodded. "Well, we close at nine, but I am here closing and cleaning until eleven. If you want to stay until then, you are welcome. I wish you could stay here all night to get out of the cold, but it's not my place."

We accepted her offer and enjoyed several cups of hot coffee and snacks still shivering in our winter coats. Eleven o'clock came too soon. We packed up our belongings and braced ourselves for another cold night in the van. The temperature was thirty degrees, but the wind made it feel colder. The van provided little to no insulation from the weather. We shivered as we lay down to sleep; morning could not come quickly enough.

We were awakened by a knock on our door. I was too groggy to be aware of what was happening, but Nick, the lighter sleeper that morning, was not.

An angry man stood outside when Nick opened the door. "You need to move your van! These parking spaces are for customers only." His voice sounded both harsh and pleading. "What will they do if they arrive and see that all the spots are full?"

As we pulled out of the parking lot, I looked back through our parted black curtains. Not a single car in the lot or at the pumps.

We ate some leftover pie before Nick and I warmed up and started our run for the day. We traveled along Highway 89 for over eleven miles before we came to a rest stop tucked into some pine trees and nestled on the side of a mountain.

We spent several nights at the rest stop utilizing the sinks, picnic tables, restrooms, and privacy before our run route brought us to the small town of Orderville. We were fascinated by the rock shops on both sides of the quiet road that led through the town. An odd one, shaped like a large, brown rock caught our attention —The Rock Stop. An old wooden fence ran in front of it, there were piles of rocks organized all around it, and old cars and ceramic dinosaurs interspersed throughout. What mostly caught our attention, though, was the huge red sign that said Espresso. We all went in, pretty skeptical of finding good coffee in Utah.

Nick ordered a test espresso drink to see if it was any good. As he took his first sip, Megan and I watched in eager anticipation. His blue eyes lit up as he handed his cup to me, then Megan.

The coffee was delicious—strong, creamy, and high quality.

"You make an incredible espresso," I told the owner.

He smiled. "I was trained by someone who worked at the Bellagio Casino in Las Vegas," he said.

"Well, that explains it." Nick took another slurp of his hot vanilla latte. Megan and I ordered hot mochas and sipped them with the deep joy of deprived coffee lovers.

The next morning was our Sabbath, so we headed straight to The Rock Stop in Orderville for more incredible coffee. He refused to let us pay and then spent hours talking with us, showing us dozens of different rocks—ones that glow under ultraviolet light, obsidian that surgeons use as an incredibly sharp blade for operations, and numerous fossils. I felt like a kid on the best field trip ever.

March arrived the next day, and with it heat we were not used to anymore. Daytime temperatures rose into the seventies as we headed through Orderville, onto Highway 9, then into Zion National Park.

Nick rode his bike as I ran next to him. The canyon walls seemed to rise from the ground out of nowhere. Patches of snow still dotted the landscape, despite the warmer weather. In early spring and still somewhat cold, the roads were free of tourists.

Nick stood up on his bike and took in the landscape. He laughed as he pedaled before looking back at me with a huge smile that even showed in his eyes. He looked so small with the canyon walls and huge rock formations rising on either side. He danced on the pedals of his bike, swaying back and forth.

"Stop, stop!" I laughed, almost crying. "I can't run and laugh this hard at the same time."

After over seven miles, we came to a mile-long tunnel cut through a mountain. A sign at the entrance of the tunnel said no cyclists or pedestrians were allowed through the tunnel.

"Clearly we can't run any more today," Nick said. He pointed to a booth near the entrance. "There's even a security guard to enforce it. I guess we'll have to come back after dark to run this section."

Nick, Megan (not pictured), and I at a pull-off on Highway 9 cooking grilled cheese and tomato soup just before running through Zion National Park in early March 2017.

After Megan picked us up, we headed to St. George because we had been invited to attend a pregnancy center banquet. Hope Pregnancy Center in St. George, Utah, was hosting the event to raise money so they could keep providing free services for women in crisis pregnancies. Once we arrived, a host offered a place to shower before the event and stay that night.

When we walked into the banquet room, we were grateful to see so many pro-life people from all over St. George. What an honor to find our seats in the front next to the keynote speaker, Roland Warren, President of Care Net (the umbrella organization for over a thousand pregnancy centers).

At the beginning of the banquet, the hosts showed our promotional video, "Be the Voice," that our friend Andy Gwynn had made. As people applauded at the end of the video, three women approached us with presents for me, Nick, and Megan. Inside each box was a new pair of running shoes.

Roland Warren then got up to speak. He first shared how he and his wife had attended college together at Princeton. They were unmarried when they discovered they were pregnant. The nurse who administered the pregnancy test advised Roland's then-girlfriend, Yvette, to have an abortion since she could not possibly fulfill her dream of medical school with a child. Rather than take the nurse's advice, Roland and Yvette got married. Yvette, he said, did not finish medical school with one child but with two!

After hearing the speech, I realized people so often tell women that they cannot achieve their dreams if they have children, but this story showed just how wrong they are. Women are strong enough to have children and achieve their dreams. Only those who think little of women would say they have to choose between their futures and their children.

The day after the banquet, we hiked Angel's Landing before heading to the tunnel. Darkness had arrived as our old van chugged wearily, bringing us to our run spot. Seeing the security guard was gone, we placed headlamps on our foreheads and flashing lights on our arms and CamelBaks. Megan rode behind us in the van with the flashers on. The air was cool and crisp, and the thrill of night running energized us.

All seemed well. We ran at an 8:40 mile pace as a few cars built up behind the van. One driver grew tired of waiting and tried to whip around to pass, not knowing our van was shielding two runners. The car passed and cut in close, almost hitting Nick before speeding away. We kept our fast pace and tried to keep as close to the tunnel walls as we could. Soon another car passed. We hoped the driver would see us as they cut over sharply, coming extremely close to Nick before seeing him and swerving to give him room. After what felt like forever, we made it out of the tunnel.

Back on the open road we no longer needed the van to shield us, so Megan drove ahead to wait for us. A long stretch of downhill switchbacks lay before us. Our headlamps and flashing lights stood in stark contrast to the deep darkness. We descended quickly and effortlessly rounding the switchbacks with our arms extended as if we were flying through the cool night air. We finished at the bottom just under five miles.

———

We spent the next few nights van-camping in Springdale, just west of Zion in a hotel parking lot. We parked our van among the hotel patrons' vehicles, closed our black curtains, and went to sleep hoping no one would notice we were not guests.

Morning came, and I sat up sleepily and said, "I have to use the restroom, and now that we're in some sort of civilization, I don't know where to go."

"Let's use the hotel," Megan said. "Hold your head up, walk in with confidence, and they won't ask any questions."

"We'll let you in the side door," I told Nick before Megan and I crawled out of the van, smoothing our hair as best we could.

We avoided eye contact with the desk clerks as we walked into the hotel, heads high. No one stopped us, so we slipped to the side door to let Nick in so he could use the restroom as well.

The next night we camped in the parking lot again. When morning came, we again needed a restroom.

"I can go in this time," offered Nick. "I'll let you guys in the side door." He walked in the front door and was back out the same door moments later, head bowed.

The front desk clerk had questioned him as if he were talking to a criminal.

"I just need to use the restroom," Nick had said and kept walking.

"Stop! Security! Security!" the desk clerk shouted.

Almost instantly, a security guard appeared.

"You need to leave now," the security guard said, standing between Nick and the bathroom.

As Nick reached the end of his story, I fumed over the hotel staff's cruel treatment.

We drove to a nearby hotel where Megan and I let Nick in the back door so we could all use the restroom. As we sneaked out of the hotel, I saw the importance of following God's will no matter the misjudgment we faced. Although I felt wounded by the harshness of people, I also felt loved by those God had brought to care for us. As we pulled away from the hotel, I resolved to focus on the kindness of our new friends and work to forget the harshness of strangers.

21

ENTERING THE DESERT

The hot sun beat down on us as we sipped Arizona Sweet Tea on the side of the road beside a sign that welcomed us to our next state, Arizona. Our bodies dripped with sweat from running over ten miles that day, but Nick's face radiated joy. I couldn't wipe the smile off my face either. We had completed our run through Utah!

The next day we ran again, finishing Arizona and reaching Nevada. Our route took us just over thirteen and a half miles through the northwest corner of Arizona before we entered Nevada. There, Andy Gwynn temporarily joined our team. On this two-week visit, he would make another video for us.

We drove all over Utah, Arizona, and Nevada, filming in beautiful spots along our route as well as in various speaking venues. Andy wanted shots not only showing running and speaking but also shots depicting our daily life as I ran across America. We filmed late into the night around campfires, high on mountainsides, and around towns and cities.

Sleeping arrangements were tough with another team member. We spent a few nights at a host's home, but others were trickier. Andy slept in the back seat of his rental car parked alongside our van in a Walmart parking lot. When filming was over, we dropped Andy off at the airport and headed back to our route on I–15 in Nevada.

We could not wait to see the next video.

With Andy gone, we resumed running along Interstate 15, which we planned to follow the rest of the way to the ocean. Each day the southern sun increased in intensity, draining our energy and dehydrating our bodies.

Despite the difficulty, I enjoyed the desert scenery, the masses of people on the interstate, and the completely different weather. Walmarts and gas-station parking lots were our home, and quick, cheap meals at McDonald's and canned good cookstove meals sustained us. I also enjoyed waking up in my curtained room while Nick and Megan slept, so I could journal, read my Bible, and pray.

"God, could we run twenty miles today?" I prayed silently.

We ate breakfast at a diner in the Chevron before setting out on our run. Our starting point that day was at the end of the off-ramp for the Chevron. Sweat beaded on my forehead as I tried to put in a good effort during warm-up, but every exercise felt like I had weights tied to me.

"Are you even trying?" Nick said.

I'm always sensitive to correction, and this was no exception.

"Yeah," I said. *But I don't know if I can run with this tough of warm-ups.*

We walked to our run spot just before mile marker 75. My heart felt heavy as tears stung my eyes. Some days were unbearably hard, and this was one of them, but I somehow found the strength to start with Nick biking beside me.

A little over five miles passed before I asked, "Could we take a break?"

I did not want to go on. I wanted to stop and rest in some shady spot and be alone. Completely alone.

"Sure," Nick said.

We stopped at a steep, cliff-like structure on the side of I-15 where the ground had been blown out for the interstate. Nick and I rested against the steep slope as the sun beat down and caused us to squint our eyes. My partially full, purple CamelBak served as a small cushion for the rocks I leaned on.

The scenery around us was bland and almost monochromatic. I picked up some rocks and discovered some of them sparkled. They were geode-like rocks. We collected some and admired them as they glittered in the bright sunshine like transparent gold in bland tan rocks. We put some in our CamelBaks and continued running.

As we ran, I was quickly draining my CamelBak. It held a liter, but I was drinking it too fast. I intended to take a sip, but the dry heat made it difficult to ration my water, and I took a long gulp, knowing I would regret it later. Not only was I low on water, but the constant roar of the rushing interstate traffic was maddening.

As I scanned the desert scenery to distract myself, I noticed a dirt road a little way from the interstate and pointed it out to Nick. After a bit more running, I realized that the dirt road was getting closer to the interstate.

"Let's run to that road so we can get some distance from the interstate. It looks like it will run parallel for a while, and it would be nice to not be so close to the traffic," Nick suggested.

As we ran toward the road, we were stopped by a barbed wire fence that separated the two roads. I stepped on the second-to-bottom rung and carefully lifted my body over. Nick lifted his heavy bike over and set it against the fence. He looked tough with his black bandana holding back his long, sweaty hair. *He is going to jump the barbed wire fence*. He backed up a few steps and ran toward the fence. I cringed, but over he went with the ease and agility of a deer.

After clearing the fence, we ran toward the small road, Nick pushing his bike through the tough terrain and sometimes carrying it over dense bushes. When we reached the road, I checked my Runkeeper GPS. The road was Las Vegas Boulevard—the road we intended to run when going through Las Vegas.

We enjoyed the quiet as we ran. My mind wandered until I was snapped back to reality by a semi driver who approached us from the opposite direction at an alarming speed. The rig was so close to us that I braced myself as the wind pushed me and sand whipped my exposed skin.

Nick and I persevered until we reached the Love's gas station at Exit 64, our meet site with Megan. I paused my GPS at just over eleven miles, then we walked into the gas station to grab some lunch with Megan.

After lunch, Megan and Nick stayed in the gas station while I went out to the van to nap. I texted James about how my day was going, then went to sleep. I awoke an hour later, sweaty but refreshed and ready to run, though I doubted I could reach my goal of twenty miles.

As Nick and I ran, Las Vegas Boulevard pulled away from the interstate, separated by a railroad track. The road was open and quieter, providing even greater relief from the traffic. My legs carried me as my mind drifted, and soon I lost any idea of how far we had gone.

We started up a hill, and Nick said, "I think this is the last hill before dropping into the Las Vegas Valley." On his tiptoes on his bike pedals, he strained to see the valley.

"No way!" I said, with some reserve about the reality of

reaching Las Vegas on foot. We had spent so long in Las Vegas with our broken van that running there felt surreal.

I scanned the hazy horizon at the top of the hill.

"Look!" shouted Nick. "There it is. The Las Vegas skyline. And there's the Stratosphere."

I pumped my fist in the air, then ran both my hands through my hair before high-fiving Nick. We had come so far, and seeing the skyline made it tangible. Joy energized every cell in my body as we descended into the valley.

The downhill drop into the valley made the miles pass almost effortlessly. My body felt lightweight and powerful. The skyline dropped out of sight for a while as we were surrounded by small hills that were clearly a dumping ground—old tires, couches, and trash everywhere. After several more miles, we reached the Las Vegas Speedway. When we finally stopped, I checked my GPS.

"Look, Nick!" I held out the Runkeeper GPS. "We ran twenty-one miles. Even more than I prayed for this morning."

Nick hugged me.

I was proud of my accomplishment, but I was even more grateful that our great God answered my prayer.

We celebrated our success that evening by exploring more of the Las Vegas strip. We rode the tram and toured casinos. We saw one that looked like a pyramid, a castle, and even one that looked like New York City. There we grabbed some New-York-style pizza and espresso drinks.

With a full stomach and happy heart, we drove to a nearby park for the night. When morning came, I prayed specifically for a host. Living in the heat without showers was even harder than living through the winter without them.

When Megan woke up, we washed our faces, brushed our teeth, and tried to tame our wild hair in a nearby park bathroom.

ANNA STRASBURG

After we filled up our water bottles in the bathroom sinks, Nick and I started our warm-up.

"This is too exhausting before a long run," I said.

"I don't have to train you anymore," he countered.

I regretted my bad attitude and tried to push my pride away, determining to not complain during warm-ups anymore. "No, I still want to be trained. I'm just exhausted."

"Okay, but no more complaining," Nick said.

When we reached our run spot at the speedway, Nick biked while I ran. We followed Las Vegas Boulevard as it led through a homeless tent city. As we grew nearer, people screamed profanities and yelled vulgarities at one another. Tents, tarps, and people covered most of the sidewalk, so we ran in the road when traffic was sparse.

As we approached two men screaming at each other, Nick and I hopped off the sidewalk to run in the road, but a car was coming up behind us, forcing us onto the sidewalk near the men. The taller man threw a rock at the shorter one; the shorter one retaliated with a loud slap across the taller man's face. They were only feet from us as they gripped each other's shirt and wrestled.

We moved as far away from them as we could and kept running.

Just after the tent city we came to the Stratosphere, where we met Megan. Nick loaded the bike on the back of van so he could run the Las Vegas Strip with me. We got coffee and lunch, then took in the craziness of Las Vegas, knowing we would be back in the lonely desert soon. We finished our run at the iconic Welcome to Fabulous Las Vegas sign. I stopped my Runkeeper GPS—just over twenty miles. We were all smiles after another long day of running, and a fun one at that.

I thought the night couldn't get any better, but then Mike Simmons II, a friend of ours from college, messaged me and offered to let us stay with him and his family. Once again, God had answered my morning prayer.

I was exhausted from running for close to four hours, so I knew it would be hard for me to carry on a conversation with the Simmons. They were extremely considerate, though, and told us to make ourselves comfortable by using the shower and going straight to bed if we wanted. I was so worn out I went straight to bed, thankful to be clean, to be out of the van, and to serve a good God who daily answered prayers.

22

THE WILD, EMPTY LAND

"It's only a quarter mile to the border," I said, my voice heightened with frustration. "Can we just keep going?"

The sun beat down on us, souring my mood. Salty sweat poured down our bodies as Nick and I bickered. My usual upbeat personality had been dampened as I battled not only a physical battle of running but also a spiritual one. A layer of intense pressure seemed to sit on me squelching my joy, dousing my passion, and amplifying my emotions.

"I guess." Nick said through gritted teeth before he started running again.

I followed behind him, feeling like I could scream but also feeling mute, unable to communicate the pressure I constantly felt. Sweat caked our limbs and faces as we continued. After a few more minutes, we saw a medium-sized blue sign. Welcome to California was written on it in yellow cursive beside three yellow flowers.

We stared at the sign. I couldn't believe it. We had made it to the last state of the western portion. It had been incredibly hard, even the last quarter mile, but all the frustration and stress melted away as we crossed the border.

We celebrated at the Circus Circus hotel, after we picked up candy and pop. Settled in our room, we played every song about California we could think of.

In mid-April 2017, Nick and I ran through the intense heat and deep sand of California next to Interstate-15.

The next day we were eager to start the California run. The earth was hard and cracked for several miles but then switched to hot, deep sand. Every step proved to be a trial. The California Department of Transportation had denied us access to run on I-15, so we were forced to run just north of it through the desert. My feet sunk several inches and were buried with every step. Nick tried to bike, but the sand was too deep, so he dragged his bike.

When we came to a ditch where water had washed away the dirt, we climbed in and out of the ditch—all the while Nick lugged his bike. We panted, dirt mixing with our sweat as we pushed on.

Before long, we encountered another ditch, then another. *I can hardly run this. I wonder how Nick is managing with that bulky bike.*

Exhausted and mentally defeated, I thought it could not get any worse. Then the lonely road added yet another obstacle: barbed-wire fences. We crossed one and then another. When I checked my Runkeeper GPS, our mileage was so low it seemed we weren't progressing at all.

Nick stopped. "It's too difficult," he said after he caught his breath. "We should run on the interstate."

"We were told we couldn't," I replied between pants.

"The California Department of Transportation said we couldn't, but the Highway Patrol said we could, so I think we should."

I shook my head, too weary to speak.

Nick threw up his hands. "You're being stubborn. I'm going to switch and ride on the interstate while you run through this terrible terrain."

With that, we parted ways. I watched him drag his bike toward the interstate, tears running down my cheeks.

Determined to conquer the arduous landscape, I kept running. The terrain became more treacherous as I ascended and descended hills where explosives had been used to blow out a level path for the interstate. The cacti became dense and cut my legs repeatedly. As I ran up the hills, rocks loosened and crashed down. Obstacle after obstacle caused my feet to give way again and again. I climbed the hills so slowly that I hardly felt like I was running. The wind blew in strong, continuous bursts, whipping the saliva out of my mouth and the moisture out of my eyes.

I reached the top of yet another hill and began descending. The footing was uncertain, and the hills so steep that I was scared of falling.

And then I did.

I tumbled down, hitting rocks and thorny cactus as I went. I came to a stop in the bottom of a washed-out ditch. Dust rose in a cloud around me. Fresh cuts on my arms and legs burned with the unforgiving combination of sweat and dirt. Blood seeped out of numerous cuts on my filthy arms and legs. I was completely alone in a ditch. *No one knows where I am, and I doubt if anyone cares.*

With a choked voice, I cried out to God, "Is this worth it? Am I making a difference? Does anybody care about the hardships I'm facing?" Tears flowed down my dirt-caked cheeks. The sun beat on my hunched and bleeding body. I wept aloud with my face in my hands.

Then it dawned on me: The war to end abortion would not be won in one day or one run. Just like my run across America, there would be great triumphs as well as defeats. Victory would not come to the faint of heart but to those who persevered. And in that moment, I determined to persevere. No matter how steep the mountain or how barren the desert, I would carry on. I would keep fighting. God would be my strength, and abortion would end.

My fall convinced me to switch to the shoulder of the interstate. I met Nick, weak and humbled. We called and asked Megan to pick us up in one mile.

I could do one mile more.

I had already consumed the last of my water supply, so my tongue felt like dry sand in my mouth. My sweat formed salt crystals on my forehead and arms, and thick, white, dried saliva formed a goopy layer around my mouth and on my lips. On Nick and I pushed for about another mile until our old red van came into view.

My Runkeeper GPS read ten miles, but all I could think of was water. I grabbed a bottle, closed my eyes, and chugged and chugged, water streaming down my face and neck as I drank, as if my thirst could never be quenched.

"Do you think you could you run three more, Anna?" Nick asked.

I opened my eyes and turned my head to look at him. Surely,

he was kidding. "There's no way, Nick. There's just no way," I said, eyes watering and frustration mounting in my chest.

Nick persisted, and after much negotiating, we decided to run one more mile—on the interstate. To my amazement, I forced my weary body to run once more, though still exhausted. My mind drifted and somehow the miles passed, not with ease, but without the toll the first ten had taken.

After quite some time, I pulled out my tracker. Twenty miles! Only God could take a weary, weak girl, and enable her to continue not just one mile more, but *ten* more.

I turned to Nick and hugged him, almost leaning on him in exhaustion.

"Thank you for pushing and encouraging me. I never could have done it without you."

He patted my shoulder. "Of course." His smile told me how proud he was.

I called my mom after the run, and she brought the comfort only a mother can bring. We didn't know anyone in California, and we had no hosts. I explained the difficult desert, the deep sand, the spiritual warfare, the loneliness, the strife, and how tired we were of the strenuous life we led. She listened for a long while.

"Mom, I feel alone. We have no hosts, no showers, and my joy is gone. I'm tired of running. I'm tired of feeling a constant pressure to succeed. I want a shower. I want a drawer to put my clothes in. I want to do my hair and wear normal clothes. I don't want to be shunned anymore for being dirty. I want a bed. I want privacy. I want a bathroom and not a bush. I want my family."

"Oh honey, those are perfectly fine things to want."

"I feel selfish even saying them, but it's been over nine months since I've had those things. And Mom, I want to see James." As I talked, I felt relief.

"You'll see him soon. You're so close to finishing the first portion. Ask God, and He will give you peace." She paused and her voice got higher and happier when she continued. "When do you think James might propose?"

"Oh, I don't know." I said with a giggle I did not expect. We continued talking, guessing at possible dates like a couple of schoolgirls. My mood had shifted from defeated to giddy when I hung up the phone—a feat only my mom could accomplish. The conversation spurred Megan and me to spend way too much time giggling, chatting, and looking at engagement rings on her phone.

While Megan and I chatted, Nick was engaged in more serious business: buying new CamelBaks that could hold two liters. He was tired of running low on water, so he consulted me on what color I wanted (I picked blue), and then he placed the order, having it shipped to a post office close to our route.

The next week consisted of large Denny's breakfasts in the morning, running in sweltering heat, dinners on our Coleman stove, and *Treasure Island* just before van-camping. Slowly, we made our way across California.

One day as I ran, Nick biked on a dirt road close to the interstate for relief from the traffic noise and hard pavement. He removed his shoes to run barefoot and push his bike. I couldn't resist joining him, and soon I too was running barefoot as he pushed his bike with our shoes neatly tied on the handlebars. Running barefoot was normal for Nick, but for me it was an adventure. I felt proud as my toes sank into the sand with each step. Though I was enjoying myself, Nick still struggled to push and drag his bike through the deep sand.

Lizard prints and sidewinder snake marks decorated the ground around us. Soon the heat of the sand made barefoot running painful. I picked up my feet to examine them. My toes were covered in blisters from the heat. I had no way to bandage them, and I didn't want to interrupt the day's run by calling

Megan, so I put my shoes back on and kept running. We sank deeper into the sand as we trudged forward. Each step became a brutal task. After eight miles of the sun baking the tops of our heads and the sand pulling at our feet, we switched back to the interstate.

From then on, we ran only on the interstate. Too soon we realized that our CamelBaks were dry again, and the Gatorades Nick carried on his bike were drained. Nowhere near our goal, we craved water. Ahead we saw a tall, whimsical tree that gently swayed its yellow blossoms next to the chaos of the interstate. We sat in its shade a few minutes before continuing.

Even swallowing my spit was difficult in the heat. The miles passed slowly but not nearly as slow as the miles in the sand. With an uphill finish, we were spent. Reaching the van, we hooked up the bike, then I grabbed a gallon water container and began chugging, hardly pausing to breathe. I felt nauseated until we ate dinner at a McDonald's in Barstow.

Barstow, California, was one of the worst places I had ever been. Many houses were boarded up and graffitied. The whole town seemed to be in shambles. Nonetheless, we were excited to be there because it meant more ground had been covered. We parked in a Ramada Inn parking lot, and I was fast asleep almost instantly.

The next day was our Sabbath, and we all looked forward to sleeping in, but the sound of something ripping awakened me early the next morning. It seemed to come from the vicinity of the bike rack attached to our van.

Perplexed and groggy, I crawled to the back window. When I parted the black curtains, my face was only a foot away from that of a homeless man undoing the Velcro that held Nick's bike in place. I dropped the curtain, jumped back, and yelled, "Nick, Nick, Nick! Someone is trying to steal our bike."

213

In a moment, Nick was beside me, but I had already startled the homeless man—if you can call it startled—because he sauntered away pushing an overflowing shopping cart as calmly as a man on a morning stroll.

Nick and I tried to go back to sleep, but trains kept making regular passes and whistle blows. As another train rumbled past, we heard what sounded like a group of people talking, hooping, and hollering. Nick and I sat up again and crawled to the back window, but when we opened our curtain, a single homeless man was looking under bushes as he carried on a conversation with himself.

With no hope of sleeping there any longer, Nick drove the van to a park where we went back to sleep awhile. Later, Nick and I climbed out of the van to enjoy some sunshine on a nearby park bench while Megan continued sleeping. We soaked up some sun, alternating between conversation and silence as we ate chocolate bars.

Not every day was as peaceful and pleasant as that one. The next morning I woke up in a bad mood. I grumbled as we tried to figure out where to eat before our run. Eventually, we decided on a Jack in the Box, but I ate my food in the van alone.

Are we really making a difference? The pressure mounted, and I felt like carrying on was impossible. Satan used my circumstances to plant lies. My mind raced with doubt. How could God use a simple Math Education major from Kansas to make difference? Who would listen to a young girl in her twenties? Maybe God was wrong to call me to such difficulty. Maybe dedication, perseverance, and faith in God was not enough to change something as monstrously wrong as abortion.

My mind was clouded as I sat in the van in misery. More running, rarely showering, van-camping lay ahead. Normalcy was now a distant memory.

The pre-run workout was tough (a core and arms day), then the fifteen miles we ran were hard as well. My mind remained bogged down and my body weary, but finally, the run was over.

The day brought no epiphany or encouragement. No speeches, interviews, or special meetings. Still the day was monumental: fifteen miles closer to reaching the nearly three-thousand-mile goal.

Sometimes that's how life is: tough. You have to push through and know that if God has called you to the task, then no recognition, epiphany, or monumental event is necessary. You just put your feet to the pavement, and follow God—no matter how wild, empty, or hard it is.

23

SAND, SWEET SAND

We felt more alone than ever.

California provided no hosts. The desert was unending, the road barren, the hills high, and the heat insufferable. Mile after mile, I told myself again and again, "Just one more step, one more hill, and one more mile."

Our water supply was low, despite the new, larger CamelBaks we wore. Weary and thirsty, Nick and I rested on the roadside under a tree's few leafless branches. Our lips were cracked, and our throats begged for water in the oppressive heat. Sweat poured down our aching backs as we sipped what remained in our CamelBaks.

An occasional car sped past us, but most of the time we sat alone in the desert. Then an old, beat-up car slowed and pulled up to us.

A young man covered in tattoos rolled down the window and asked, "Are you okay?"

"Yeah, just out running," Nick said with a dry, worn voice.

"Would you like some water?"

"We'd love some!" I said.

The guy got out and searched his car. Face red, he looked at us and said, "I'm so sorry. I thought I had some water." He then grabbed a partially empty bottle of blue Gatorade and held it out to us. "This is all I have."

We accepted it gratefully and watched him pull away. As he drove out of sight, Nick and I gulped the blue liquid as fast as we could. Even when we were seemingly alone in the desert, God sent someone to care for us. God knew we needed someone to come alongside us. I was reminded of the importance of coming alongside the preborn even when it seems that no one else cares about them.

We booked a hotel about once a week to shower, but most nights we slept in the van. After several days, we stopped at a playground to spend the night and do our morning workout. When we awoke, we went to the restrooms to freshen up. Megan and I shared a foggy mirror in the ladies' restroom, tamed our hair, and held down the sink handles for each other to wash our faces.

In walked a lady and her early-elementary class. Her eyes opened wide as horror spread across her face.

She yelled at her students, "Against the wall."

After a couple seconds of eying us, she again shouted to her class, "Back out of the bathroom! Quickly, children, quickly!" The kids scrambled to get away from us.

I looked at Megan and then in the mirror. My stomach sank at the sight of us, two dirty women doing our best to bathe in a bathroom sink.

The teacher then took them to the men's restroom, assuming it was unoccupied. If she thought two girls were scary, just wait until she saw a man with long, scraggly hair!

Nick told us he that when he came out of the stall to wash his hands, he startled the woman. "Oh!" she gasped, then collected herself well enough to yell, "Out! Children outttt!"

When we met up outside the bathroom, Megan and Nick's faces were red. I felt the heat of embarrassment in my face too.

The teacher stared at us, her nose scrunched in disgust as she kept her class a safe distance away from us. After we moved away from the bathroom, she took her kids into the restroom to wash their hands. When the children had finished, they marched to the nearby basketball court. As they ate their lunch, we did our playground routine of three hundred jump ropes, monkey bars, balancing, and more.

As we prepared to leave, the teacher yelled at the gardener, telling him we should be kicked out of the playground. We heard "two women in the bathroom" and "a long-haired man," and "the van."

I planned to ignore it and leave, but Nick approached them and asked what the problem was.

"I-I-I wasn't talking about you," she stammered.

Before we started the day's run, we ate breakfast at Denny's. To combat exhaustion, I had hash browns and eggs but afterward felt nauseous. At our run spot, Nick led the warm-ups, but each arm circle drained more energy out of my head and neck. Lightheaded, I drank some water and continued with the warm-ups, but I did not feel better. We took a ten-minute break to rest before running, so I consumed more water.

By the time we hit just over six miles, my face was red and swollen. "You look like a watermelon." Nick said, almost laughing.

I called Megan and asked her to bring PowerAde. I guzzled it, then set a ten-minute timer for a nap in the front seat of the van.

I awoke with a river of sweat streaming down my neck. Despite my weariness, we ran again. Mile after mile, I felt more exhausted and more defeated. Every step was an act of concentrated discipline. Thick white film formed on my mouth and inside my lips.

I stopped, hunched over, breathing heavily, and then resumed. I made it another quarter mile before stopping and resting. Then another quarter mile, then another. Nick was patient and encouraging, both of us determined to keep going until we reached the day's goal of fifteen miles. We finished just over that mark.

At McDonald's, I asked Megan and Nick to order dinner for me and slumped in a booth. Before they returned with the food, my stomach churned, so I rushed to the bathroom. A bunch of girls stood in front of the door, and an excuse for cutting in line tumbled out of my lips before I realized that vomit might be its companion.

Thankfully, I made it to the toilet. I hunched over, leaning on the nasty toilet seat as my body was wracked with dry heaves. I choked as tears filled my eyes, and I leaned on the toilet, trying to catch my breath. I heaved again, but this time actually threw up. My nose and throat stung as I continued to support myself on the toilet. After a moment, I was hit by another round of dry heaves. When they passed, I staggered out of the stall and headed to the sink. I washed my hands and arms past my elbows, then splashed water on my face.

Back at the table with Nick and Megan, I couldn't think about or even look at food.

"Could you save it for me? I just threw up, and I feel awful. I'm gonna nap in the van." I fell asleep as soon as I lay down. A few hours had passed when I awoke. I felt sick but not awful. I ate a bit of my burger and smoothie, then threw the rest away.

Megan booked us a hotel for the night.

Over the next few days, we persevered through arduous runs—all over twenty miles. Our bodies struggled in the desert climate. We van-camped, conditioned, did our runs, and practiced self-defense. Each day brought us closer to the ocean.

When we were roughly thirty miles from the ocean, everything within me ached to reach it and jump in. The air had changed—I could smell the salt, feel the ocean breeze. My heart beat faster, my legs stretched farther. Every step I anticipated seeing and hearing the waves lapping.

Nick had warned me over and over to maintain a reasonable mileage, but pacing myself was hard when the ocean was so near. I felt like I had wings, and I ached to finish the western portion of my cross-country run.

The desert climate finally gave way to a beach climate. Rain fell, but that didn't faze Nick or me. Exhilaration pumped through my veins. We ran through neighborhoods with mega houses and huge hills, on a trail with rolling hills and long grasses, and past a densely wooded area with steep hills.

Then I saw it.

The Pacific Ocean lay ahead of us. Burning, joyful tears stung my eyes. Excitement grew as the distance to the ocean shrank. Nick and I crossed a busy street and reached the sand less than a quarter mile from the beach. Our joints ached, but on we pushed.

Megan was there to greet us.

Sand, sweet sand. We could see it, then we were on it! Off came our CamelBaks as we strode toward the rough waves. The day was cloudy and dark and the water intimidating, but my heart soared. My legs kicked up the cold, rough sand with every joyful, exhausted step.

The water!

Nick dove in first with graceful agility. I clumsily dove on top of him, but I didn't care.

We had run 28.53 miles that day.

The western run was finished.

Nick and I hugged, panting, as a wave crashed over us, knocking me off balance and under the water. We both came up gasping for air as the rough waves continued to hit us. The pull of the water was strong, and my body was too drained to fight it.

I hugged Nick again. Another even bigger wave hit us again and I fell once more, the waves pulling me under. Then Nick's strong, protective arms pulled me toward the surface.

I gasped for air as he shouted above the sound of the waves,

"We should head for shore!" As we tried to run through the water, I fell again, and Nick once more pulled me out. I coughed, my lungs burning with salt water.

The waves still crashed with ferocity as the three of us sat on the shore. The air was cold and damp. Nick put his arm around me, and I pulled Megan in for a hug.

We made it!

Approximately 1,700 miles. Countless steps. Six States. Prairies, mountains, canyons, and deserts. Mosquitoes, cops, and strangers. Camping, hosts, and homelessness. Friends, loneliness, and perseverance.

We made it. By God's grace, we made it.

On May 6, 2017, Nick and I jumped in the Pacific Ocean just north of the Santa Monica Pier after running approximately 1,700 miles all the way from the Kansas-Missouri border to Santa Monica Beach, California.

24

MY WINGS WERE GONE

Daylight filled the room. I squinted, trying to clear my blurry vision. Sarah-Marie's face came into focus. She smiled as she finished parting the curtains to the old nursery of my parents' house. I sat up in bed as she turned and placed a large tray with an egg, potato burrito, and a cup of coffee on my lap. I smiled back.

I was finally home.

After the rush of finishing the first half of the run across America had passed, time seemed to crawl. We had planned to take a week off for rest, but my body did not feel rejuvenated. Instead, it showed the wear and tear of the last ten months. Not only was I exhausted and hardly able to get out of bed, but my knees also ached whether I sat, squatted, bent over, or walked.

During the last week of the western portion, Nick had warned me to take the mileage slowly, but being so close to the Pacific had given me wings. Now those wings had been clipped, and my body suffered the consequences.

Day after day, I hoped for recovery. I prayed for recovery. I dreamed of recovery, but I only felt pain. *Would I be able to complete the other half of the cross-country run?*

Despair, sadness, and fear settled over me like weighted blankets. My sadness was heightened because Nick would not be part of my team anymore. He felt called only to run the first portion with me. Even though we were both living in my parents' home, I already missed him as my run companion. I already missed his strength, determination, protection, and faith.

For the eastern portion, the team would have four members: Besides Megan and me, Sarah-Marie was returning to the team for the whole trip, and Ben Burke, a friend of ours from Mt. Rainier, was joining for a six-week period. Brown-haired and brown-eyed, Ben was a charismatic man of twenty-two. He arrived excited to help the team in any way he could, and we quickly put him to work. Megan, Sarah-Marie, and Ben went to a coffee shop to work on the logistics of hosts, speaking engagements, finances, and routing for the last 1,200 miles of our journey.

Days passed in Kansas City.

My knees continued to ache, but my desire to keep running never stopped. My heart was set on finishing the cross-country trip, but I wondered if I could run another mile. The days dragged until June arrived, marking almost a month since my last run.

Feeling stagnant, I decided to run despite my pain. I set out where I had begun so many months prior on the Kansas-Missouri border, but this time headed East. The temperature was moderate as I ran that evening, and I felt good for the first few paces. Encouraged, I continued, but I stopped at two miles—upset and in pain. Over the next few days, I managed two ten-mile runs, but my knee pain persisted.

A few days later, Megan told me, "A news station wants to interview you running your route tomorrow!"

The next morning we headed out to run and do the news interview, despite my pain. We drove to the run spot, but as I was stretching and warming up, Megan's phone rang. I stopped stretching and watched her expressions to see if I could guess the reason for the call. Disappointment filled her face as she listened, then said goodbye. "I guess the producers aren't pro-life," she said. "They canceled when they found out what you're running for."

"Some news coverage," I said, kicking the ground lightly. "They're not willing to tell a story that doesn't fit their narrative." I looked up. "Since we already made the drive, I'll go ahead and run anyway." But as soon as I started running, my knee pain returned. I pushed through five miles before the pain became unbearable.

The canceled interview was disappointing and the run discouraging, but our evening didn't end that way. Lisa Drake (who had sent me packages of running clothes and gear during the western portion) and her husband invited us to their home. They presented me with more running clothes and another pair of running shoes.

"Thank you so much," I said. "You have no idea how much this encourages me and makes me feel taken care of."

Lisa's faithfulness throughout the entirety of Project If Life reminded me of God's goodness throughout the western run, and I was comforted by the many ways I had seen His faithfulness before my injury.

After the time with Lisa, Megan again came to me with exciting news: "Guess what? I have you scheduled for another news interview with Natalie Davis on KCTV5."

"No way! Another interview?"

"Yep!" said Megan with a proud giggle.

The next day, I wore my running shorts and one of our team's pro-life shirts. We commuted back to my last run spot and met up with Natalie. She had light blonde hair and a bubbly personality. She chatted effortlessly as she set up, but my nerves kept me from saying much as I reminded myself to smile. She began recording. I wanted to stand still and look professional, but nerves made me sway and shuffle my feet. To my relief, her energy and kindness soon made the interview easy and smooth.

After the interview portion, she asked, "We'd like a few shots of you warming up, would you mind going through your routine?" I began stretching and doing different skips to warm up.

After a few minutes, she said, "Okay, I think we have enough." She smiled. "Now could we get some shots of you running?"

I nodded and began running, feeling much more at ease as she recorded. I ran until she was out of sight. After my run, my knees hurt, but Megan and I headed home to watch the 5:00 p.m. news segment.

We all crowded into my family's basement and turned to the right channel just in time to hear a classic male newscaster voice begin, "A local woman is lacing up her running shoes for an epic run across the country."

The other newscaster was female. Her energetic voice finished the introduction to the video: "As KCTV 5's Natalie Davis explains, 'It's not about the run but about the cause.' All new, at 5."

My stomach fluttered as the clip switched to Natalie's now familiar face, then to me warming up, being interviewed, and running. The clip was less than a minute and a half but explained the run well.

"How neat!" Sarah-Marie said. "And they did such a fantastic job too." Sarah-Marie had an eye for quality, and her enthusiasm made me smile.

On June 13, 2017, Natalie Davis with KCTV 5 News interviewed me about running across America. This image was taken from the news segment.

A few days later, I headed over to Third Space, a local coffee shop to ask if I could use their space for an event. The cozy coffee shop had a modern farmhouse feel. The drinks, pastries, and lunch menu were fantastic, and best of all, it was owned by a Christian couple. I had talked to one of the owners, Amy, a few times when I had been there planning Project If Life.

Amy was a kind lady with short blonde hair, a keen memory for names, and a way of making people always feel welcome. Her warm smile and familiar greeting made me feel more confident as we talked. I had told her about Project If Life, and she was enthusiastic and encouraging.

"I want to tell as many people as I can about the goodness of God during the first part of our run and about the pro-life cause. We need a venue, so I was wondering if we could use yours?"

"Of course!" she said. "We'd love to support a pro-life cause."

We got to work setting up the event and inviting everyone we could think of. When the night arrived, we set up our trifold display board and various flyers. When I was ready to begin, the chairs were filled with many moms of students from Maranatha Christian Academy, my old high school.

I shared about what we had done so far and what we hoped to accomplish. I talked about God's goodness and faithfulness during the first half of the run, and our trust that He would see us through the last roughly 1,200 miles. When I finished, the ladies enthusiastically greeted me, donated, and promised prayer.

Over the next several days, I could hardly run. With my mileage remaining low, we invested time in some area events. We prayed at Planned Parenthood. When we pulled up in our van, angry men with long, scraggly beards, starched white-collared shirts, and wide black suspenders scowled at us. I felt deeply uncomfortable as we got out of the van and walked toward the sidewalk where we were going to pray. The scowling continued, and I could see fierce hatred in their eyes.

Sweat formed on my forehead as my discomfort grew—they thought we were there to have an abortion. They approached us quickly and coldly handed us pamphlets. The pamphlet showed terrifying images of demons killing children. It was so violent and disgusting that I ripped it up. I felt awful, and I wasn't even there for an abortion.

Again, I realized the importance of love. The importance of meeting people where they were and guiding them to the truth, not hating and shaming them. My cheeks flushed as I thought of the men's scowls and hatred. How could they possibly think they were helping? As we stood and prayed a short distance away from them, we tried to ignore their presence.

Finally able to get them out of my mind, I prayed. I looked at the modern gray building with its perfectly cut grass and the huge blue lettering of Planned Parenthood across it. I prayed, all the while being horrified that only a few feet beyond locked and closed doors, children were being killed legally—poisoned, dismembered, and suctioned to death. The horror of being that close gripped me as I pondered the disturbing fact that not only was this happening but also people defended it as a human right.

I prayed silently, "God defend these children even today. Raise up people to come alongside these mothers and fathers as they face an unplanned pregnancy. Take their shame and fear and replace it with courage. Bring people to partner with these parents and show them that they are capable of having children and achieving their dreams. Silence those who say children are a burden. Lift up those who can encourage these struggling parents with words, money, time, baby items, or prayer. Also show these mothers the humanity of their children. Let their eyes be opened to see that they would never kill a child outside the womb, so they shouldn't kill children inside the womb. God, I know you are grieved by abortion, so I ask you to use me and my team to end this. Please raise up leaders all across our nation to make the merciless and violent killing of our children unthinkable. In Jesus's name, Amen."

My run after the visit to Planned Parenthood was reflective. I was proud of myself for running over seven miles and making it to Route 50 in Missouri, but to my dismay, those were the last miles I was able to run for a while. Another wave of exhaustion hit, bringing with it frustration and stress. It felt like every day was passing and I couldn't do anything to slow it down—almost like waking up and discovering the day was already over.

Slowly, I became less involved with the details of Project If Life and slept more. As the team went to work each day, I found myself so exhausted that I cried, discouragement magnifying my lethargy. My knees ached endlessly, making me doubt my ability to ever run again.

Five days had passed since my last run, and I was tired of facing my injuries, fears, and shame alone. It was time to tell my team what I was dealing with. I called a team meeting in my parents' dimly lit garage. Megan, Ben, and Sarah-Marie looked at me calmly, waiting for me to speak. Under the weight of their eyes, I felt I would burst. I was so embarrassed to be struggling. Tears came for no other reason than to increase my embarrassment. Despite the tears, I somehow managed to begin.

"I'm exhausted. I'm ... I'm afraid of continuing. I'm scared my knees won't heal. I'm nervous to live in a van again and be snubbed, unshowered, and worn-out," I said. All my words tumbled out on top of one another.

When I finished, I could hardly lift my gaze to meet theirs, but when I did, they each looked at me with understanding and compassion.

Sarah-Marie was the first to speak, "Oh, Annie," she said, "We understand." Megan and Ben echoed her sentiments. She continued, "We need to trust God's timing, even with your injury. Know that God is working."

"I've been learning to trust God. I know God works all things for good, even when I'm afraid. I've been so scared of not being able to continue that my fear has begun to control me. But now I know I must trust God."

After that meeting, I knew no matter what happened, I would keep going. But we had more obstacles than my injury. We didn't think our old red van could take any more cross-country trips. I hadn't even sought God's guidance about it, though. I just knew He would provide. A few days later, God answered the prayer I hadn't even formulated into words: new transportation for the second half.

My boyfriend's family, the Strasburgs, came through in a way I did not expect. They offered the use of their van—a purple 2000 Dodge Ram. It was in great shape and much newer than our old van. We accepted the offer, but before they dropped it off, James and his dad did extensive repairs to ensure it was roadworthy.

Borrowing the Strasburgs' van also meant seeing James. I sat in my parents' front-facing living room waiting for the first sight of him. When I saw a purple van pull into our driveway, I flung open the front door of my parents' house and ran to meet him. He hardly had time to step out of the van before I jumped into his arms, hugging him tightly. He was so giddy to show me the van that he quickly pulled me by the hand to the back of the van. He opened the back doors, and I couldn't believe my eyes: two custom-built beds, several neat, sturdy storage compartments, and so much room.

After a thorough tour of the van, I soaked up time with James. He was his usual joyful, laughing, kind self, but more than that, he was my best friend. He knew I had been struggling over the past weeks, but again he sat and listened, knowing the importance of being there in person to hear my heart. I shared with him all I was fearing and thinking. When I had described everything I felt and thought, he put his arm around me, pulled me close so my head could rest on his shoulder, and leaned his head on mine. His presence and confidence in me calmed me.

"God can still work good out of your injury," he said. We sat silent for a while before he continued, "I really think you should see a doctor about your knees."

He must have sensed my anxiety, because he said, "Knowing what's wrong with your knees doesn't mean you're quitting, but it can definitely give insight as to why you're in pain. Just get them looked at, then see what to do after that."

I agreed to go to a doctor. *No need to be afraid,* I reminded myself.

After a few days, James had to return home for work. He had just graduated college and was saving money to begin grad school. I hugged him tightly and said a difficult goodbye before dropping him off at the airport. As he walked into the terminal and disappeared into a crowd of people, I again wondered when I would see him next.

Several days later, I sat in the doctor's office as the doctor pulled up my x-rays. After she studied them, her eyes met mine. I sat on the edge of the x-ray table, swinging my legs back and forth, my hands folded in my lap to still their nervous shaking.

"The x-rays don't show anything wrong with your knees," she said. "But based on what you've told me about your pain, and your high level of activity ..." Her voice trailed off, followed by a long silence. Finally she continued, "Basically, if you don't stop running now, I don't think you'll ever run again. My advice is rest and switch to cycling."

My heart sank as memories of the western portion's approximately 1,700 miles played through my mind—Monarch

Pass, the Burr Trail, reaching California. I had pushed through the most difficult physical, mental, and emotional pain I had ever experienced. And now I was to quit? I was to just give it up and hop on a bike?

No. Not me.

All this passed through my mind but never showed on my face. I simply nodded at the doctor and hopped off the table. I couldn't make this decision by myself, so the next step was to ask my parents and our board members, the Becks, for advice.

First, I asked my parents. I trusted them wholeheartedly. Their faith was deep, which enabled them to lean on God more than anyone else I knew. But until I had begun Project If Life, I had mostly taken their faith for granted. My whole life they had told me to seek and trust God, then follow, so when I told them about my plan to run across America to end abortion, they didn't object. They just listened, gave wisdom, and let me go.

When I told my mom and dad about my knees, they prayed with me. My mom said, "God knows what's best, Anna. He will show you what to do."

"But people will think I'm a quitter. I told everyone I would do this run, and now I just quit and switch to cycling?" My voice was shaky. "I feel ashamed even thinking about cycling. It's nowhere near the difficulty, but more importantly, it's not what I said I would do."

"Annie, people will understand your injuries," my dad said. "Trust God that if the door for running is closed, He'll open a new one with cycling. God really can work good from your injury." I hugged them and thanked them. Hearing Dad's advice to switch to cycling was less painful than listening to the doctor say it.

For the first time, I asked God about switching to cycling. I tried to surrender my fears and shame of quitting. Maybe He could work something good out of my injuries.

The next people to consult were the Becks. They invited me into their cozy home, where we enjoyed muffins and coffee. I slowly opened up about my injuries.

After a pause, they told me with confidence, "People will understand you're injured. Switch to cycling, and trust God."

Six weeks of struggling with exhaustion and injuries had passed. It was now mid-July, and I was ready to begin cycling. Unfortunately, Ben's time as a team member had ended, and though I was disappointed we hadn't been able to leave my parents' house while he was a team member, I was grateful for his time and dedication. To see him off, we had a huge brunch with lots of decorations to make him feel special and appreciated.

The decision to cycle required me to lean on God in a way I had never expected: it forced me to trust that although God had called me to run, He could use cycling the eastern portion to complete my mission just as much as running it. I had to trust Him even if I had to stop running—the very thing He first called me to do.

With the western portion of the run across America complete, it was time for me to begin the eastern portion—beginning on the Kansas-Missouri border and running on Highway 50 to Washington, DC. I began the eastern portion on June 6, 2017, re-running a little bit of Kansas from my parents' house until I reached Highway 50. This map shows many of the stops along the way.

25
GOODNESS FROM INJURY

The day was hot but bearable as I mounted my gray Trek bike. I forced a smile for the camera and began the first few pedals of the second half. Tears ran down my cheeks, but I pedaled onward. I had officially switched to cycling.

I was a runner through and through, so I daily mounted my $30 garage-sale bike with confidence—running shoes and no cycling gear. Other cyclists gave me odd looks. I didn't realize they thought I looked funny without the so-called necessary gear, though I quickly discovered the importance of padded shorts.

I was extremely sore the first day from sitting on the tiny, hard bike seat. When I dismounted, I could hardly walk without feeling bow-legged, so the team stopped at a cycling store. I was greeted by a male cashier, but as we explained our journey, his demeanor changed. He looked me up and down—my shoes, my outfit, and my bike— then pursed his lips with disbelief.

"You're planning to ride all the way to the East Coast on that?" he scoffed, gesturing at my bike. "And wearing that?" He pointed at my running clothes and running shoes and raised his eyebrows. "You'd better just go home." After a long pause, he added in a gentler tone, "Maybe just go home and fundraise."

Go home? I didn't care how ridiculous I looked or how snobby the cycling community was. God had called me to this task, and He would make a way. That man had no idea what I had already overcome.

I bought the padded shorts and left.

With the new shorts, everything else was functional, even if atypical for cyclists. The miles passed quickly and rather effortlessly. I covered in three days what would have been an incredibly hard week of running. My old bike was not a road bike, but it was easy and fast compared to running.

On July 12, 2017, in Lone Jack, Missouri, I smiled for the camera and held back tears while mounting a bike to continue the eastern portion.

A few days later, we were thrilled to receive amazing news from Megan's dad, Mr. Maier. He was going to loan me his road bike. He sent it down from Chicago—a black-and-blue Northrock.

Although it was a man's bike, I was thrilled to have a road bike built for speed.

Before I knew it, I had cycled through Warrensburg and Sedalia and into Jefferson City, Missouri—a joyous occasion because I spent much time there as a child on my grandpa's 500-acre farm, located just outside the city. We drove down the long, winding gravel roads until we reached a sign above his quarter-mile driveway reading Mengwasser. We pulled up to his old, red-brick house and settled into some of the many bedrooms.

Shortly after we arrived, my grandpa came in the side garage door with his usual cowboy hat, white cotton t-shirt, jeans, and work boots. Although his words were few, his smile showed his delight as we each hugged him. We made spaghetti and garlic bread for dinner, then went to sleep.

Our time at the farm was delightfully busy. Speaking engagements and a meeting with the governor of Missouri arose, opportunities for interviews on TV and the radio came, I met with LifeRunners, and I was introduced on the Missouri Senate floor by Representative Paul Curtman. In addition to all the meetings, I was happy that each day after cycling, I was less exhausted, though still in some pain.

As I cycled through Jefferson City, I was more encouraged by what greeted me there than the attention and publicity starting to surround the eastern portion of Project If Life. My Aunt Julie—a woman with blonde, curly hair and green eyes—met me in Jefferson City. When I spotted her, my heart swelled with joy.

She cheered as I approached. "Woo-hoo! Go, Anna!" she yelled, stretching the syllables of my name as she celebrated. When I reached her, I dismounted my bike and hugged her.

"I'm so proud of you," she said. "I took time off from work in hopes I could see you as you rode through."

"Thank you, Aunt Julie. Your encouragement means so much to me." When I said goodbye and kept cycling, I rode quicker and felt lighter because of her support.

The next day we ate a hearty farm breakfast with my grandpa before Megan and I headed to my start spot. Rain fell, making everything appear gray and the visibility low. I wasn't used to cycling, so I had no idea if riding in the rain was safe.

After Megan and I did an internet search about cycling in the rain, we purchased flashing lights for my bike. I put on my helmet and my CamelBak and began pedaling. The rain persisted. I watched the ground pass below my tires, fearful of losing traction on the shoulder of Highway 50. Rain pelted me, running down my face, arms, and legs, but I felt rejuvenated as I rode up and down the Missouri hills. My thighs and calves pumped, putting new muscles to work. Several miles passed, and I felt powerful.

The rain abated, and the sun peeked through the clouds, making the day hot and humid, but manageable. After over thirty miles, I arrived in the small town of Linn. I was tired but doing well when I came around a long, sharp turn.

To my surprise, standing on the side of the road in front of a McDonald's were my cousins: ten-year-old Madison, fourteen-year-old Emily, and eighteen-year-old Andrew. As I got closer, I heard their enthusiastic cheering and appreciated the pro-life signs they held. "Yay! Go, Anna, go!" and "You can do it!"

Their support made me feel like I was in an actual race. I dismounted and hugged each of them, then rode through Linn—a small town with a few buildings, a small park, and a local bank.

Several hot rides passed before the commute back to my grandpa's farm became too long. We were sad to leave my family but eager to keep going. Megan had been working on connections, hosts, and speaking engagements, so I wasn't surprised that she had arranged another host—our friend and former resident assistant during college, Amber Morton. She lived in the St. Louis area very near our route on Highway 50.

Amber was out of town when we arrived at her apartment, but she left us a key. I was amazed. Very few people opened their homes to us while they were there, let alone while they were gone.

The next day I planned to ride through St. Louis. Sarah-Marie joined me on the gray Trek bike. The August sun shone brightly and intensely as we began our route. St. Louis had a reputation for being dangerous, so I was grateful for a riding companion. We crossed through most of St. Louis and took pictures with the famous arch in the background.

On August 3, 2017, Sarah-Marie (not pictured) and I cycled past the St. Louis Arch in Missouri.

Sarah-Marie and I set out for our second ride in St. Louis the next day. What had been easy and peaceful ended as we cycled through East St. Louis. We were alarmed to see the houses alongside the road progressively become more dilapidated. Many were abandoned and boarded up. As we rode, we passed a burned-down house, more abandoned or dilapidated ones with broken windows, and to our surprise, another burned-down one. We saw so many fire-damaged homes that I started counting them —about one in seven had been burned. Trash was strewn all over the roadside, and we passed many strip clubs with packed parking lots, despite it being midafternoon.

Sarah-Marie and I exchanged nervous glances as we pedaled through the area as quickly as we could. Soon, we were passing abandoned buildings rather than homes, which made us even more eager to leave the area. We approached a large, scary-looking building, its garage doors open. We peered inside and could see nothing but darkness. Something about the building made us feel scared—like people inside watched us from the shadows.

There were train tracks directly ahead of us. To our surprise, the crossing bell sounded and the mechanical arms lowered. We did not want to remain, but the train's whistle signaled its approach. We stopped, resting our feet on the ground. Sweat beads formed on my skin, then trickled down my back. Fear grew as I peered into the deep darkness of the garage and yet saw nothing.

A fancy sports car drove up the closest street toward us and slowed while the driver stared at us, then pulled away slowly. Time seemed frozen as we waited for the train to pass.

"We gotta get out of here." Sarah-Marie looked from side to side quickly and nervously.

"Yeah. I feel sick to my stomach being stopped here."

Finally, the last train car passed, the bells rang once again, and the arms blocking our way rose. We pedaled away, eager to put distance between us and the abandoned buildings and burned homes.

After several more miles, we crossed into Illinois. After only eight rides and about 260 miles, Missouri was behind me, and I was starting to enjoy cycling. Sarah-Marie and I hugged as we took in our surroundings. The land around the Missouri-Illinois border was forested with many winding roads, which led to numerous rolling hills.

We took a rest day, then Megan and I set out to cycle some of Illinois together. We relaxed in the beauty of the countryside, despite the intense exercise. The weather that day was comfortable for August—slightly cooler than previous days, like the first kiss of fall.

There were fewer hills, and the road was wide enough for us to ride side by side sometimes. We crossed a bridge and admired the water underneath us, decorated with lily pads and lilies. We maintained a comfortable speed and enjoyed chatting as we cycled.

After Megan and I crossed the bridge and entered more open country, we saw dozens of butterflies on the side of the road. They created a beautiful picture as they flitted in the wind. After we put in several miles of riding and talking, Sarah-Marie brought us lunch, and made it lovely in her unique way. She brought delicious gyros and warm chocolate chip cookies. We enjoyed them on the side of the road in the warm sunshine.

A week of cycling and staying at Amber's apartment passed before she came home. She walked into the apartment with a big smile, and though it had been a while since we had seen her, she immediately made us laugh. Her goofiness came out more and more as we laughed, talked, ate pizza, and listened to her hilarious stories.

Sunday arrived, and I was invited to briefly speak in Amber's church. As I looked out at the audience, they seemed engaged as my eyes met theirs. I concluded by challenging them to stand alongside God's precious children. Tears flowed down many cheeks, and many sniffles rippled through the audience. The pastor took up a love offering for our team and then directed his church to meet us in the back to hear more about our ministry.

I stood next to our trifold board with our flyers and a set of baby models, telling people about our journey so far. As I greeted people, twin three-year-old girls peeked at my fetal models. I pulled them out of their case and placed one in the arms of each girl. They cradled them tenderly and gently, in a motherly way.

I knelt beside them. "This is what babies look like in their mommies' tummies. Isn't that amazing?" They nodded in a childlike fashion, smiles beaming from their little faces. "God made these babies special, and we always have to protect them and make sure they're taken care of, right?" They responded with more smiles and nods.

As I greeted many people, the enticing smell of a church potluck filled the church. After we had talked with everyone, we headed to the church basement to join them for their weekly lunch. Although the congregation wasn't large, it was welcoming and wonderful like a family.

As we got our food, we saw a familiar face: Paul Curtman, who had introduced me on the Missouri Senate floor.

Paul was a dark-haired man with a clean-shaven face and a reserve that quickly faded into animated smiles and stories. He introduced us to his wife, Ruth, and their toddler son, Oliver. Beautiful, blonde-haired Ruth was pregnant. As we talked, they invited us to have dinner with them that evening.

When we arrived at their house, we immediately felt like we were among friends. Paul was wise, experienced, and well read.

As we talked about various stories (Megan, Amber, Paul, and I shared the same college alma mater), Paul reminded me very much of my dad. Hundreds of books filled his bookshelf, he had clearly studied history and government in depth, he was passionate about our Founding Fathers, and he shared his wisdom in an unaffected, humble way. When the evening ended, we were sore from much laughter and satisfied from much good conversation.

When we had finished dinner with the Curtmans, we said goodbye to Amber to head to our next host home.

"Can you believe it?" I said. "We've been on the road for weeks, and we haven't spent one night in our van!"

Our next hosts, the Thomases, lived in Greenville, Illinois, and they too were out of town but had willingly opened their home for us to use even though we were strangers. We pulled up in our purple van and admired their beautiful, large home. When we let ourselves in with the key, we admired the lovely interior. We made our way to the spacious guest rooms and settled in, then explored the main area of the house. We were delighted to see a large porch outside attached to an above-ground pool.

Our time staying at the Thomases' home was busy and blessed. Radio interviews, news interviews, and speaking engagements came, and it was a true delight to see the pro-life message spread. Although many stations refused to interview us once they knew our cause, I was proud of the ones that did because they were fearless and undeterred by the pressures of our society to keep silent about abortion. I thought of Luke 12:8: "And I tell you, everyone who acknowledges me before men, the Son of Man also will acknowledge before the angels of God, but the one who denies me before men will be denied before the angels of God" (ESV). This verse made it so much more important to be willing to speak about abortion, an issue undoubtedly close to God's heart.

I was covering so much ground so quickly that we were ahead of our scheduled speaking engagements and hosts, so we took a day off from riding and worked from home. I wrote thank-you letters to donors, worked on speeches, and updated social media. In the afternoon, we swam in the pool, relishing every minute at our luxurious host home. Later we all returned to the kitchen area, planning to work until dinnertime.

I was deeply absorbed in my work when I looked up and, to my complete surprise, James stood a few feet from me in the kitchen. I dropped my pen and jumped up to hug him.

"Wha-a-a-t? How are you here?" I said.

"I had to see you on my way down to grad school. I planned it with Megan and Sarah-Marie and got permission from your hosts to stay here. Do you want to go on a date with me?"

We set out right away. We grabbed burgers at a local place and shared a bench as we ate. Not seeing each other regularly made me want to have my arm always wrapped around him and his around me. We laughed and talked for over an hour before James realized we had to take dinner to Megan and Sarah-Marie.

Back at the house, we watched TV while they ate their burgers and then went to bed. I woke up early the next morning, excited to spend time with James. In the living room, his tall frame looked cramped on the couch, a small throw blanket only partly covering him. He awoke when I walked into the room and sat up with a tired, happy smile.

"Do you wanna make chocolate chip pancakes with me?" I hugged him good morning.

"Sounds like fun to me."

After breakfast, James offered, "I can ride with you today to give Megan and Sarah-Marie a break. I brought my bike."

Megan dropped us off. Ahead of me, James's back was bent with perfect posture, and he looked sleek and professional despite his bike being old. As I admired him riding so well, I wished I looked as perfectly postured. He rode quickly and effortlessly, and I couldn't keep up. Several times, I asked him to slow down when he got caught up in covering ground and the thrill of riding.

The next day, Mr. and Mrs. Thomas, our hosts, came home and introduced us to a youth pastor named Greg Groves, a tall, lean, middle-aged man with salt-and-pepper hair, though more salt than pepper. He was known all over the area as an incredible cyclist, but more importantly, for taking his youth group on several hundred-mile journeys each year. Since he constantly worked with novice cyclists, I was the perfect pupil for him.

"Go ahead and mount your bike. I want to see how you pedal and your leg extension." He watched closely. "Okay, we need to raise your seat up so your knee can extend further, but not hyper-extend. That will help prevent injuries. Put your heel down just a little too." He adjusted my bike. "Now go ahead and try again." He seemed pleased with my attempt. "If you straighten your back more and lean into the handles, that will help too."

I absorbed his instruction eagerly. "Thank you so much for all of this advice. I really have no idea what I'm doing."

"You're doing great!"

Over the next few days, Mrs. Thomas proved to be a doting hostess—fixing meals, constantly brewing more coffee, and cleaning up everything.

I was extremely sad when James had to leave for school. I hugged him tightly, realizing I probably wouldn't see him again until I finished Project If Life. After our goodbyes with James, we spent the rest of the day chatting with Mrs. Thomas, enjoying brownies, and watching a movie.

The leisure, joy, and attention surrounding the second portion confirmed in me that the mission to protect the preborn had not ended merely because I had switched to cycling. This realization calmed my heart and made me grateful to God for enabling me to continue, even if it was not on foot.

2 6

UNEXPECTED COMPANY

P *op!* My tire blew, making a loud, unnerving sound. I careened to one side and lost control but somehow managed to dismount as I fell and avoided injury. Sarah-Marie stopped, and we called Megan for a new bike tube as Sarah-Marie and I struggled on the side of the road to get the tire off. Cars passed, leaving us little room to remove the tube.

As we worked to get it off, Megan arrived. She quickly had success and put a new tube in the tire. A brown-haired, athletic man in his mid-thirties approached on a bicycle, seemingly out for a training ride.

He stopped and introduced himself as Richard. We then told him about our project.

"That's a neat journey," he said.

"Thank you. What are you training for?" I asked.

"I am trying to get fit to climb Mt. Rainier."

"What? I climbed Rainier in 2014 when I lived there for a summer job."

"That's so cool! I love just about any sport. You know, this may seem unusual, but my wife and I are going out of town. You're welcome to stay in our house while we're gone. There will be no one there, but someone will be dropping off our dog in the morning."

"That would be great!" Megan said.

"Here's the key, and here's the address. I'm glad my wife and I can help." He wrote down the address, then took off on his bike.

When my cycling was done for the day and Sarah-Marie and Megan's work was completed, we headed to the house. It was a massive structure, basically in the middle of nowhere. When we pulled up, we marveled at the beauty of the house and well-kept lawn that overlooked a small, lovely lake. We let ourselves in and admired the huge windows, which filled one living room wall and provided a stunning view of the meticulously landscaped grounds and sparkling lake. In front of the windows was a large TV.

As we unpacked our stuff and got situated for the night, a huge rainstorm rolled in. The sky grew dark, and the rain came in almost wave-like bursts. We made pizza and sat on the couches facing the giant windows so we could watch the storm. The storm intensified and lightning flashed, illuminating the darkness outside.

We decided to watch *Pride and Prejudice* as we enjoyed the beauty of the storm. We each wrapped our hands around a mug of hot cocoa and got lost in one of our favorite movies. The lightning continued to flash followed by lovely, cracking thunder. Freshly showered and comfortable with my sister and best friend in a luxurious home, I wondered if this kind of pampered life would be the norm for the eastern portion.

The next morning, I awoke early. Slamming cabinet doors and the sound of a chainsaw made me sit straight up in bed. As the banging and roaring sounds continued, Sarah-Marie quietly opened my door, her eyes wide with fear. Megan was in a room across the house, so I texted her to see if she knew what was going on.

No response.

No one was supposed to be home.

The noises continued as we worked up the courage to peek downstairs. We made it only a few steps down the stairs when a large brown dog charged the stairs at us and bared his fierce teeth. A deep growl rumbled in his throat as he continued to snarl and creep closer. His body was low to the ground, ready to lurch at us.

We backed up toward my room as he inched forward. He snapped his teeth and ascended the stairs. As we backed away from him, he quickened his pace. Sarah-Marie and I both reached the top of the stairs, but he was closing the gap. We were almost at my door when he reached the top of the stairs, only a few feet from us. We slipped in my room and slammed the door. Breathless, my heart pounded. The dog continued snapping and growling outside the door.

I grabbed my phone and called Megan. She said she would come in through the kitchen and see what she could do. We heard the kitchen door open, and the dog—perfectly calm—retreated from our door and headed down the stairs toward Megan.

We came down behind the dog and saw him meet her happily with his tail wagging. We watched cautiously, still fearful, but he approached us happily as if he had not just cornered us in my room.

Megan laughed at us. "He's so friendly. Why were you scared?"

"He was growling and had cornered us in our room. Just because he's calm now doesn't mean he wouldn't have ripped our legs off earlier."

As I spoke, I realized that our confrontation with the dog had made me forget about the dull chainsaw noise and the banging cabinets. Now that we were in the kitchen, we could investigate. The explanation was quite comical: a noisy robot vacuum was repeatedly running into cabinets. We all laughed heartily.

Over the next several days, cycling continued to go extremely fast, and soon I had ridden through Illinois and entered the small town of Vincennes, Indiana. States were passing so quickly, it hardly felt real.

Our next hosts were Scott and Brenna Moreland. Scott pastored Westminster Presbyterian Church. They let us stay with them for a night, fed us, and treated us extremely well. The next morning, Brenna offered to take us to the local pregnancy center called Heart to Heart to meet the director, Diana Willis.

Diana had short brown hair and a high-pitched, sweet voice. Her eyes seemed to view people through one lens: what could she do to help them. After giving us a tour of the pregnancy center, she invited us to sit at the long conference room table.

She smiled, then asked, "Would you share your whole story with me?"

I laughed a little, thinking of how long our story was, but I realized she didn't want the short version when she looked at me kindly but seriously and leaned forward, placing her folded hands on the table.

I started out shyly, but with Diana's gentle and eager prodding, Megan, Sarah-Marie, and I were soon taking turns as we shared God's miraculous provision. Delight covered Diana's whole face as she listened.

"Here, take this." She handed me a $500 check. "I'm also going to give you every contact I have between here and Washington, DC." She laughed. "And I sure know a lot of people."

By the time we left, I felt like I had known Diana my whole life. She walked us to the door of her center and smiled at us again as she paused in front of the door. She clasped her hands in front of her chest like a delighted child and said, "I'd also like to pay for you guys to take your bikes to the local shop to have them fixed or at least tuned up."

We hugged our new friend goodbye. She hugged us back enthusiastically and wished us God's best.

Once we were almost back to the van, Sarah-Marie said, almost whispering with childlike joy, "It feels like Christmas!" And it truly did.

We headed directly to the bike shop for much-needed tune-ups. We pushed our bikes through the doorway and were greeted by a lady with an athletic build and shoulder-length, dark hair. She put my Northrock bike on a repair stand to assess it. We chatted as she began repairs.

"What brings you to Vincennes?" she said in a flat but pleasant tone.

"I'm cycling across America as we all spread the pro-life message," I responded.

"Coast to coast?" she asked, her voice less dull as her interest was sparked. As she spoke, she switched the bikes and began working on our Trek.

"Well, I started with running, but I injured both my knees after the first seventeen hundred miles. That's when I switched." I told her many stories of our journey as she worked.

"Wow!" she said. "I love that you're doing this. I rarely see women in this sport." She worked quickly and then pulled the Trek bike off the stand and pushed it toward us. "No charge," she said with a half-smile. "I'm just so glad you're doing this."

We each shook her hand firmly and gratefully before we left.

That night, we met Megan's parents at a nearby hotel to stay the night and have dinner. They had helped us since the beginning of Project If Life, and their company was always welcome. Mrs. Maier was a sweet Filipino woman who loved to mother—sharing everything we posted, messaging encouraging texts constantly, and calling to see how we were doing. Mr. Maier was a tall, dark-haired businessman, and I treasured every bit of his advice as he explained different ways to make our ministry actually sustainable, different speeches I should be prepared to give, and how to engage people in what we were doing.

As we enjoyed dinner, we shared stories of the good and bad encounters, basking in their company and kindness. We finished off the evening with ice cream and more conversation.

We spent two nights in the hotel before Sunday, a day of opportunity and blessing, arrived. Sunday school was held in the basement of Pastor Scott's church. The small room had white cinder-block walls and was filled with tan folding chairs. I was provided with a black music stand and gratefully set my notes on it.

I started with my usual nervousness and then warmed up. In my conclusion, I was encouraged when I looked out into the small audience and saw Megan and Sarah-Marie, my ever-faithful team, teary-eyed.

Their congratulations, applause, and excitement for a speech meant more to me than anyone else's, and they never stopped cheering for me, no matter how many times they heard me speak.

After Sunday school, we headed to the main church area for the service. Pastor Scott led everyone as we stood to sing. The church sang songs straight from the Psalms that were put to a cappella music. We tried to sing the unfamiliar songs as we followed along in the hymnal.

That evening we headed to Calvary Church. Their service was extremely different from the morning one, which had been so conservative. All around us, people prayed out loud, spoke in tongues, and worshiped while lying on the floor. The contrast between the churches was stark, but both congregations served the same God and welcomed the message of the sanctity of life.

The church members were amazingly kind, enthusiastic, and encouraging about our journey and my message. They also collected a generous donation, paid for another hotel room, and invited us to join them for dinner. We were thrilled by all of it, but one small encounter made us see that God was not only our provider but also cared about our heart's desires like a true Father would.

A woman named Teresa Pena approached. "Do you have glasses for the upcoming eclipse?" she asked. "Your eyes will get damaged if you look at it without glasses," she warned.

"We don't have any," Megan said, "but we've been looking for some to wear."

"Here are three pairs. You know we're in the perfect part of the US to see it, right?" She handed them to Megan.

"Yeah, we do, but we thought we wouldn't get to without the glasses," I said. "I've been praying for some. Thank you so much!"

We headed to the hotel after church, and I was asleep in moments. We were awakened the next morning by a circus of sounds from dogs yapping to doors slamming. None of us could sleep any longer, so we headed to breakfast.

After a hearty breakfast and many cycled hills, Megan and I sat cross-legged on the side of road, squinting into the sun to see history in the making. The sun was brilliant, almost blinding, even with the glasses helping to tint its brightness. We were forced to look down and wait a little longer for the eclipse.

We looked back up a few moments later as the moon started to cross the sun. We took periodic glances up at the eclipse, and little by little, the sun was hidden behind the moon—only a bright, red ring showed the sun was still there.

The media called it the Great American Eclipse, and it definitely lived up to its name.

We mounted our bikes once more and rode some challenging hills where pedaling seemed almost impossible.

As we rode, we spotted a creek—a perfect place for a swim. We pulled our bikes over a guardrail and into some woods, then carefully inched our way down a muddy, slippery riverbank. I plopped into the water happily, as I was prone to do. Megan waded in behind me, and we relaxed.

We soon mounted our bikes again and rode a little more until we hit twenty-seven miles. Megan was exhausted, so Sarah-Marie picked her up in the van. I rode another thirteen before I too was exhausted. The hills were becoming steeper and steeper as we approached the Appalachians.

Our next host was Megan's friend Jonnah. She invited us into her home with a high-pitched voice, a broad smile, and kind eyes. Dreadlocks cascaded down her back. She set up sleeping bags in her living room for us to use as her Pomeranian yipped and dashed around the room.

She clearly loved the work we were doing, and her excitement about the project was encouraging. We settled in as Jonnah told us she had scheduled me to speak at a potluck dinner in her church.

When the day of the event arrived, we drove over to her church to set up. We walked into her church's gymnasium to find tables and chairs already set up as well as two long rectangular tables for food. People were already entering and setting their dishes on the table for our potluck.

As more and more people entered, I tried to greet them with a smile, but I became disconcerted as they warmly greeted Jonnah, said nothing to my team and me, then left.

Though many tables were set up and there was lots of food, only about seven people stayed for my speech. I wondered if the others had left because of my presentation's topic.

I went to Jonnah and asked, "Should I still speak?"

"Oh yes! Please do," she said.

I moved my stand closer to the two tables that held people and began to speak, though the size of the group made me uncomfortable.

Soon I warmed up as my usual passion for my topic overtook me. Afterward, I spoke with the people in the audience.

"I have to tell you that I was undecided about being pro-life or pro-choice until I heard you speak. Your presentation completely convinced me to be pro-life," said a girl about our age.

"Wow! Thank you so much for telling me," I said as I shook her hand.

"I heard you mention getting involved with a pregnancy center. I would love to."

Here Jonnah chimed in. "I can get you started with that!"

I was pleased with the response of those who stayed for my presentation, and I was reminded that no matter the size of the audience, God had a plan and purpose for each person he brought.

In Late August 2017, I spoke at a potluck at Asberry United Methodist in Indiana.

A couple days later, Megan and I rode together again. When we saw an abandoned house on the side of the road, we pulled our bikes up to explore it.

"I found a way in! Look at this partially open door." I climbed up some rubble, then squeezed through the door. Megan entered behind me.

The place looked like a museum from the early '90s—clothes hung on racks, newspapers sat on a desk, pictures hung on the wall, shelves were filled with knickknacks. Other than added junk someone had clearly stored there, the home seemed as if it was left untouched. We looked at all kinds of things, including an extremely old typewriter. I climbed up on an old desk to get a better view of the museum-like home, then my stomach dropped.

Through a partially covered window, I could see a stern man sitting on a riding lawn mower pointing a gun at me.

Our eyes met.

"Get out of there!" he yelled. He screamed profanities as he motioned with his gun for me to come out.

My face flushed with fear and embarrassment as I hopped down. We clambered clumsily out of the house through the partially opened door we had entered through as quickly as we could, fearful that we were going to be shot.

"Get out here!" he screamed as we came around the house toward him with our hands in the air above our heads. The man's face was red with fury as we met his gaze.

After a few more moments passed, hands in the air and fear pulsing through my body, the man's face softened—clearly relieved to see two non-threatening girls.

He was still furious, though, as we cautiously approached him. He had stationed himself on his riding mower next to our bikes. We took a few more cautious steps with our hands in the air. He lowered his gun slightly, but a fierce look remained in his eyes as he said, "What are you doing on my property?"

Sweat beaded on my forehead. "We're so sorry! We saw an old, abandoned house and didn't realize anyone owned it." My hands shook with fear as I tried to remain respectful and calm.

He must have seen I meant no harm because as I spoke his gun lowered and his face looked less angry. In a calmer, though still stern voice, he explained, "I just recently had some people attempt to break into my house." He gestured with his gun in the direction of a small driveway leading into some woods where his house must have been. "And when I saw your bikes, I assumed it was the same people."

"We're so sorry," I said again emphatically, feeling awful for causing him so much fear.

"Well, you'd better get on your way," he answered, almost kindly.

"Sorry again," Megan said.

We grabbed our bikes, mounted them quickly, and pedaled off, convinced never to trespass again.

After a few miles, Sarah-Marie picked up Megan. I continued cycling, planning to meet them at the Ohio border. The miles passed quickly until I saw a sign which brought joy to my whole being: Ohio! Megan and Sarah-Marie were there waiting for me at the border as I rode past the sign.

I checked my GPS—over thirty-seven miles. I proudly dismounted my bike and pushed it back to the van. Another state done, and though we had met with some fearful encounters, God had given us wonderful hosts, abundant provision, and opportunities to spread the pro-life mission. He'd also answered the simple desires of our hearts.

27

DEPENDENCE DESPITE FEAR

Cars whipped past me at seventy mph as I rode alone. Their slipstream almost knocked me over. I was still soaked from the earlier rainstorm, but that was the least of my worries. The semi-quiet Highway 50 had crossed with I-71 and I-75 in Ohio. My only option was to pedal as fast as possible through the chaotic area.

As I approached an on-ramp followed by an off-ramp, I applied my brakes, stopping just before the merging and exiting cars. I looked back over my right shoulder to gauge when to cross. Finally, what seemed like a sufficient gap appeared, and I stood on my bike pedals to accelerate. My heart throbbed as I crossed the small stretch of threatening road. Exit after exit, I jammed on my brakes to avoid being hit by cars. They came so quickly I hardly mounted my bike and started cycling again before another one was dangerously close.

Again and again I thought about trying a different route, but I convinced myself the traffic would soon subside.

After I crossed several exits without a collision, the exits became even closer together. I had had several near misses, but I had no other choice.

Heat, fear, and the drive to persevere clouded my reason, and I decided to cross numerous lanes of traffic because there were no off-ramps on the left side of the road. Trembling, I waited for an opportunity to cross. Cars, trucks, and semis flew by with unbelievable speed.

After some time, a large enough gap in the traffic flow gave me an opportunity to cross all the lanes. With my bike in a low gear, I stood once more, pedaling furiously.

I feared being hit at any moment but managed to safely reach the other side of the interstate. Although I was relieved there were no exits, this side seemed scarier because cars drove even faster in the left lane and the left shoulder was narrower than the right shoulder.

My mind replayed the same thought: *I'm going to be hit, I'm going to be hit.*

I felt nauseated and weak. The wind continued to make my bike sway side to side as vehicles sped past me. Just ahead I saw some wood boards on the shoulder that must have fallen off someone's truck.

I'm going to have to ramp these boards. There's just no way I'll survive this.

The first board came, and I stood up on my bike to help maintain balance. I tried my best to pick up the front of my bike as I rode to "ramp over it." My bike's thin tires clumsily thudded over the board, and I swayed toward the traffic lane. Cars were so close to me that their slipstream was pushing me over, making it almost impossible to keep my balance. Another board lay ahead of me. I ramped up over it again, almost teetering sideways into traffic again. In the same way, I successfully crossed the remaining boards.

Fear of imminent death had never been so intense, and my stomach seemed to climb into my throat. *Just a little farther, and it'll all be over.*

The thought hardly passed through my mind when another unavoidable obstacle appeared: tons of glass shattered all across the shoulder. I gulped and pedaled through it, half expecting my tire to blow.

Finally, the three roads diverged, and I was able to follow Highway 50 out of Cincinnati and into calmer traffic. My heart remained in my throat for the remainder of my ride. When I was finished, Sarah-Marie and Megan picked me up and asked how my ride had been. I barely responded because I was so shaken up about it.

They cheered me up by taking me back to the coffee shop where they had been working. I ordered a huge hot cocoa and, feeling like a child, asked for extra whipped cream on top. The barista did not disappoint: the whipped cream was mounded so high that my nose touched it as I sipped the cocoa. It was a delightful way to decompress after my terrifying ride.

The next day my knees ached and shot pain up through my hips. Again I wondered if I could finish the eastern portion. But I had to! We were planning our finish event, which reminded me the end was near. We had decided to reserve the Lincoln Memorial in Washington, DC, so I could give a speech there.

A few days later, I received an invitation to speak at the national Care Net Conference, the organization of Roland Warren, whom we had met back in St. George, Utah. We rented a small blue car and began the long drive to Washington, DC, where the conference was to be held. I drove the whole way, delighted to spend so much time with Megan and Sarah-Marie. As we listened to our typical playlist, Megan worked on receipts and connections while Sarah-Marie worked on articles.

When we arrived, we met up with our dear friend, Diana Willis, who had been so helpful to us in Vincennes, Indiana. Her pregnancy center was part of Care Net. Diana graciously stayed with a friend so we could use her hotel room at the Wardman.

The next day, Diana introduced us to Representative Hostetler, a former Congressman, who offered to take us on a tour of the Capitol Building. He told us much of the building's history as we walked through it. He then took us in the tunnels under it and told us more stories. I felt like we were escaping some massive threat to our country as we wandered the dimly lit halls.

After our tour, we went to the banquet. It was held in a large room with seating for hundreds of people representing 1,500 pregnancy centers. We wandered through the tables until we found ours right in the front. I felt deeply honored as we took our seats and also jittery with the excitement of sharing about the run across America.

When the time came for me to speak, I mounted the stairs of the stage and smiled shyly as they played the video Andy Gwynn had made. The audience cheered when the video ended, and their appreciation grew louder and louder. I stepped up to the microphone to begin, but the cheering increased even more, followed by a standing ovation. I couldn't believe it: the leaders of pregnancy centers, whom I so admired and saw as true heroes of the pro-life movement, were cheering for me.

When the applause died down, I shared briefly about the hardships of running across America and thanked the centers for their work on the front lines every day. People clapped again as I walked off of the stage.

After the banquet concluded, I spotted Roland and Yvette Warren. Megan and I hugged them and reminisced about the last several months before introducing Sarah-Marie to them.

As we talked, Yvette said, "You're welcome to stay with us when you get to the DC area."

"That would be wonderful!" Megan said.

Back in our hotel that night, we talked like schoolgirls about the success and honor of the occasion.

"I can't believe you're going to be the keynote speaker at several banquets," said Megan.

"I can't either," I said. "What a night! There's nothing like being surrounded by a whole room of like-minded pro-lifers who love

God."

Megan and Sarah-Marie nodded in agreement before we all headed to bed.

On our drive back to Cincinnati, I reflected on all the meetings, trips, and speeches that had filled our days and weeks since I switched to cycling, including the Care Net Conference. During that drive, I better understood the goodness of God.

Though my injury was a disappointment and a trial, there was no way I would have had the energy or time to attend the multitude of meetings and to give all the speeches that had arisen and were arising daily. I thought back on those long, hard six weeks of suffering and debating the switch to cycling, and I thanked God for them. He had taken something as weak and human as an injury and used it for so much good.

In early September, we returned to Cincinnati so I could continue cycling. Megan had scheduled hosts that were the parents of one of my college friends, Josh Hall. Though Josh was not there when we went through the city, his parents, Pastor Steve and Deb, and sister, Abigail, welcomed us warmly.

On Sunday, I spoke in the women's Sunday school service at the Halls' church, Hope Baptist. After Sunday school, the Halls took us out for something Cincinnati was famous for: Skyline Chili. I had never heard of it, but they said it was a must if you visit Cincinnati. We entered the Skyline restaurant, and our hosts ordered for us: Skyline hotdogs and Skyline spaghetti.

When the food came out, one dish looked like a chili dog and the other looked like spaghetti noodles topped with chili and a massive mound of cheddar cheese. It smelled sweet with a hint of cinnamon. I took my first bite. It was awful. As I tried to eat my food, the Halls offered to top it with Tabasco sauce and oyster crackers. I passed.

How could I add any other flavor to this odd mix? And how could I possibly eat two chili-mounded hot dogs?

Pastor Hall saw my plight, laughed, and said, "Don't feel like you have to finish it."

After dinner, Mrs. Hall and Abigail took us out to an ice cream place called Graeter's Ice Cream. We all ordered double scoops, enjoying the rich, high-quality ice cream. With ice cream in hand, they gave us a mini tour of the city. The Labor Day fireworks, a splendid view of the Ohio River, and the bustle of the city topped off the evening.

After our visit with the Halls ended, my day's ride brought me to the Appalachian Mountains, which was thrilling to say the least.

When Megan picked me up, she said, "I have the most incredible news! You remember Pastor Weaver who gave advice about the Navajo Reservation? He found a bike for you to use. A really nice one!"

"I definitely remember him. And no way! This is the most perfect timing— just as I'm reaching the Appalachians, the toughest cycling portion."

"I'm so excited for you. He's on his way down to meet us at a local Dairy Queen."

We drove to meet him. I hopped out of our van and shook Pastor Weaver's hand, "It's nice to finally meet you."

Pastor Weaver was a man of medium height with a full head of light brown hair, a kind smile, and a strong handshake, marking his many years of construction work.

After a brief hello, he unloaded one of the loveliest things I had ever seen: a white Cannondale, originally $2,000!

On September 16, 2017, Pastor Neil Weaver provided a Cannondale bike for me to borrow for the remainder of Project If Life.

"You can use this until you complete your journey," he said. "Go ahead," he prodded. "Give it a spin."

I hopped on and rode it around the small parking lot. "It's so smooth, and incredibly fast," I said as I pulled back up to him and dismounted. "And so light!" I lifted the bike with one hand.

Pastor Weaver laughed, pleased I was so delighted.

I shook his hand again, unable to stop smiling. "I can't wait to ride it tomorrow."

The Connors family hosted us the next few days. I spoke at St. Timothy's Catholic Youth Group, launched our second video made by Andy Gwynn, toured Heartbeat International (another umbrella organization for pregnancy centers), and attended an Ohio Supreme Court Case on abortion.

The best event, though, was a surprise Megan and I arranged

for Sarah-Marie. We had contacted *Live Action News*, our all-time favorite pro-life news source, and given them an article Sarah-Marie had written. Sarah-Marie's pieces were so well-written and convicting that we wanted more people to read them, so we asked *Live Action* to republish one of them, and they had agreed. Megan and I were eager to surprise her with the re-publication, so we bought sparkling juice to make the announcement special.

"Sarah-Marie, guess what?" I said.

Megan finished for me. "You've been officially re-published by *Live Action News!*"

"Wait, what?" she said. "Really?"

"Yep," I said, smiling and patting her knee.

"Oh guys, this is one of the best gifts I've ever received. Thank you so much."

"Well, you deserve it. Your writing is phenomenal and *needs* to be read." I poured each of us a glass of sparkling juice and we clinked them together.

Several busy days passed before we reached West Virginia and our next host family, the Lindamoods. Mr. Lindamood was a tall man with short, fairly black hair and a huge heart. Mrs. Lindamood was an elementary teacher with short, curly hair and the characteristic sweetness of those who work well with young children.

As soon as we entered their home, we felt welcome. Our first night, Mr. Lindamood whipped up a batch of chocolate chip cookies. By the time we were ready for bed, we had consumed all of the cookies.

"Do you need another batch to take to bed with you?" he said with a broad grin and a wink.

"They're so good, I think we could eat more than you can bake," I said.

"I doubt it," Megan chimed in making us all laugh.

The next evening after cycling, we came back to our host home, and Mr. Lindamood produced another huge batch of homemade chocolate chip cookies. "You guys sure like your cookies," he said as we helped ourselves to more. For the rest of our stay, he joked with us about how fast we ate the cookies each time he baked them.

The days seemed to pass as fast as the cycling miles did: speaking engagements all over the country were opening up. The places that asked me to speak also paid for me to get there, which I found incredible. As Megan booked more speeches and interviews, I again realized how God was using my knee injury and cycling for good. Since cycling was so easy and quick, I was able to drive or fly to so many different locations for events and maintain high mileage without exhaustion. God's perfect plan was clear.

Sadly, the time came for us to leave the Lindamoods' home. We said a difficult goodbye. So many of our hosts felt like family, even after a short visit.

After I had cycled that day, we were grateful to find a coffee shop in Clarksburg, West Virginia, called Stonewall Coffee. We arrived late, just before it closed. We ordered drinks and enjoyed them, passing the time and relaxing. We were about to leave when we started a conversation with the owner.

We told her all about our journey, and she replied, "I'm a Christian too, and I'm pro-life!" After talking with us for a while, she asked, "Have you guys had supper? I made chili for my employees, and there's plenty for you."

"We actually haven't," Sarah-Marie said.

"But we would love some," Megan finished.

We took Styrofoam bowls and ladled large helpings into them. As I ate the chili, I thanked God for providing a dinner when we had none.

Over the next several days, I continued to cycle as the leaves changed into hundreds of magical shades. Autumn in the Midwest was beautiful, but I had never experienced fall in the Appalachians. The yellows, reds, and browns made the mountains seem as if they were on fire.

While I rode my bike through the steep hills, the road constantly turned sharply and disappeared behind the brightly colored trees and large, mossy rocks. The turns through the mountains were so sharp and on such steep hills that I squeezed my brakes tightly to stay on the road. Eventually, I got the hang of the terrain.

Our next hosts were the Jordans, relatives of the Lindamoods. We arrived at their rural West Virginia home, which had a lovely view of a river. The backyard was a steep downhill to a dock that jutted into the dark, fast-flowing water.

When we walked into our hosts' home, Mrs. Jordan led us into a bedroom with a king-size bed and a queen-size, blow-up mattress at the foot.

Oh no. Are we going to sleep in the same room with our hosts?

My discomfort disappeared when she said, "Mr. Jordan and I will stay in the basement." I felt overwhelmed by their kindness when I realized they would be sleeping upright in recliners so we could use their room for the night.

The next day was our Sabbath, and we were happy to relax in their home. I had been longing to swim, and the Jordans' river home was the perfect answer to my unspoken prayer. After a delicious waffle breakfast, I wandered down the steep hill and onto their dock. The dark, murky water had a seemingly safe current. I sat on the edge of the dock, my feet splashing gently in the warm water as I debated if I would jump in.

My adventurous side won, and I sprinted down the short dock. At its edge, I bent into a dive. I shallow dove and resurfaced almost immediately, blowing a little water out of my mouth. I caught my breath and half swam, half treaded water as I fought the current.

As I enjoyed the water, Sarah-Marie came down to enjoy the fall sunshine. We talked as I dipped in and out of the water, peering into the murkiness below the surface. After my swim, we packed up to leave. Mrs. Jordan eagerly handed us soaps, lotions, hair spray, and other toiletry items as gifts.

When evening came, we had nowhere to stay. Every day we had been living by faith that God would provide, and again and again He did. We had not spent a single night in our van or a tent the entire eastern portion, but we were out of money, so a hotel was not an option. We had regularly been receiving money every week or so to support us, but the last couple weeks, it had not come in. We seemed to be at the end of God's provision.

We again recited the phrase that had helped bring us so far: "If we run out of money, we know we have done all God has called us to, and we will go home."

With nowhere to stay and uncertain what to do, we made up the van beds that James and his dad had built and prepared for bed. Megan was texting with Pastor Weaver.

When Pastor Weaver learned we were out of money, he called Megan and said, "Come up to my house here in Pennsylvania to stay. We will help you out, and we'd love to have Anna speak at our church."

"If we drive there," Megan admitted, "we won't have enough money to get back to our route."

"Don't worry about anything," he said. "I can take care of paying for your gas when you get here, and then we'll see what else we can do. Just come on up, and we'll help you out."

"We'll head up tomorrow morning since it's already so late. Thank you so much."

The next day, I rode another thirty miles before we took the two-hour trip to the Weavers' home in Pennsylvania. Once we arrived, they showed us an RV in their backyard, set up comfortably for us to use.

I relaxed even more when Mrs. Weaver said, "Please feel free to stay with us as long as you need and join us for meals too."

That evening, we joined the Weavers and five of their seven children for dinner. Mrs. Weaver had prepared a huge, homecooked meal that smelled delicious. We enjoyed the energy and joy of their large family. They shared stories of being missionaries on the Navajo Reservation, adopting kids in addition to their seven, and God's provision.

On Sunday, Pastor Weaver allowed me to speak in his church. I was nervous, like always, but the Weavers lived in such a faithful, joyful way that I felt more comfortable than usual. The words flowed effortlessly, and the congregation seemed to believe in our mission as much as we did.

I stepped off the stage, and Pastor Weaver shared his belief in our mission and the importance of protecting the preborn. He concluded by taking up an offering to keep us on the road. When I greeted people after the service, they talked about our mission as if it was their own.

Pastor Weaver counted the money the church of only about fifty people had given—the exact amount Megan had calculated we would need to finish! Mrs. Weaver had not known the amount we were praying for, but she too had prayed for the exact amount we needed to finish.

God's miraculous provision continued throughout the rest of our stay with the Weavers: *Answers in Genesis* wrote an article on our ministry; a family, the Holderbaums, outfitted me with cold weather cycling clothes and gear for the cold weather ahead; we received a second grant from the Templeton Foundation. I was also invited to several more speaking engagements.

In addition, we received a huge package from my friend from college, Lexy Elmaksoud. We opened it at the RV's kitchen table. We took turns pulling out items: three lovely dresses, lotion, soap, nail polish, and so many other girly things. Lexy's love for gift-giving was so evident in the contents of the package.

The Weavers were one of the most generous, thoughtful, and

faithful families we encountered. Their lifestyle of faith encouraged us trust to God even more. It was amazing to me how much God used so many families and churches to be His hands and feet and take care of us.

If I could have planned the journey from the beginning, we would have been fully funded and stayed in hotels the whole way, but God had a different plan that enabled my team and I to be loved and cared for by His people. My faith grew as it was daily tested as we waited for what bed we would sleep in, who would feed us, and where I would share our message. People say that God works in mysterious ways, and I saw that in how intricately He had planned our journey. He knew the lessons my weak faith needed to grow strong, especially when it came to living each day in total dependence on God.

28

THE LAST RIDE

S peeding through the mountains on my Cannondale bike, I once again felt like I had wings taking me not just *one mile more* but many more miles than I could have hoped.

Due to the speed of my new bike, I rode alone, taking in the beauty of a thousand shades of fall foliage. My legs had become muscular and accustomed to the mountains, and I seemed to ascend them with relative ease. The narrow, steep roads turned and snaked. As I cycled up the hills, I stood to get better leg power. When I descended the hills, my speedometer reached as high as 40 mph as I wound my way down mountains I had just climbed. The wind whipped my face, and I bent lower to get more speed. I had come so far from that first ride in Missouri when hitting twenty miles was a struggle.

As I reached the crest of another hill, the downhill ahead of me was full of wild, difficult turns that both excited and terrified me. I leaned into the turns and hunkered down for more speed.

The roar of an engine signaled a motorcycle approaching behind me. The rider cautiously passed me, probably wary of potential oncoming traffic and sharp turns. After he passed, two more motorcycles passed me. I heard the approach of a fourth motorcycle, but I was going so fast down the winding turns and not too far behind the first three motorcycles, that the fourth one stayed behind me.

A smile spread across my face as I increased my speed: I was part of a biker gang! I felt tough as I rode with them down the twists and turns of the mountain. Even with the air whipping past me, I gave no thought to how wildly fast I was riding. When I made it to the bottom of the hills, my speed decreased and the fourth motorcycle passed me. I was once again alone but elated.

When I was finished, Megan and Sarah-Marie met me with Chobani hazelnut yogurt. As we sat and snacked, I enjoyed the October weather. They chuckled through my animated account of being a biker chick for a few minutes.

Over the next couple days, I rode through West Virginia, a tiny bit of Maryland, and then back into West Virginia again before entering Virginia, the final state in my cross-country adventure. I couldn't believe I had made it that far.

After my ride, we headed to the home of our next hosts, Roland and Yvette Warren (from Carenet). We walked through their beautifully landscaped backyard to a two-story 1850's brick cabin. The rainy day made me feel both sleepy and comfy inside the exposed brick-and-stone structure filled with vintage rocking chairs, tables, and bed frames along with a giant, inviting hearth.

The Warrens left us to settle into the cozy cabin. We felt like we had stepped into a Jane Austen novel, so we decided to watch the film version of *Emma*. Yvette had stocked the refrigerator with goat cheese, sparkling water, grapes, croissants, honey, different teas, nectarines, orange jam, and dark chocolate. We each made ourselves a plate that looked like elegant charcuterie boards before we settled on a bed to enjoy our movie.

We left the Warrens' home as I neared the end of my route in Virginia. I rode along a mostly quiet road. Long driveways led to massive mansions with large pillars and immaculate, stately landscaping. I loved the speed of my bike, but the serene beauty around me made me wish I could slow my pace. As I drew near DC, the silence subsided.

I crossed into the city on a beautiful bridge over the Potomac River that was part of Highway 50. The autumn air was warm, and I smiled as I took in the famous monuments, the waterway, the buildings, the traffic, and the knowledge that I was almost done. My goal for the day was to make it to the Lincoln Memorial. As I neared the famous monument, the streets were clogged with traffic, and I struggled to maneuver through them. I had been cycling for two months, but never in such a busy city.

About a quarter mile from the Lincoln Memorial, I came to an intersection. As I waited to cross the street, vehicles flew past. Finally there was a gap, so I pedaled quickly to cross. Pop! My tire blew, but I managed to maintain control of my bike and reach the sidewalk.

Once on the sidewalk, I took a deep breath, trying to collect myself and decide what to do. I was so close to the monument, and I didn't want to call Megan and Sarah-Marie for a tire change. After some thought, I decided to push my bike and run the last bit until I reached the Lincoln Memorial.

I texted Megan and Sarah-Marie to let them know I was almost to the monument, but I would be running because my tire was flat. I began jogging and pushing my bike. After only a few minutes, I saw them.

We hugged joyfully when I reached them. I was so close to finishing, but I would wait to run up the steps of the Lincoln Memorial after I finished my speech in a few days.

"Can you believe it? We're finally here!" I said, relishing the moment.

For so many years I had talked about finishing at the Lincoln Memorial. I looked up at Abraham Lincoln, seated high in the white monument with its stately support pillars. Hundreds of people wandered around me. At the base of the monument, the reflection pool stretched toward the Washington Monument. All that lay between me and the completion of my journey was my finishing speech, and one last thirty or so mile ride so I could jump in the Atlantic Ocean.

Over the next few days, I had numerous speaking engagements in DC and the surrounding areas. I spoke at Patrick Henry College, and I table-hosted an event for the Family Research Council, which provided us with housing in the heart of DC the whole time we were in the area. What a blessing to have a free place to stay without needing to commute into the bustling, expensive city!

The day of my last ride came, but before I mounted my bike, we met with two Congressmen, a staffer, recorded a radio interview, and had an interview with *Lifesite News* (strong advocates of the pro-life movement). As if squeezing all that excitement into one day wasn't enough, I kept thinking of riding for the last time.

After all the busyness of the day had passed, I hopped on my bike for the final time and started my ride at the Lincoln Memorial just beyond the steps I had saved for the finish event. I would have to ride in the dark, but I did not care. All I wanted was to jump into the Atlantic Ocean and be finished.

I rode quickly and covered about twenty-five or so miles. I knew I was close, but the sun had set, so I was nervous. There was no shoulder to ride on and lots of construction. A light rain fell and fog made visibility low. I stopped, turned on my flashing lights, and pedaled onward.

Cars passed me aggressively and closely at about forty mph. Many of the drivers blared their horns at me. I assumed they were frustrated that I was on the side of the road until someone angrily yelled, "Turn your lights on!"

I pulled off the road to check, and sure enough, my lights were off. I had been riding for who knows how long on a narrow shoulder with no lights. *How in the world did they turn off?*

I turned them back on, checked my GPS to see how close the water was, and continued riding. After riding almost thirty-two miles into Annapolis, Maryland, I arrived at a small private beach. Sarah-Marie and Megan met me there and pulled out glow sticks to help me stand out in the darkness. They put the yellow, green, and pink glow sticks around my neck, arms, legs, and on my head.

Megan and Sarah-Marie spoke quickly, their voices full of excitement, and I couldn't contain my joy either.

In the darkness, I ran down the cold, sandy shore. The air was chilly as I kicked up rough, brown sand. I reached the water and bent to shallow dive. I quickly came up for air, gasping from the frigid water. I hugged myself tight as I shivered.

I hugged Megan and Sarah-Marie.

I had made it.

I splashed and jumped and laughed. By God's strength, I had run approximately 1,700 miles and biked 1,200 miles—from coast to coast!

On October 12, 2017, I cycled 31.74 miles from the Lincoln Memorial to Beverly Beach, concluding the cycling portion of Project If Life.

29

HOW DID I GET HERE?

S arah-Maire and Megan seemed to giggle about everything. I attributed it to the joy of finishing Project If Life. It was Thursday, so we got dolled up like we normally did for our Sabbaths, but still they seemed eager to look extra lovely. I put on a long, white lace dress and pulled my hair out of French braids so it would be wavy.

"Can you believe it?" I said, putting my finishing touches on my hair. "I jumped in the Atlantic Ocean last night!"

"We're so proud of you, Annie," Sarah-Marie patted my shoulder.

"I've got to get you a bumper sticker with 2,900 miles written on it so people can know how far you've run and biked!" Megan said.

We headed to a restaurant called Paul for lunch and dessert. Paul was a lovely building with black paint on the front and red brick on the sides. We entered to see a pastry case grander than I had ever seen: rows and rows of freshly made bread and artistic pastries. After a long deliberation, we ordered salmon sandwiches and chocolate-filled, circular pastries with coffee.

"Let's go see some monuments!" suggested Megan when we had finished eating.

"Yeah! Let's!" chimed in Sarah-Marie. "Would you guys want to see the DC War Memorial? It's more obscure, but it's supposed to be lovely!"

We soon arrived at an open-air structure with a large, white dome supported by pillars.

"Let's take pictures. It's just so lovely." said Megan. "Anna, you go first."

"Okay." I walked to the center of the memorial. "I never know how to pose." I swayed a bit and tried to place my hands where they might seem natural for a photo.

"You're fine," Megan said. I smiled and stood shifting to find a position, then realized Megan wasn't looking at me but beyond me. As I wondered why she wasn't looking at me, I felt strong arms wrap tightly around my waist and smelled James's woodsy cologne.

"What on earth? How are you here?" I turned to face him.

"I'm here to surprise you for the end of Project If Life," he said, still hugging me.

"I had no idea when you were coming." I laughed. "I guess I've been so distracted, I didn't have time to think about what day."

"I've been talking with Megan and Sarah-Marie for weeks about coming."

"He has." Megan confirmed. "Now you two go have a date."

"That sounds amazing," I replied.

After Megan and Sarah-Marie left, James and I walked around DC, holding hands. I had never felt so happy.

After a lot of exploring on foot, James asked, "Do you want to see the National Cathedral?"

"Sure!" I said. I could not have cared less about what we saw, as long as I was with him. James ordered a ride share to the National Cathedral, and once we arrived, we walked through a large doorway into a beautiful garden of roses and meticulous landscaping that seemed unending.

We wandered through the garden down seemingly ancient stone steps surrounded by roses and old, mossy trees before taking more steps past a trickling fountain. We stopped at an old stone gazebo covered in vines. James motioned for me to sit beside him on a bench and then read a letter about how much he loved me.

He said, "Anna, I want to spend the rest of my life with you."

My mind could hardly process the moment as James knelt on one knee. He was shaking and laughing and stumbling over his words as he worked to appear calm.

He took a deep breath, looked up at me, and opened a small red box. Inside was the loveliest diamond ring I had ever seen. I looked up from the box into his green eyes. He said, "Anna, will you marry me?"

James proposed to me in the gazebo at the National Cathedral in Washington, DC, on October 12, 2017.

Everything around me was a blur.

Finally, "Yes, yes, yes!" poured out of my mouth.

My hand trembled as he slipped the ring on my finger. I moved my finger up and down to admire the diamond catching the radiant sunlight. He took my face in his hands, kissed me, and then wrapped his arms tightly around me.

When I became aware of my surroundings again, I spied Sarah-Marie and Megan in jackets with their hoods up taking photos from behind bushes. They had been in on it the whole time. I smiled at them, and then James and I wandered around joyously hugging, kissing, and laughing. He picked me up and spun me around as I laughed and laughed, clinging to the man who had made me the happiest woman in the world.

Three days later, we held our finish event at the Lincoln Memorial. That evening, about a hundred people who had supported us all across America came to hear me speak. I took photos with my parents, my brother Nick, James's family, Mr. Beck, Mr. Clarke, the Weavers, many of my best friends, college friends, and people who had helped us all along the way.

Everyone took their seats and waited for me to run the final steps of my journey. It felt surreal as I stood at the base of one set of steps of the Lincoln Memorial. I was about to run the last physical steps I would take on my whole fifteen-month, roughly 2,900-mile journey. Though the thought of running the last steps was monumental, the symbolism of running the steps of the Lincoln Memorial pressed on my mind—the steps that led to the statue of Abraham Lincoln who had worked to free slaves, the steps that Martin Luther King Jr. spoke on during the Civil Rights movement, and now the steps I would speak on to proclaim the oppression of yet another group: the preborn.

I wore my running shoes and a red tank top with our team's logo on it. As I waited for my dad to introduce me, thoughts of ending abortion filled my mind. How long would we have to fight? When would this injustice finally come to an end? Would people ever realize the only way to end the slaughter of the preborn children is to rise and fight?

My dad concluded with "And now Annie is going to run up the steps. These will be the very last steps to complete her run across America."

My heart raced. The steps were effortless and almost a blur. Cheers broke out from the audience, a smile spread across my face, and hot, happy tears filled my eyes. Everything was surreal.

I stood at the top of the memorial, relishing the moment as people continued to cheer and clap.

I turned and jogged to the bathroom attached to the Lincoln Memorial. I changed into a lovely red dress and heels, then let my hair out of the bun so my curls fell onto my shoulders. I took a few deep breaths and walked back to the steps. I took my seat on the front row until it was my turn to speak.

My brand-new fiancé, James, stood up to sing the National Anthem. Holding the microphone and standing with his signature perfect posture and confidence, the words of the National Anthem flowed from of his mouth. Like magic, people all around the memorial stopped and put their hands over their hearts. James then took his seat beside me. He held my hand tight, clearly calming his nerves. I patted his hand as we listened to Mr. Clarke read Scripture and representatives from Americans United for Life and Family Research Council speak.

The sun had set, and lights were turned on and directed toward the microphone. I was ready to speak. I looked calmly out at the audience of so many faithful friends and family members. Thankfulness and love filled my heart. The eyes I met belonged to those who had believed in me when no one else would, and it only seemed right to stand before them and tell them about their faithfulness and the faithfulness of God.

I first shared about battling loneliness on the plains of Kansas and asking God, "How did I get here?" Next, I shared about my fight with fear on the heights of the Rocky Mountains, the difficulty of the barren desert, my painful knee injury, and the slopes of the Appalachian Mountains.

"How did I get here?" The answer was by trusting God's faithfulness and knowing He would provide the strength for me to run *one mile more*. I concluded my speech by saying,

This week I reflect on our last fifteen months. We now experience news interviews almost every day, speaking engagements scheduled into next year, many meetings with elected officials, and so many people across America who have been successfully activated into the pro-life movement.

So now, on the steps of the Lincoln Memorial, officially a USA crosser, having spoken all across America, I ask myself again, "How did I get here?"

Because of God and because you were willing. Willing to act on behalf of those that are voiceless. To act on your call to defend the defenseless. You have provided prayer, vehicles, hosts, donations, encouragement, materials, counsel, packages, clothes, bikes, gifts, and so much more. I am here today, and my team is here today, officially having completed the task that God has called us to— saving the lives of the preborn.

I want to conclude tonight by saying the biggest thank you. Thank you to those that made the journey here. Thank you for being pro-life in your own way. Thank you for defending the lives of the weakest of our society—the preborn. And thank you for being the ones who made it possible for us to complete our calling. Because of you here tonight and many more watching, we have been able to fulfill our calling. Defending the lives of the preborn has been our greatest privilege.

Tears filled my eyes as Megan's Dad, Mr. Maier, stood up to close the event in prayer. As he prayed, I couldn't help but see the clusters of people who had stopped and joined our event as I spoke, now with heads bowed in prayer. Once again, the miracle-working God of the Bible was with us, and He was working.

On October 15, 2017, I concluded Project If Life at the Lincoln Memorial in front of about a hundred people, many of whom had helped make the journey possible.

EPILOGUE

The next few days in DC were packed with numerous interviews (including CBN with John Reid and EWTN with Catherine Szeltner), amazing meetings, becoming an honorary senator with Kansas Senator Pat Roberts, and the thrill of making a difference to end abortion.

The cross-country adventure had ended, and yet somehow I knew that season had rightly come to a close, and God had different things in store. July 15, 2016–October 15, 2017 had been the hardest fifteen months of my life but also the most incredible.

Trusting God week to week to survive, being miserably homeless, running across the Rockies, being rejected, seeing modern-day miracles, running through desert sands, jumping in the Pacific, facing injury, seeing constant provision, achieving success and recognition, and jumping into the Atlantic were all part of this incredibly hard journey.

But everything the team and I faced, good or bad, was worth it to stand for the preborn.

Sadly, the war to end abortion has not been won, but no matter what hardships we face—whether seemingly insurmountable like mountains or seemingly barren like deserts, or seemingly unbeatable like an injury—our God is greater and He will make a way to end abortion.

We must keep running this race to end abortion.

Hebrews 12:1–3 says, "Therefore, since we are surrounded by so great a cloud of witnesses, let us also lay aside every weight, and sin which clings so closely, and let us run with endurance the race that is set before us, looking to Jesus, the founder and perfecter of our faith, who for the joy that was set before him endured the cross, despising the shame, and is seated at the right hand of the throne of God. Consider him who endured from sinners such hostility against himself, so that you may not grow weary or fainthearted" (ESV).

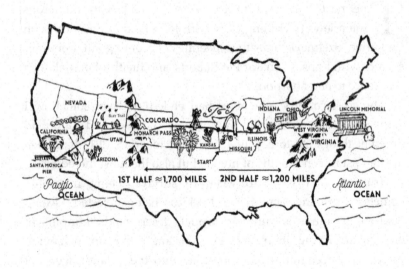

My complete route from coast to coast: approximately 1,700 miles run and 1,200 miles cycled. Started on July 15, 2016, and finished on October 15, 2017.

Where Is the Team Now?

Nicholas Hoduski is back in Kansas where he continues to adventure: running, swimming, biking, and hiking. He is an amazing man of God who remains faithful and steadfast.

Megan Maier teaches third, fourth, and fifth grade at a small Christian school in California. Though she's wildly busy, no one could do a better job than she can.

Sarah-Marie Hoduski (now Sherbon) still writes beautifully and fearlessly. She and her husband have one child and one on the way. Atticus now lives happily with the Sherbons.

I married James on June 1, 2018, and we have four children. There has been no greater honor for me than to stand for the most innocent of our time, the preborn, and no greater joy than being pregnant with and giving birth to our four children.

I still run Project If Life, now called If Life. I travel and speak across the nation spreading the pro-life message to educate and activate people into the pro-life movement, the most important cause of our time.

ABOUT THE AUTHOR

Anna Strasburg began her pro-life journey in her fifth-grade classroom of Maranatha Christian Academy where her teacher, Mrs. Linda Steinbrink, first told her about fetal development and abortion. She spent the next eight years caring about the preborn but unsure how to help end abortion.

Under her high school coach, Bianca Williams, Anna became a distance runner. During her sophomore year of college, while training for her second half-marathon, she used her training runs to seek God. During the end of a ten-mile training run, Anna asked God how to live out her care for the preborn. God called her to run across America to help bring people into the pro-life movement.

Anna started the run across America after graduating college with a degree in Math Education. She completed her journey on October 15, 2017, and now speaks nationwide. She co-founded If Life, an organization dedicated to teaching the beauty of fetal development and revealing the true horrors of abortion. Anna now lives in Pensacola, Florida with her husband and four children.

Website: If-life.org
Facebook: @Projectiflife
Instagram: @anna.strasburg, @projectiflife